EDITED BOOK OF PHARMACOLOGY – II

[According to latest syllabus of B. Pharm – V Semester of Pharmacy Council of India]

Dr. Surya Prakash Gupta

Professor & Director

Rajiv Gandhi Institute of Pharmacy

Faculty of Pharmaceutical Science & Technology

AKS University,

Satna (Madhya Pradesh)

Ms. Neha Goel

Associate Professor

Rajiv Gandhi Institute of Pharmacy

Faculty of Pharmaceutical Science & Technology

AKS University

Satna (Madhya Pradesh)

EDITED BOOK OF
PHARMACOLOGY – II

First Edition 2024

Published by:
NOTION PRESS

EDITED BOOK OF PHARMACOLOGY – II

NOTION PRESS

PREFACE

The authors feel great pleasure in presenting the first edition of the book **"Edited Book of Pharmacology – II"** for graduate and post graduate students. The present book on **Edited Book of Pharmacology – II** has been written according to the syllabus of B. Pharm – V semester of Pharmacy Council of India and covers full course of the subject.

THE SALIENT FEATURES OF THE BOOK ARE: -

- *Easy to understand style of writing* which makes the book a self-study material.
- *Each new concept has been introduced through day-today problem of interest* to the students which makes the subject matter interesting.
- *The language of the book, on the whole, is lucid and easy to understand.*
- Wherever needed *neatly labeled figures have been drawn.*

The authors hope that the students, teachers and other readers will find the book interesting and to the point covering the course. We hope that the students will receive the book warmly.

I express a sincere thank you to the Management of Rajiv Gandhi Institute of Pharmacy, Faculty of Pharmaceutical Science & Technology, AKS University for their support during the writing of this book.

Every effort is made to keep the book error free. The author will gratefully acknowledge the suggestions to improve the book to make it more useful.

Wishing our readers success in examination and life ahead. The authors feel that their efforts will be fully rewarded if the book serves the purpose for which it is written.

EDITED BOOK OF PHARMACOLOGY – II

ABOUTH THE EDITORS

Dr. Surya Prakash Gupta is a distinguished academician and currently serves as a Professor and Director at the Rajiv Gandhi Institute of Pharmacy, Constituent Unit of AKS University, Satna (M.P.). With an illustrious career spanning several years, Dr. Gupta has made significant contributions to the field of pharmacy education and research. He holds a Ph.D. in Pharmacy and is widely respected for his expertise in the field. Dr. Gupta's academic journey is marked by numerous achievements, and he has played a pivotal role in shaping the careers of aspiring pharmacists. As the Director of the Rajiv Gandhi Institute of Pharmacy, Dr. Gupta has been instrumental in implementing innovative teaching methodologies and fostering an environment conducive to research and learning. Under his guidance, the institute has achieved new heights of excellence. Dr. Surya Prakash Gupta is not only a proficient academician but also an inspiring mentor who is dedicated to the advancement of pharmacy education in India. His commitment to academic excellence and research makes him a highly regarded figure in the field.

Ms. Neha Goel is working as Associate Professor, Rajiv Gandhi Institute of Pharmacy, AKS University; Satna (M.P.). She has bagged first class academic degree M. Pharm. from premier institute. She is actively participating in academic & research work & also involved in various extracurricular activity. She has participated in various conferences & received best poster award.

With over 10 years of experience in teaching, she has established herself as a respected figure in the field of education. Her commitment to fostering a holistic learning environment underscores her dedication to the development of her students.

EDITED BOOK OF PHARMACOLOGY – II

CONTENTS

S. No.	Particular	Author name, designation, college name and address	Page number
1.	Pharmacology of drugs acting on Cardio vascular system	Dr. Surya Prakash Gupta Professor & Director Rajiv Gandhi Institute of Pharmacy Faculty of Pharmaceutical Science & Technology, AKS University, Satna (M.P.)	11
2.	Anti-hypertensive drugs	Mr. Prabhakar Singh Tiwari Associate Professor Rajiv Gandhi Institute of Pharmacy, Faculty of Pharmaceutical Science & Technology, AKS University Satna, (M.P.)	31
3.	Anti-anginal drugs	Ms. Neha Goel Associate Professor Rajiv Gandhi Institute of Pharmacy, Faculty of Pharmaceutical Science & Technology, AKS University Satna, (M.P.)	38
4.	Anti-arrhythmic drugs	Mr. Satyendra Garg Assistant Professor Rajiv Gandhi Institute of	43

		Pharmacy, Faculty of Pharmaceutical Science & Technology, AKS University Satna, (M.P.)	
5.	Anti-hyperlipidemic drugs.	Mrs. Neelam Singh Assistant Professor Rajiv Gandhi Institute of Pharmacy, Faculty of Pharmaceutical Science & Technology, AKS University Satna, (M.P.)	54
6.	Drug used in the therapy of shock	Mr. Abu Tahir Assistant Professor Rajiv Gandhi Institute of Pharmacy, Faculty of Pharmaceutical Science & Technology, AKS University Satna, (M.P.)	59
7.	Hematinic	Mr. Ashutosh Jain Assistant Professor Rajiv Gandhi Institute of Pharmacy, Faculty of Pharmaceutical Science & Technology, AKS University Satna, (M.P.)	66
8.	Pharmacology of drugs acting on cardio vascular system-II	Ms. Shikha Singh Assistant Professor Rajiv Gandhi Institute of	72

		Pharmacy, Faculty of Pharmaceutical Science & Technology, AKS University Satna, (M.P.)	
9.	Anti-platelet drugs	Mrs. Saba Ruksaar Assistant Professor Rajiv Gandhi Institute of Pharmacy, Faculty of Pharmaceutical Science & Technology, AKS University Satna, (M.P.)	84
10.	Pharmacology of drugs acting on urinary system	Dr. Surya Prakash Gupta Professor & Director Rajiv Gandhi Institute of Pharmacy Faculty of Pharmaceutical Science & Technology, AKS University, Satna (M.P.)	90
11.	Autocoids-I	Mr. Prabhakar Singh Tiwari Associate Professor Rajiv Gandhi Institute of Pharmacy, Faculty of Pharmaceutical Science & Technology, AKS University Satna, (M.P.)	117
12.	Autocoids-II	Ms. Neha Goel Associate Professor Rajiv Gandhi Institute of	131

		Pharmacy, Faculty of Pharmaceutical Science & Technology, AKS University Satna, (M.P.)	
13.	Non-steroidal anti-inflammatory agents	Mr. Satyendra Garg Assistant Professor Rajiv Gandhi Institute of Pharmacy, Faculty of Pharmaceutical Science & Technology, AKS University Satna, (M.P.)	149
14.	Anti-gout drugs	Mrs. Neelam Singh Assistant Professor Rajiv Gandhi Institute of Pharmacy, Faculty of Pharmaceutical Science & Technology, AKS University Satna, (M.P.)	155
15.	Antirheumatic drugs.	Mr. Abu Tahir Assistant Professor Rajiv Gandhi Institute of Pharmacy, Faculty of Pharmaceutical Science & Technology, AKS University Satna, (M.P.)	165
16.	Pharmacology of drugs acting on endocrine system-I	Mr. Ashutosh Jain Assistant Professor Rajiv Gandhi Institute of	190

		Pharmacy, Faculty of Pharmaceutical Science & Technology, AKS University Satna, (M.P.)	
17.	Pharmacology of drugs acting on endocrine system-II	Ms. Shikha Singh Assistant Professor Rajiv Gandhi Institute of Pharmacy, Faculty of Pharmaceutical Science & Technology, AKS University Satna, (M.P.)	204
18.	Pharmacology of drugs acting on endocrine system-III	Mrs. Saba Ruksaar Assistant Professor Rajiv Gandhi Institute of Pharmacy, Faculty of Pharmaceutical Science & Technology, AKS University Satna, (M.P.)	221
19.	Bioassay-I	Ms. Neha Goel Associate Professor Rajiv Gandhi Institute of Pharmacy, Faculty of Pharmaceutical Science & Technology, AKS University Satna, (M.P.)	249
20.	Bioassay-II	Mr. Abu Tahir Assistant Professor Rajiv Gandhi Institute of	271

		Pharmacy, Faculty of Pharmaceutical Science & Technology, AKS University Satna, (M.P.)	

CHAPTER – 1

PHARMACOLOGY OF DRUGS ACTING ON CARDIO VASCULAR SYSTEM – I

Dr. Surya Prakash Gupta

Professor & Director, Rajiv Gandhi Institute of Pharmacy, Faculty of Pharmaceutical Science & Technology, AKS University, Satna (M.P.)

ABSTRACT:

The cardiovascular system plays a crucial role in maintaining the body's overall health by ensuring the efficient circulation of blood. Understanding the electrophysiology of the heart is essential in comprehending how this system functions. The heart's electrical activity, initiated by the sinoatrial node, spreads through the atria, causing their contraction and subsequently triggering the atrioventricular node. This process results in the coordinated contraction of the ventricles, ensuring effective blood circulation. Drugs that act on the cardiovascular system are pivotal in managing various heart conditions. Congestive heart failure (CHF), a condition where the heart's ability to pump blood is compromised, is one such ailment. The pharmacological treatment of CHF includes a range of medications aimed at improving heart function and alleviating symptoms. Diuretics help reduce fluid overload, while ACE inhibitors and beta-blockers work to decrease the heart's workload and improve its efficiency. Additionally, digitalis glycosides increase the force of myocardial contractions, enhancing cardiac output. These drugs, when used appropriately, significantly improve the quality of life for patients with CHF. Understanding the intricate workings of the heart and the pharmacology of these drugs is essential for effective clinical management of cardiovascular diseases.

Introduction:

The cardiovascular system, also known as the circulatory system, is a complex network responsible for the transport of blood, nutrients, oxygen, and hormones to cells throughout the body and the removal of metabolic wastes such as carbon dioxide and nitrogenous wastes. Central to this system is the heart, a muscular organ that pumps blood through a vast network of blood vessels, including arteries, veins, and capillaries. The arteries carry oxygen-rich blood away from the heart to the body, while the veins return oxygen-depleted blood back to the heart. Capillaries, the smallest blood vessels, facilitate the exchange of oxygen, nutrients, and wastes between blood and tissues.

The cardiovascular system is critical for maintaining homeostasis, supporting the immune response, and regulating body temperature. It is divided into two main circuits: the systemic circulation, which delivers blood to the entire body, and the pulmonary circulation, which transports blood to the lungs for oxygenation. The heart itself is divided into four chambers: two atria and two ventricles, which work in a coordinated manner to ensure efficient blood flow. The right side of the heart receives deoxygenated blood from the body and pumps it to the lungs, while the left side receives oxygenated blood from the lungs and pumps it to the rest of the body. Understanding the anatomy and function of the cardiovascular system is essential for recognizing how it supports life and how various diseases can affect its performance.

Introduction of Electrophysiology of heart:

The electrophysiology of the heart refers to the study of the electrical activities that govern the heart's rhythmic contractions. These electrical impulses are critical for maintaining the heart's ability to pump blood effectively throughout the body. The process begins in the sinoatrial (SA) node, often referred to as the heart's natural pacemaker. Located in the right atrium, the SA node generates an electrical impulse that causes the atria to contract and push blood into the ventricles.

This impulse then travels to the atrioventricular (AV) node, located at the junction between the atria and the ventricles. The AV node acts as a gatekeeper, slowing down the electrical signal before it passes into the ventricles. This delay ensures that the atria have enough time to fully contract and empty their blood into the ventricles before the ventricles themselves contract.

Following the AV node, the electrical impulse travels through the bundle of His, which divides into right and left bundle branches, and then into the Purkinje fibers. These fibers spread throughout the ventricles, ensuring a coordinated and rapid contraction of the ventricular muscle, which propels blood into the pulmonary and systemic circuits.

The heart's electrophysiology is intricately regulated by the autonomic nervous system, with the sympathetic nervous system increasing heart rate and the parasympathetic nervous system decreasing it. Any disruptions to the normal electrical pathways can result in arrhythmias, which are abnormal heart rhythms that can affect the efficiency of the heart's pumping action. Understanding the electrophysiology of the heart is essential for diagnosing and treating these conditions, as well as for developing interventions like pacemakers and defibrillators that can help manage abnormal heart rhythms.

Types of Electrophysiology of heart:

Electrophysiology of the heart encompasses various types that focus on different aspects of the heart's electrical activity and its regulation. These include surface electrocardiography (ECG), intracardiac electrophysiology studies (EPS), and Holter monitoring, among others. Each type provides unique insights into the heart's function and is used for different diagnostic and therapeutic purposes.

1. **Surface Electrocardiography (ECG):**

- **Description**: The ECG is a non-invasive test that records the electrical activity of the heart using electrodes placed on the skin. It provides a visual representation of the heart's electrical impulses as they travel through the heart.
- **Applications**: ECGs are used to diagnose arrhythmias, myocardial infarction (heart attack), and other heart conditions. They can detect abnormalities in the heart's rhythm, conduction pathways, and overall electrical activity.
- **Discussion**: ECGs are widely used in clinical practice due to their simplicity, non-invasiveness, and ability to provide quick and valuable diagnostic information. They are often the first step in evaluating heart conditions.

2. **Intracardiac Electrophysiology Studies (EPS)**:
   - **Description**: EPS involves the insertion of catheters with electrodes into the heart through blood vessels. These catheters are used to map the electrical activity inside the heart and to induce and analyze arrhythmias.
   - **Applications**: EPS is used to diagnose and treat complex arrhythmias, evaluate the effectiveness of antiarrhythmic medications, and guide catheter ablation procedures to treat abnormal electrical pathways.
   - **Discussion**: EPS is a more invasive but highly detailed method that allows precise mapping of the heart's electrical activity. It is essential for diagnosing and treating arrhythmias that cannot be fully assessed with surface ECG alone.
3. **Holter Monitoring**:
   - **Description**: Holter monitoring involves wearing a portable ECG device for 24 to 48 hours to continuously record the heart's electrical activity.

- **Applications**: This method is used to detect intermittent arrhythmias that may not be captured during a standard ECG. It is useful for evaluating symptoms like palpitations, dizziness, and syncope (fainting).
- **Discussion**: Holter monitoring provides a more comprehensive picture of the heart's activity over an extended period, making it valuable for diagnosing transient arrhythmias and assessing the effectiveness of treatments.

4. **Event Monitoring**:
   - **Description**: Similar to Holter monitoring, event monitors are worn for longer periods, typically 30 days. Patients activate the device to record their heart's activity when they experience symptoms.
   - **Applications**: Event monitoring is used for detecting infrequent arrhythmias and correlating them with specific symptoms.
   - **Discussion**: This type of monitoring is beneficial for patients with sporadic symptoms, as it allows for targeted recording of abnormal events.
5. **Signal-Averaged ECG (SAECG)**:
   - **Description**: SAECG is a specialized form of ECG that averages multiple heartbeats to detect subtle abnormalities in the heart's electrical activity.
   - **Applications**: It is used to identify patients at risk for ventricular arrhythmias and sudden cardiac death.
   - **Discussion**: SAECG enhances the sensitivity of traditional ECG by revealing low-amplitude signals that may indicate the presence of abnormal myocardial substrates.

6. **Tilt Table Testing**:
   - **Description**: This test evaluates how the heart and blood pressure respond to changes in body position, typically from lying down to standing up.
   - **Applications**: It is used to diagnose conditions like vasovagal syncope and orthostatic hypotension.
   - **Discussion**: Tilt table testing helps identify the cause of unexplained fainting by simulating the conditions that lead to syncope.

DRUGS USED IN CONGESTIVE HEART FAILURE

Congestive heart failure (CHF) is a condition in which the heart is unable to pump blood effectively, leading to a buildup of fluid in the lungs and other parts of the body. There are several classes of drugs used in the treatment of congestive heart failure, and they are often used in combination to manage the condition effectively. Some of the common drugs used in the management of congestive heart failure include:

1. **Diuretics:** These drugs help the body get rid of excess fluid and reduce the symptoms of fluid retention, such as swelling and shortness of breath. Common diuretics used in CHF include furosemide (Lasix), hydrochlorothiazide, and spironolactone.
2. **Angiotensin-Converting Enzyme (ACE) Inhibitors**: ACE inhibitors help relax blood vessels, reduce blood pressure, and decrease the workload on the heart. Common ACE inhibitors include enalapril, lisinopril, and captopril.
3. **Angiotensin II Receptor Blockers (ARBs):** ARBs work similarly to ACE inhibitors by relaxing blood vessels and reducing blood pressure. Common ARBs include losartan, valsartan, and candesartan.
4. **Beta-Blockers:** Beta-blockers slow the heart rate and reduce the force of heart contractions, which can be helpful in CHF. Common beta-blockers used include metoprolol, carvedilol, and bisoprolol.

5. **Aldosterone Antagonists:** Medications like spironolactone and eplerenone are used to block the effects of aldosterone, a hormone that can worsen heart failure.
6. Inotropes: These drugs, such as dobutamine and milrinone, can be used in severe cases of CHF to improve the heart's pumping ability.
7. **Digoxin**: Digoxin is a medication that can be used to increase the strength of the heart's contractions and slow down the heart rate.
8. **Hydralazine and Isosorbide Dinitrate:** This combination of drugs is used in certain cases to relax blood vessels and reduce the workload on the heart.
9. **Sodium-Glucose Cotransporter 2 (SGLT2) Inhibitors:** Medications like empagliflozin and dapagliflozin, originally designed for diabetes management, have shown benefits in reducing hospitalization and mortality in heart failure patients.
10. **Vasodilators**: These medications, like nitroglycerin, can help relax blood vessels and reduce the workload on the heart.

CLASSIFICATION OF DRUGS USED IN CONGESTIVE HEART FAILURE

Drugs used in the management of congestive heart failure (CHF) can be classified into several categories based on their mechanisms of action and therapeutic goals. Here are some common drug classes used in the treatment of CHF, along with examples of specific medications within each class:

1. **Diuretics:**
    a. These drugs help reduce fluid retention, which is common in CHF. They decrease the workload on the heart by promoting the excretion of excess salt and water.
    b. **Example:** Furosemide (Lasix), Hydrochlorothiazide (HCTZ).
2. **Angiotensin-Converting Enzyme Inhibitors (ACE Inhibitors):**

a. These drugs dilate blood vessels and reduce the strain on the heart. They also help reduce the levels of certain hormones that can worsen heart failure.

b. **Example:** Enalapril (Vasotec), Lisinopril (Prinivil, Zestril).

3. **Angiotensin II Receptor Blockers (ARBs):**
    a. ARBs work similarly to ACE inhibitors by blocking the effects of angiotensin II, a hormone that constricts blood vessels.
    b. **Example:** Losartan (Cozaar), Valsartan (Diovan).
4. **Beta-Blockers:**
    a. These drugs reduce the heart rate and decrease the force of contraction, which can be beneficial in CHF to improve the heart's efficiency.
    b. **Example:** Carvedilol (Coreg), Metoprolol (Toprol-XL).
5. **Aldosterone Antagonists:**
    a. These drugs block the effects of aldosterone, a hormone that can contribute to fluid retention and cardiac remodeling in CHF.
    b. **Example:** Spironolactone (Aldactone), Eplerenone (Inspra).
6. **Digoxin:**
    a. This medication increases the strength of the heart's contractions and helps control the heart rate. It is used less frequently today than in the past.
    b. **Example:** Digoxin (Lanoxin).
7. **Hydralazine and Isosorbide Dinitrate:**
    a. This combination can help reduce the workload on the heart and dilate blood vessels.
    b. **Example:** Hydralazine/Isosorbide dinitrate (BiDil).
8. **Inotropes:**

a. These drugs can increase the strength of heart contractions. They are reserved for severe cases of heart failure not responding to other therapies.

b. **Example:** Dobutamine, Milrinone.

9. **Sodium-Glucose Cotransporter-2 (SGLT2) Inhibitors:**

a. These relatively newer medications have shown benefit in heart failure by reducing hospitalizations and improving symptoms.

b. **Example:** Empagliflozin (Jardiance), Dapagliflozin (Farxiga).

Furosemide (Lasix):

1. **Mechanism of Action:**

a. Furosemide is a loop diuretic that acts on the thick ascending limb of the loop of Henle in the nephron of the kidney.

b. It inhibits the reabsorption of sodium and chloride ions, leading to increased excretion of these electrolytes in urine.

c. Furosemide's action results in a significant diuretic effect and also causes the excretion of water, leading to decreased blood volume and reduced fluid retention.

2. **Pharmacokinetics:**

a. Furosemide is typically administered orally, intravenously (IV), or intramuscularly (IM).

b. It has a rapid onset of action when given intravenously, making it useful in acute situations.

c. The duration of action is relatively short, requiring multiple daily dosing in most cases.

d. Furosemide is metabolized in the liver but primarily excreted unchanged in the urine.

3. **Clinical Uses:**

a. Furosemide is used to treat conditions characterized by excessive fluid retention, such as congestive heart failure, edema, and hypertension.

b. It is often used to manage acute pulmonary edema and in chronic heart failure to alleviate symptoms related to fluid overload.

Hydrochlorothiazide (HCTZ):

1. **Mechanism of Action:**
    a. Hydrochlorothiazide is a thiazide diuretic that acts on the distal convoluted tubules in the nephron.
    b. It inhibits the reabsorption of sodium and chloride ions, leading to increased excretion of these electrolytes in urine.
    c. Unlike loop diuretics, thiazides have a milder diuretic effect and are less effective at promoting water loss.
2. **Pharmacokinetics:**
    a. Hydrochlorothiazide is typically administered orally.
    b. It has a slower onset of action compared to loop diuretics.
    c. The duration of action is longer, allowing for once-daily dosing in most cases.
    d. Hydrochlorothiazide is excreted primarily in the urine.
3. **Clinical Uses:**
    a. Hydrochlorothiazide is used to treat hypertension and edema associated with various conditions, such as congestive heart failure, kidney disorders, and liver disease.
    b. It is often used as a first-line treatment for essential hypertension and is generally well-tolerated.

Enalapril (Vasotec):

1. **Mechanism of Action:**
    a. Enalapril is an ACE inhibitor that acts on the renin-angiotensin-aldosterone system (RAAS). It inhibits the conversion of angiotensin I to angiotensin II, a potent vasoconstrictor.

b. By blocking the formation of angiotensin II, Enalapril leads to vasodilation (relaxation of blood vessels) and reduces aldosterone secretion, ultimately decreasing blood pressure.

2. **Pharmacokinetics:**
   a. Enalapril is typically administered orally in its prodrug form and is converted to its active metabolite, enalaprilat, in the liver.
   b. The onset of action is within one hour, and the duration of action allows for once-daily dosing.
   c. Enalaprilat is primarily eliminated by the kidneys.
3. **Clinical Uses:**
   a. Enalapril is used to treat hypertension, congestive heart failure, and to improve survival following myocardial infarction (heart attack).
   b. It is also used in patients with left ventricular dysfunction and a reduced ejection fraction to reduce the risk of heart failure symptoms and hospitalization.

Lisinopril:

1. **Mechanism of Action:**
   a. Lisinopril is another ACE inhibitor that works by blocking the conversion of angiotensin I to angiotensin II.
   b. Similar to Enalapril, Lisinopril reduces vasoconstriction, lowers blood pressure, and decreases aldosterone secretion.
2. **Pharmacokinetics:**
   a. Lisinopril is administered orally.
   b. It has a longer duration of action than Enalapril, allowing for once-daily dosing.
   c. Lisinopril is primarily eliminated by the kidneys.
3. **Clinical Uses:**
   a. Lisinopril is used for the treatment of hypertension, heart failure, and post-myocardial infarction.

b. It is also prescribed for diabetic nephropathy (kidney disease) in patients with diabetes.

Losartan (Cozaar):

1. **Mechanism of Action:**
    a. Losartan is an angiotensin II receptor blocker that selectively blocks the action of angiotensin II on its receptors.
    b. By blocking angiotensin II, Losartan dilates blood vessels, reduces aldosterone secretion, and lowers blood pressure.
    c. It is particularly selective for the AT1 subtype of angiotensin II receptors.
2. **Pharmacokinetics:**
    a. Losartan is orally administered and is metabolized in the liver to its active metabolite, E-3174.
    b. The active metabolite has a longer half-life and contributes to the drug's antihypertensive effects.
    c. Losartan and its metabolites are primarily excreted in the urine and feces.
3. **Clinical Uses:**
    a. Losartan is used to treat hypertension and may also be prescribed for patients with type 2 diabetes to reduce the risk of diabetic nephropathy (kidney disease).
    b. It can also be used for heart failure, although ACE inhibitors are often preferred in heart failure treatment.

Valsartan (Diovan):

1. **Mechanism of Action:**
    a. Valsartan is also an angiotensin II receptor blocker that selectively blocks angiotensin II receptors, primarily the AT1 subtype.

b. It has a similar mechanism of action to Losartan, leading to vasodilation, reduced aldosterone secretion, and lowered blood pressure.

2. **Pharmacokinetics:**
    a. Valsartan is administered orally and is rapidly absorbed from the gastrointestinal tract.
    b. Its elimination half-life is relatively short, which allows for twice-daily dosing.
    c. Valsartan is primarily excreted in the feces and urine.
3. **Clinical Uses:**
    a. Valsartan is used to treat hypertension and can be part of combination therapy with other antihypertensive drugs.
    b. It may also be used in heart failure treatment, especially when ACE inhibitors are not well-tolerated by the patient.

Carvedilol (Coreg):

1. **Mechanism of Action:**
    a. Carvedilol is a non-selective beta-blocker. It blocks beta-1 and beta-2 adrenergic receptors and also has alpha-1 adrenergic blocking activity.
    b. By blocking beta-1 receptors, it reduces heart rate and contractility, decreasing the workload of the heart.
    c. By blocking beta-2 receptors, it dilates blood vessels, lowering blood pressure.
    d. The alpha-1 blocking activity leads to vasodilation and reduces peripheral resistance.
2. **Pharmacokinetics:**
    a. Carvedilol is typically administered orally.
    b. It undergoes extensive metabolism in the liver, primarily by the CYP2D6 enzyme, into active metabolites.

c. The elimination half-life of Carvedilol is relatively short, requiring multiple daily dosing.

3. **Clinical Uses:**

   a. Carvedilol is used for various cardiovascular conditions, including hypertension, congestive heart failure, and post-myocardial infarction (post-heart attack) management.

   b. It is also used to reduce the risk of hospitalization and death in patients with chronic heart failure.

Metoprolol (Toprol-XL):

1. **Mechanism of Action:**

   a. Metoprolol is a selective beta-1 adrenergic receptor blocker, meaning it primarily affects the beta-1 receptors in the heart.

   b. By blocking beta-1 receptors, Metoprolol reduces heart rate, contractility, and cardiac output, which can lower blood pressure and reduce the heart's workload.

2. **Pharmacokinetics:**

   a. Metoprolol is available in both immediate-release (Metoprolol tartrate) and extended-release (Metoprolol succinate, e.g., Toprol-XL) formulations.

   b. The extended-release form allows for once-daily dosing and provides more stable blood levels.

   c. Metoprolol is mainly metabolized in the liver, and its elimination half-life varies depending on the specific formulation.

3. **Clinical Uses:**

   a. Metoprolol is used to treat hypertension, angina (chest pain), and to manage certain arrhythmias (irregular heart rhythms).

   b. It is also prescribed after a heart attack to improve survival and reduce the risk of recurrent events.

Spironolactone (Aldactone):

1. **Mechanism of Action:**
    a. Spironolactone is a non-selective aldosterone receptor antagonist. It competes with aldosterone, a hormone that promotes sodium reabsorption and potassium excretion in the kidney.
    b. By blocking the effects of aldosterone, Spironolactone promotes the excretion of sodium and water while conserving potassium, leading to diuresis and natriuresis.
2. **Pharmacokinetics:**
    a. Spironolactone is orally administered and is metabolized in the liver to its active metabolite, canrenone.
    b. It has a relatively long duration of action and requires once-daily dosing.
    c. Spironolactone is excreted in the urine.
3. **Clinical Uses:**
    a. Spironolactone is used for various conditions, including the management of hypertension, edema (fluid retention), and heart failure.
    b. It is particularly effective in heart failure, as it helps reduce fluid overload, improve symptoms, and decrease the risk of hospitalization and mortality.
    c. Spironolactone can also be used to treat primary aldosteronism (a condition where the adrenal glands produce too much aldosterone).

Eplerenone (Inspra):

1. **Mechanism of Action:**
    a. Eplerenone is a selective aldosterone receptor antagonist. It primarily blocks the effects of aldosterone on the mineralocorticoid receptor, especially in the kidneys.

b. By selectively inhibiting aldosterone receptors, Eplerenone promotes sodium and water excretion while conserving potassium, similar to Spironolactone.

2. **Pharmacokinetics:**
   a. Eplerenone is orally administered and has a shorter duration of action compared to Spironolactone.
   b. It is mainly metabolized in the liver, and its elimination half-life allows for once- or twice-daily dosing.
   c. Eplerenone is excreted in the urine.
3. **Clinical Uses:**
   a. Eplerenone is used primarily for the management of hypertension.
   b. It is also employed in the treatment of heart failure after a myocardial infarction (heart attack) to reduce the risk of cardiovascular events and improve outcomes.

Digoxin:

1. **Mechanism of Action:**
   a. Digoxin is a cardiac glycoside. Its primary mechanism of action is to inhibit the sodium-potassium pump (Na+/K+ ATPase) in cardiac myocytes.
   b. Inhibition of the sodium-potassium pump leads to an increase in intracellular sodium, which, in turn, affects calcium handling within the cell.
   c. The net result is an increase in intracellular calcium levels, which enhances myocardial contractility.
   d. Digoxin also has effects on the electrical conduction system of the heart, slowing down the heart rate and potentially controlling certain arrhythmias.
2. **Pharmacokinetics:**
   a. Digoxin is typically administered orally.

b. It has a relatively long half-life, which allows for once-daily dosing.
c. It is primarily eliminated by the kidneys.

3. **Clinical Uses:**
    a. Digoxin is used in the treatment of congestive heart failure, particularly to improve symptoms and reduce hospitalizations.
    b. It may also be used in the management of certain atrial arrhythmias, such as atrial fibrillation and atrial flutter.
    c. Monitoring of blood levels (serum digoxin concentrations) is crucial, as Digoxin has a narrow therapeutic window, and toxicity can occur if levels become too high.

Hydralazine/Isosorbide Dinitrate (BiDil):

1. **Mechanism of Action:**
    a. Hydralazine is a direct-acting vasodilator that primarily relaxes arterioles, reducing peripheral vascular resistance.
    b. Isosorbide dinitrate is a nitrate that primarily dilates veins, reducing preload on the heart.
    c. The combination of these two drugs reduces the workload on the heart and improves blood flow, especially in the coronary arteries.
2. **Pharmacokinetics:**
    a. Hydralazine/Isosorbide dinitrate is available in a fixed-dose combination tablet.
    b. The pharmacokinetics of each component differs, but they are usually administered orally.
3. **Clinical Uses:**
    a. The combination of Hydralazine and Isosorbide dinitrate is used to treat heart failure in African American patients and other populations with reduced ejection fraction who are already on standard heart failure therapies (like ACE inhibitors and beta-blockers).

b. This combination is particularly beneficial in improving exercise tolerance, reducing symptoms, and reducing the risk of hospitalization in heart failure patients.

Dobutamine:

1. **Mechanism of Action:**
    a. Dobutamine is a synthetic catecholamine that primarily acts as a beta-1 adrenergic receptor agonist.
    b. It increases the strength of cardiac contractions and improves cardiac output by increasing myocardial contractility.
    c. Dobutamine also has some beta-2 receptor activity, leading to peripheral vasodilation.
2. **Pharmacokinetics:**
    a. Dobutamine is typically administered intravenously (IV).
    b. It has a rapid onset of action, making it suitable for acute situations.
    c. Dobutamine is metabolized in the liver and excreted in the urine.
3. **Clinical Uses:**
    a. Dobutamine is used in acute settings, such as the management of acute decompensated heart failure and during stress testing to evaluate heart function.
    b. It can also be used in patients with severe heart failure to improve cardiac output and symptoms while awaiting further interventions.

Milrinone:

1. **Mechanism of Action:**
    a. Milrinone is a phosphodiesterase III inhibitor that primarily works by increasing cyclic adenosine monophosphate (cAMP) levels in cardiac and smooth muscle cells.
    b. Elevated cAMP levels result in increased contractility of the heart muscle and peripheral vasodilation.

c. Milrinone has both inotropic (increasing contractility) and vasodilatory effects.

2. **Pharmacokinetics:**
    a. Milrinone is administered intravenously (IV).
    b. It has a rapid onset of action and a relatively short duration of action.
    c. Milrinone is primarily eliminated by the liver.
3. **Clinical Uses:**
    a. Milrinone is used in the treatment of acute decompensated heart failure when a positive inotropic effect is needed.
    b. It may also be considered in patients who do not respond to dobutamine or other conventional heart failure therapies.
    c. Milrinone is not typically used as a long-term therapy due to potential side effects.

Empagliflozin (Jardiance):

1. **Mechanism of Action:**
    a. Empagliflozin inhibits the sodium-glucose co-transporter 2 (SGLT2) in the renal tubules of the kidney.
    b. SGLT2 is responsible for reabsorbing glucose from the renal tubules back into the bloodstream. By inhibiting this transporter, Empagliflozin reduces the reabsorption of glucose, leading to increased glucose excretion in the urine.
    c. This mechanism helps lower blood glucose levels in individuals with type 2 diabetes.
2. **Pharmacokinetics:**
    a. Empagliflozin is typically administered orally.
    b. It is well-absorbed in the gastrointestinal tract and reaches peak plasma concentrations within 1.5 to 2 hours.
    c. The drug is metabolized in the liver, primarily through glucuronidation, and is eliminated primarily through the urine.

3. **Clinical Uses:**
    a. Empagliflozin is used to improve glycemic control in adults with type 2 diabetes, either as monotherapy or in combination with other antidiabetic medications.
    b. It has also demonstrated cardiovascular benefits by reducing the risk of cardiovascular events in patients with type 2 diabetes and established cardiovascular disease.

Dapagliflozin (Farxiga):

1. **Mechanism of Action:**
    a. Dapagliflozin, like Empagliflozin, inhibits the SGLT2 transporter in the renal tubules.
    b. By blocking SGLT2, Dapagliflozin increases the excretion of glucose in the urine, thus lowering blood glucose levels in individuals with type 2 diabetes.
2. **Pharmacokinetics**:
    a. Dapagliflozin is typically administered orally.
    b. It is rapidly absorbed after oral administration and reaches peak plasma concentrations within 2 hours.
    c. Dapagliflozin undergoes minimal hepatic metabolism and is mainly excreted unchanged in the urine.
3. **Clinical Uses:**
    a. Dapagliflozin is indicated for the treatment of type 2 diabetes to improve glycemic control.
    b. Like Empagliflozin, it has shown cardiovascular benefits, reducing the risk of major adverse cardiovascular events in certain patients with type 2 diabetes and established cardiovascular disease.

CHAPTER – 2

ANTIHYPERTENSIVE DRUGS

Mr. Prabhakar Singh Tiwari

Associate Professor, Rajiv Gandhi Institute of Pharmacy, Faculty of Pharmaceutical Science & Technology, AKS University Satna, (M.P.)

ABSTRACT:

Antihypertensive drugs are a diverse group of medications used to treat hyper tension, a condition characterized by persistently high blood pressure. Hypertension is a major risk factor for cardiovascular diseases, including stroke, heart attack, and heart failure, making effective management crucial for reducing morbidity and mortality. The pharmacological treatment of hypertension involves various classes of drugs, each targeting different mechanisms to lower blood pressure. Diuretics, such as thiazides, help reduce blood volume by promoting the excretion of sodium and water, thereby lowering blood pressure. Angiotensin-converting enzyme (ACE) inhibitors, like enalapril and lisinopril, inhibit the production of angiotensin II, a potent vasoconstrictor, leading to vasodilation and reduced blood pressure. Angiotensin II receptor blockers (ARBs), such as losartan and valsartan, block the effects of angiotensin II at its receptor, providing similar benefits to ACE inhibitors without some of the associated side effects. Calcium channel blockers, including amlodipine and diltiazem, relax blood vessels by inhibiting the influx of calcium into vascular smooth muscle cells. Beta-blockers, such as metoprolol and atenolol, reduce heart rate and the force of contraction, decreasing the cardiac output and subsequently lowering blood pressure. Additionally, aldosterone antagonists like spironolactone help reduce blood pressure by blocking the effects of aldosterone, a hormone that promotes sodium and water retention. Direct vasodilators, such as hydralazine, directly relax the smooth muscles of blood vessels, leading to decreased resistance and lower blood pressure. Alpha-blockers, including prazosin, inhibit the action of norepinephrine on alpha receptors, causing vasodilation. Central alpha agonists, like clonidine, work within the central nervous system to reduce sympathetic outflow, thereby lowering blood pressure. The choice of antihypertensive therapy is tailored to individual patient needs, considering factors such as age, comorbidities, and the presence of other cardiovascular risk factors. Effective blood pressure control often requires a combination of these medications to achieve optimal results. Regular monitoring and lifestyle modifications, including diet and exercise, complement pharmacological treatment in managing hypertension. By addressing the various underlying mechanisms contributing to high blood pressure, antihypertensive drugs play a crucial role in preventing the complications associated with hypertension and improving overall cardiovascular health.

Introduction:

Antihypertensives are medications used to manage high blood pressure (hypertension), a major risk factor for cardiovascular diseases, including stroke, myocardial infarction, and heart failure. They work through various mechanisms to lower blood pressure by affecting cardiac output, systemic vascular resistance, or both. Here's a detailed look at antihypertensives:

1. Classes of Antihypertensive Drugs:

a. Diuretics

Diuretics help reduce blood pressure by decreasing blood volume through increased excretion of sodium and water.

1. **Thiazide Diuretics:**
    i. **Examples:** Hydrochlorothiazide, Chlorthalidone, Indapamide.
    ii. **Mechanism of Action:** Inhibit the reabsorption of sodium and chloride in the distal convoluted tubule of the nephron, leading to increased excretion of these electrolytes and water.

iii. **Use:** First-line treatment for hypertension, often combined with other antihypertensives. Also used for heart failure and edema.
iv. **Adverse Effects:** Hypokalemia, hyponatremia, hyperuricemia (risk of gout), and hyperglycemia.

2. **Loop Diuretics:**
   i. **Examples:** Furosemide, Bumetanide, Torsemide.
   ii. **Mechanism of Action:** Inhibit the Na-K-2Cl cotransporter in the ascending limb of the loop of Henle, leading to potent diuresis and reduced blood volume.
   iii. **Use:** Used for severe hypertension, heart failure, and renal impairment.
   iv. **Adverse Effects:** Hypokalemia, hypomagnesemia, dehydration, and ototoxicity.
3. **Potassium-Sparing Diuretics:**
   i. **Examples:** Spironolactone, Eplerenone, Amiloride, Triamterene.
   ii. **Mechanism of Action:** Either antagonize aldosterone (e.g., spironolactone) or block sodium channels (e.g., amiloride), leading to reduced potassium excretion.
   iii. **Use:** Often used in combination with other diuretics to prevent hypokalemia. Also used in conditions like heart failure and hyperaldosteronism.
   iv. **Adverse Effects:** Hyperkalemia, gynecomastia (with spironolactone), and metabolic acidosis.

b. Angiotensin-Converting Enzyme (ACE) Inhibitors

ACE inhibitors lower blood pressure by preventing the conversion of angiotensin I to angiotensin II, a potent vasoconstrictor.

1. **Examples:** Enalapril, Lisinopril, Ramipril, Captopril.

2. **Mechanism of Action:** Inhibit the enzyme ACE, leading to decreased levels of angiotensin II and reduced vasoconstriction. Also increase bradykinin levels, which promotes vasodilation.
3. **Use:** First-line treatment for hypertension, heart failure, diabetic nephropathy, and chronic kidney disease.
4. **Adverse Effects:** Cough (due to bradykinin accumulation), angioedema, hyperkalemia, and renal impairment.

c. Angiotensin II Receptor Blockers (ARBs)

ARBs block the action of angiotensin II at its receptors, leading to vasodilation and reduced blood pressure.

1. **Examples:** Losartan, Valsartan, Candesartan, Irbesartan.
2. **Mechanism of Action:** Block the AT1 receptor, which mediates the vasoconstrictor and aldosterone-secreting effects of angiotensin II.
3. **Use:** Alternative to ACE inhibitors, especially in patients who cannot tolerate ACE inhibitors. Used for hypertension, heart failure, and diabetic nephropathy.
4. **Adverse Effects:** Similar to ACE inhibitors but generally less risk of cough and angioedema.

d. Calcium Channel Blockers (CCBs)

CCBs reduce blood pressure by blocking calcium entry into vascular smooth muscle cells and cardiac myocytes.

1. **Examples:** Amlodipine, Nifedipine, Diltiazem, Verapamil.
2. **Mechanism of Action:**
   i. **Dihydropyridines (e.g., Amlodipine, Nifedipine):** Primarily affect vascular smooth muscle, leading to vasodilation and reduced blood pressure.
   ii. **Non-Dihydropyridines (e.g., Diltiazem, Verapamil):** Affect both vascular smooth muscle and the heart, reducing cardiac output and peripheral resistance.

3. **Use:** Used for hypertension, angina, and some arrhythmias. Non-dihydropyridines are also used for certain arrhythmias.
4. **Adverse Effects:** Dihydropyridines can cause peripheral edema, flushing, and dizziness. Non-dihydropyridines can cause bradycardia, heart block, and constipation.

e. Beta-Adrenergic Blockers

Beta-blockers reduce blood pressure by blocking beta-adrenergic receptors, leading to reduced heart rate and cardiac output.

1. **Examples:** Metoprolol, Atenolol, Carvedilol, Propranolol.
2. **Mechanism of Action:**
    i. **Selective Beta-1 Blockers (e.g., Metoprolol, Atenolol):** Primarily block beta-1 receptors in the heart, reducing heart rate and cardiac output.
    ii. **Non-Selective Beta-Blockers (e.g., Propranolol):** Block both beta-1 and beta-2 receptors, affecting the heart and bronchial smooth muscle.
    iii. **Alpha and Beta Blockers (e.g., Carvedilol):** Block both alpha-1 and beta-adrenergic receptors, leading to reduced vascular resistance and cardiac output.
3. **Use:** Used for hypertension, heart failure, angina, and arrhythmias. Also used post-myocardial infarction.
4. **Adverse Effects:** Bradycardia, fatigue, depression, and bronchospasm (with non-selective beta-blockers).

f. Alpha-1 Adrenergic Blockers

Alpha-1 blockers reduce blood pressure by preventing the action of norepinephrine at alpha-1 receptors on vascular smooth muscle, causing vasodilation.

1. **Examples:** Prazosin, Doxazosin, Terazosin.

2. **Mechanism of Action:** Block alpha-1 receptors, leading to relaxation of smooth muscle and vasodilation.
3. **Use:** Used for hypertension and symptoms of benign prostatic hyperplasia (BPH).
4. **Adverse Effects:** Orthostatic hypotension, dizziness, and headache.

g. Central Alpha-2 Agonists

These drugs act on the central nervous system to reduce sympathetic outflow, thereby lowering blood pressure.

1. **Examples:** Clonidine, Methyldopa.
2. **Mechanism of Action:** Stimulate alpha-2 adrenergic receptors in the central nervous system, leading to reduced sympathetic nervous system activity and lower blood pressure.
3. **Use:** Used for hypertension, often as a second-line treatment. Methyldopa is also used in pregnancy-induced hypertension.
4. **Adverse Effects:** Sedation, dry mouth, and rebound hypertension on discontinuation.

h. Direct Vasodilators

Direct vasodilators relax vascular smooth muscle, leading to vasodilation and reduced blood pressure.

1. **Examples:** Hydralazine, Minoxidil.
2. **Mechanism of Action:** Directly relaxes arterial smooth muscle, reducing systemic vascular resistance.
3. **Use:** Used for hypertension, often in combination with other antihypertensives. Minoxidil is also used topically for hair growth.
4. **Adverse Effects:** Reflex tachycardia, fluid retention, and headache. Often used in conjunction with diuretics and beta-blockers to mitigate these effects.

2. Clinical Considerations:

a. **Combination Therapy:** Often, multiple antihypertensive agents are used in combination to achieve better blood pressure control and to minimize adverse effects. For example, combining a diuretic with an ACE inhibitor or an ARB is common.
b. **Patient-Specific Factors:** The choice of antihypertensive medication depends on individual patient characteristics, such as the presence of comorbid conditions (e.g., diabetes, heart failure), age, and potential side effects.
c. **Monitoring:** Regular monitoring of blood pressure and side effects is essential to ensure effective management and to adjust therapy as needed.

CHAPTER – 3

ANTIANGINAL DRUGS

Ms. Neha Goel

Associate Professor, Rajiv Gandhi Institute of Pharmacy, Faculty of Pharmaceutical Science & Technology, AKS University Satna, (M.P.)

ABSTRACT:

Antianginal drugs are a class of medications used to alleviate the symptoms of angina pectoris, a condition characterized by chest pain or discomfort resulting from insufficient oxygen supply to the heart muscle. Angina is often a manifestation of underlying coronary artery disease (CAD), where the coronary arteries become narrowed or blocked, restricting blood flow to the heart. The primary goal of antianginal therapy is to reduce the frequency and severity of angina attacks, improve exercise tolerance, and prevent complications such as heart attacks. Nitrates, such as nitroglycerin, are the cornerstone of antianginal therapy. They work by dilating the coronary arteries and veins, reducing the heart's workload and oxygen demand, and increasing blood flow to the myocardium. Nitrates are available in various forms, including sublingual tablets, sprays, and transdermal patches, providing rapid relief during acute angina episodes and long-term prophylaxis. Beta-blockers, including metoprolol and atenolol, are another key class of antianginal drugs. They reduce heart rate, contractility, and blood pressure, thereby decreasing the oxygen demand of the heart. By improving the balance between oxygen supply and demand, beta-blockers help prevent angina attacks and improve exercise capacity in patients with chronic stable angina. Calcium channel blockers, such as amlodipine and diltiazem, are effective in both stable and variant angina. They inhibit calcium influx into cardiac and smooth muscle cells, leading to vasodilation and reduced myocardial oxygen consumption. Calcium channel blockers are particularly useful in patients who cannot tolerate beta-blockers or have contraindications to their use. Ranolazine, a relatively newer antianginal agent, works by inhibiting late sodium currents in the heart, thus reducing intracellular calcium overload and improving myocardial relaxation. It is often used in combination with other antianginal drugs to enhance symptom control in patients with refractory angina. In addition to pharmacological treatment, lifestyle modifications and risk factor management, such as smoking cessation, weight control, and regular exercise, play a crucial role in the comprehensive management of angina. Antianginal drugs, by improving the oxygen supply-demand balance and relieving myocardial ischemia, significantly enhance the quality of life for patients with angina, reducing the burden of symptoms and preventing adverse cardiovascular events.

Introduction:

Antianginal drugs are used to manage angina pectoris, a condition characterized by chest pain due to insufficient blood flow to the heart muscle. These drugs work through various mechanisms to improve blood flow to the heart, reduce myocardial oxygen demand, or both. Here's a detailed look at antianginal drugs:

1. Classes of Antianginal Drugs:

a. Nitrates and Nitrites

Nitrates and nitrites are vasodilators that primarily affect venous return to the heart, reducing preload and myocardial oxygen demand.

1. **Nitroglycerin:**
   i. **Mechanism of Action:** Nitroglycerin is converted to nitric oxide (NO) in the body, which leads to the relaxation of smooth muscle cells and dilation of veins. This reduces venous return to the heart (preload), decreasing myocardial oxygen demand.
   ii. **Forms:** Sublingual tablets, sprays, transdermal patches, and intravenous infusion.
   iii. **Use:** Acute management of angina attacks, prevention of angina in chronic stable angina, and management of acute coronary syndromes.

iv. **Adverse Effects:** Headache, dizziness, hypotension, and tachycardia.

2. **Isosorbide Mononitrate and Isosorbide Dinitrate:**
   i. **Mechanism of Action:** Similar to nitroglycerin, these drugs release NO, causing vasodilation and reducing preload. They have a longer duration of action compared to nitroglycerin.
   ii. **Forms:** Oral tablets, extended-release formulations.
   iii. **Use:** Prophylactic treatment of angina, particularly in chronic stable angina.
   iv. **Adverse Effects:** Similar to nitroglycerin, including headache, dizziness, and hypotension.
3. **Amyl Nitrite:**
   i. **Mechanism of Action:** Volatile nitrite that releases NO, causing rapid vasodilation. Used mainly in emergency settings.
   ii. **Use:** Acute treatment of angina attacks, particularly in cases of severe angina.
   iii. **Adverse Effects:** Headache, dizziness, and hypotension.

b. Beta-Adrenergic Blockers

Beta-blockers reduce myocardial oxygen demand by decreasing heart rate, contractility, and blood pressure.

1. **Examples:** Metoprolol, Atenolol, Propranolol, Carvedilol.
2. **Mechanism of Action:** Block beta-adrenergic receptors in the heart, reducing heart rate and contractility, which lowers myocardial oxygen demand and workload.
3. **Use:** Chronic management of angina, especially in patients with stable angina or after a myocardial infarction. They are also used in heart failure and hypertension.
4. **Adverse Effects:** Bradycardia, fatigue, depression, and bronchospasm (particularly with non-selective beta-blockers).

c. Calcium Channel Blockers (CCBs)

CCBs reduce myocardial oxygen demand and improve oxygen supply by dilating coronary arteries and reducing cardiac contractility.

1. **Dihydropyridines:**
   i. **Examples:** Amlodipine, Nifedipine, Felodipine.
   ii. **Mechanism of Action:** Primarily affect vascular smooth muscle, leading to arterial dilation and reduced systemic vascular resistance. This decreases myocardial oxygen demand by reducing afterload.
   iii. **Use:** Used for chronic angina and hypertension.
   iv. **Adverse Effects:** Peripheral edema, flushing, dizziness, and headache.
2. **Non-Dihydropyridines:**
   i. **Examples:** Diltiazem, Verapamil.
   ii. **Mechanism of Action:** Affect both vascular smooth muscle and cardiac muscle. They reduce heart rate and contractility, which decreases myocardial oxygen demand, and also dilate coronary arteries.
   iii. **Use:** Effective for both angina and certain arrhythmias. Useful in chronic stable angina and for rate control in atrial fibrillation.
   iv. **Adverse Effects:** Bradycardia, heart block, and constipation.

d. Sodium Channel Blockers

Sodium channel blockers like Ranolazine help reduce angina by affecting cardiac muscle cells' ion channels and altering metabolism.

1. **Ranolazine:**
   i. **Mechanism of Action:** Modulates sodium channels in cardiac myocytes, reducing late sodium current and myocardial calcium overload. This leads to improved cardiac efficiency and reduced

anginal symptoms. It does not significantly affect heart rate or blood pressure.

ii. **Use:** Used for chronic stable angina, often in combination with other antianginal agents.

iii. **Adverse Effects:** Dizziness, headache, constipation, and nausea. Can also affect QT interval on ECG.

2. Clinical Considerations:

a. **Combination Therapy:** Antianginal drugs are often used in combination to achieve better control of angina symptoms. For example, nitrates can be combined with beta-blockers or CCBs to enhance therapeutic effects and manage different aspects of angina.

b. **Patient-Specific Factors:** The choice of antianginal medication depends on individual patient factors, including the type of angina (stable vs. unstable), comorbid conditions, and potential drug interactions.

c. **Tolerance:** Chronic use of nitrates can lead to the development of tolerance, reducing their effectiveness over time. To mitigate this, nitrate-free intervals are often recommended.

3. Monitoring and Management:

a. **Effectiveness:** Regular monitoring of angina frequency, severity, and duration is essential to evaluate treatment efficacy. Adjustments to therapy may be needed based on patient response.

b. **Side Effects:** Monitoring for and managing side effects is important to ensure patient safety and adherence to therapy. Adjusting doses or switching medications may be necessary if adverse effects are significant.

CHAPTER – 4

ANTI – ARRHYTHMIC DRUGS

Mr. Satyendra Garg

Assistant Professor, Rajiv Gandhi Institute of Pharmacy, Faculty of Pharmaceutical Science & Technology, AKS University Satna, (M.P.)

ABSTRACT:

Anti-hyperlipidemic drugs are medications designed to lower lipid levels in the blood, particularly cholesterol and triglycerides, to reduce the risk of cardiovascular diseases such as heart attack, stroke, and atherosclerosis. These drugs work through various mechanisms to reduce the production of lipids, enhance their removal, or inhibit their absorption from the digestive tract. Statins, such as atorvastatin and simvastatin, are the most commonly prescribed anti-hyperlipidemic drugs. They inhibit HMG-CoA reductase, an enzyme involved in cholesterol synthesis in the liver, effectively lowering LDL cholesterol levels. Other classes include fibrates like gemfibrozil and fenofibrate, which primarily reduce triglyceride levels and can increase HDL cholesterol. Bile acid sequestrants, such as cholestyramine and colesevelam, bind bile acids in the intestines, preventing their reabsorption and prompting the liver to use more cholesterol to produce bile acids, thereby reducing blood cholesterol levels. Ezetimibe, a cholesterol absorption inhibitor, blocks the absorption of cholesterol from the small intestine, complementing the action of statins. PCSK9 inhibitors, including evolocumab and alirocumab, are newer agents that enhance the liver's ability to remove LDL cholesterol from the blood. Niacin, also known as vitamin B3, can reduce LDL cholesterol and triglycerides while raising HDL cholesterol. The choice of anti-hyperlipidemic therapy depends on the patient's lipid profile, risk factors, and tolerance to medications. By effectively managing blood lipid levels, anti-hyperlipidemic drugs play a crucial role in preventing cardiovascular events and promoting overall heart health.

Introduction:

Antiarrhythmic drugs are used to manage abnormal heart rhythms, or arrhythmias, which can range from benign to life-threatening. These drugs work by modifying the electrical activity of the heart, affecting ion channels, and altering conduction pathways. Antiarrhythmics are categorized based on their mechanisms of action and effects on the cardiac action potential. Here's a detailed look at antiarrhythmic drugs:

1. Classifications of Antiarrhythmic Drugs:

a. Class I: Sodium Channel Blockers

Class I antiarrhythmics are divided into three subclasses based on their effects on sodium channel blockade and action potential duration:

1. **Class IA: Intermediate-acting Sodium Channel Blockers**
    i. **Examples:** Quinidine, Procainamide, Disopyramide.
    ii. **Mechanism of Action:** Block sodium channels in the open and inactivated states, which slows conduction velocity and prolongs the action potential duration. They also have varying effects on the repolarization phase of the action potential.
    iii. **Use:** Used for atrial fibrillation, atrial flutter, and ventricular arrhythmias.
    iv. **Adverse Effects:** QT prolongation (risk of torsades de pointes), anticholinergic effects (disopyramide), and gastrointestinal symptoms (quinidine).
2. **Class IB: Fast-acting Sodium Channel Blockers**
    i. **Examples:** Lidocaine, Mexiletine, Tocainide.
    ii. **Mechanism of Action:** Block sodium channels primarily in the inactivated state, leading to a reduction in conduction velocity with minimal effect on action potential duration. They preferentially affect ischemic or depolarized tissues.

iii. **Use:** Mainly used for ventricular arrhythmias, particularly during acute myocardial infarction. Lidocaine is also used for post-myocardial infarction arrhythmias.

iv. **Adverse Effects:** CNS effects such as tremors, seizures, and dizziness. Minimal cardiac toxicity compared to Class IA.

3. **Class IC: Slow-acting Sodium Channel Blockers**

   i. **Examples:** Flecainide, Propafenone, Lorcainide.

   ii. **Mechanism of Action:** Strongly block sodium channels, significantly slowing conduction velocity and having minimal effect on action potential duration. They are potent inhibitors of conduction.

   iii. **Use:** Used for atrial fibrillation, atrial flutter, and certain ventricular arrhythmias.

   iv. **Adverse Effects:** Risk of exacerbating arrhythmias, especially in patients with structural heart disease. Can also cause dizziness, blurred vision, and gastrointestinal disturbances.

b. Class II: Beta-Adrenergic Blockers

1. **Examples:** Metoprolol, Atenolol, Propranolol, Esmolol.
2. **Mechanism of Action:** Block beta-adrenergic receptors, reducing the effects of sympathetic stimulation on the heart. This decreases heart rate, conduction velocity through the AV node, and myocardial contractility.
3. **Use:** Effective for controlling ventricular rate in atrial fibrillation and atrial flutter, preventing ventricular arrhythmias, and managing tachycardias.
4. **Adverse Effects:** Bradycardia, fatigue, depression, and bronchospasm (with non-selective beta-blockers).

c. Class III: Potassium Channel Blockers

Class III antiarrhythmics primarily prolong the action potential duration and refractory period by blocking potassium channels responsible for repolarization.

1. **Examples:** Sotalol, Dofetilide, Dronedarone, Amiodarone.
2. **Mechanism of Action:** Block various potassium channels involved in repolarization, leading to prolongation of the action potential duration and refractory period. Sotalol and Dofetilide specifically block the rapid component of the delayed rectifier potassium current (IKr).
3. **Use:** Used for atrial fibrillation, atrial flutter, and ventricular arrhythmias. Amiodarone is also used for life-threatening arrhythmias and in various types of arrhythmias.
4. **Adverse Effects:**
    i. **Sotalol:** QT prolongation, risk of torsades de pointes, and renal impairment.
    ii. **Dofetilide:** QT prolongation and risk of torsades de pointes.
    iii. **Amiodarone:** Pulmonary toxicity, thyroid dysfunction, hepatic toxicity, skin discoloration, and corneal deposits.

d. Class IV: Calcium Channel Blockers

1. **Examples:** Verapamil, Diltiazem.
2. **Mechanism of Action:** Block L-type calcium channels, primarily affecting the conduction through the AV node and the rate of depolarization. This reduces the heart rate and slows conduction in the AV node.
3. **Use:** Effective for controlling ventricular rate in atrial fibrillation and atrial flutter, and for certain supraventricular tachycardias.
4. **Adverse Effects:** Bradycardia, hypotension, heart block, and gastrointestinal disturbances.

e. Other Antiarrhythmics

1. **Adenosine:**
    i. **Mechanism of Action:** Activates adenosine receptors, leading to a decrease in cAMP levels, which slows AV node conduction and can terminate certain types of supraventricular tachycardias.

ii. **Use:** Used acutely to convert paroxysmal supraventricular tachycardia (PSVT) to normal sinus rhythm.

iii. **Adverse Effects:** Transient flushing, chest pain, and dyspnea.

2. **Digoxin:**

i. **Mechanism of Action:** Inhibits the Na+/K+ ATPase pump, increasing intracellular calcium and enhancing vagal tone. This slows conduction through the AV node and increases the refractory period.

ii. **Use:** Used for rate control in atrial fibrillation and atrial flutter, and for heart failure with reduced ejection fraction.

iii. **Adverse Effects:** Nausea, vomiting, visual disturbances (yellow-green halos), and potential for digitalis toxicity.

2. Clinical Considerations

a. **Indications:** The choice of antiarrhythmic medication depends on the type of arrhythmia, patient comorbidities, and specific characteristics of the arrhythmia.

b. **Monitoring:** Antiarrhythmic drugs often require close monitoring for efficacy and side effects. This includes ECG monitoring for QT prolongation and arrhythmias, as well as routine laboratory tests for drug levels and organ function.

c. **Drug Interactions:** Many antiarrhythmics have significant interactions with other drugs and can affect or be affected by changes in liver function and renal function.

Heart Failure Medications:

Heart failure (HF) is a complex clinical syndrome where the heart is unable to pump sufficient blood to meet the body's needs. The treatment of heart failure involves a combination of lifestyle changes, medical therapies, and sometimes surgical interventions. Medications play a crucial role in managing heart failure by improving symptoms, reducing hospitalizations, and extending survival.

Here's a detailed look at the main classes of medications used in the management of heart failure:

1. Diuretics:

Diuretics help reduce fluid overload by promoting diuresis (increased urine production), which helps alleviate symptoms of congestion and edema.

a. **Loop Diuretics:**

   i. **Examples:** Furosemide, Bumetanide, Torsemide.

   ii. **Mechanism of Action:** Inhibit the $Na^+/K^+/2Cl^-$ cotransporter in the thick ascending limb of the loop of Henle, leading to increased excretion of sodium, potassium, and chloride.

   iii. **Use:** Effective for acute and chronic management of fluid overload in heart failure, particularly when edema is present.

   iv. **Adverse Effects:** Electrolyte imbalances (hypokalemia, hypomagnesemia), dehydration, hypotension, and renal dysfunction.

b. **Thiazide Diuretics:**

   i. **Examples:** Hydrochlorothiazide, Chlorthalidone.

   ii. **Mechanism of Action:** Inhibit the Na^+/Cl^- symporter in the distal convoluted tubule, leading to increased excretion of sodium and chloride.

   iii. **Use:** Often used in combination with loop diuretics for added diuretic effect or in cases where loop diuretics alone are not sufficient.

   iv. **Adverse Effects:** Electrolyte imbalances (hypokalemia, hyponatremia), hyperglycemia, and hyperuricemia.

c. **Potassium-Sparing Diuretics:**

   i. **Examples:** Spironolactone, Eplerenone, Amiloride, Triamterene.

ii. **Mechanism of Action:** Inhibit aldosterone or act as sodium channel blockers in the distal nephron, reducing potassium excretion while promoting sodium excretion.

iii. **Use:** Used to counteract hypokalemia caused by other diuretics and in the treatment of chronic heart failure.

iv. **Adverse Effects:** Hyperkalemia, gynecomastia (spironolactone), and renal dysfunction.

2. ACE Inhibitors

Angiotensin-converting enzyme (ACE) inhibitors are crucial in the management of heart failure by reducing afterload and preventing the progression of heart failure.

a. **Examples:** Enalapril, Lisinopril, Ramipril, Captopril.

b. **Mechanism of Action:** Inhibit the enzyme that converts angiotensin I to angiotensin II, leading to vasodilation, reduced aldosterone secretion, and decreased blood pressure. They also reduce cardiac remodeling and improve symptoms.

c. **Use:** First-line treatment for heart failure with reduced ejection fraction (HFrEF) and for reducing mortality and morbidity.

d. **Adverse Effects:** Cough, hyperkalemia, hypotension, and angioedema. Renal function should be monitored regularly.

3. Angiotensin II Receptor Blockers (ARBs)

ARBs provide similar benefits to ACE inhibitors but are often used when ACE inhibitors are not tolerated.

a. **Examples:** Losartan, Valsartan, Candesartan.

b. **Mechanism of Action:** Block the angiotensin II type 1 receptor, preventing the effects of angiotensin II, including vasoconstriction and aldosterone release.

c. **Use:** Used for heart failure with reduced ejection fraction (HFrEF), particularly in patients who cannot tolerate ACE inhibitors.

d. **Adverse Effects:** Similar to ACE inhibitors but generally less cough. Hyperkalemia and renal dysfunction can still occur.

4. Angiotensin Receptor-Neprilysin Inhibitors (ARNIs)

ARNIs combine an ARB with a neprilysin inhibitor to enhance efficacy in heart failure management.

a. **Example:** Sacubitril/Valsartan (Entresto).

b. **Mechanism of Action:** Sacubitril inhibits neprilysin, an enzyme that breaks down natriuretic peptides, bradykinin, and angiotensin II. Valsartan blocks angiotensin II receptors. This combination improves cardiac function and reduces mortality.

c. **Use:** Used for chronic heart failure with reduced ejection fraction (HFrEF).

d. **Adverse Effects:** Similar to ARBs, with additional risks of angioedema and hypotension. Should not be used with ACE inhibitors due to the risk of angioedema.

5. Beta-Adrenergic Blockers

Beta-blockers are used to reduce the workload on the heart and improve outcomes in heart failure.

a. **Examples:** Metoprolol succinate, Carvedilol, Bisoprolol.

b. **Mechanism of Action:** Block beta-adrenergic receptors, reducing heart rate, myocardial contractility, and cardiac output. They also reduce neurohormonal activation and cardiac remodeling.

c. **Use:** Beneficial in heart failure with reduced ejection fraction (HFrEF) and in improving survival and reducing hospitalizations.

d. **Adverse Effects:** Bradycardia, fatigue, dizziness, and potential worsening of heart failure symptoms initially.

6. Mineralocorticoid Receptor Antagonists (MRAs)

MRAs help manage heart failure by blocking the effects of aldosterone, which can contribute to fluid retention and cardiac remodeling.

a. **Examples:** Spironolactone, Eplerenone.
b. **Mechanism of Action:** Inhibit aldosterone binding to its receptor, reducing sodium and water retention while preserving potassium.
c. **Use:** Used in chronic heart failure with reduced ejection fraction (HFrEF) and in combination with other heart failure therapies.
d. **Adverse Effects:** Hyperkalemia, renal dysfunction, and gynecomastia (spironolactone).

7. Inotropic Agents

Inotropic agents are used to improve cardiac contractility, particularly in acute heart failure or in cases of severe heart failure with reduced ejection fraction.

a. **Examples:** Digoxin, Dobutamine, Milrinone.
   i. **Digoxin:**
      1. **Mechanism of Action:** Inhibits the Na+/K+ ATPase pump, increasing intracellular calcium and improving cardiac contractility. It also has a vagomimetic effect, which slows the heart rate.
      2. **Use:** Used for rate control in atrial fibrillation and to improve symptoms in chronic heart failure.
      3. **Adverse Effects:** Digitalis toxicity, nausea, vomiting, visual disturbances.
   ii. **Dobutamine:**
      1. **Mechanism of Action:** Stimulates beta-1 adrenergic receptors, leading to increased myocardial contractility and cardiac output.
      2. **Use:** Used in acute heart failure and cardiogenic shock.
      3. **Adverse Effects:** Tachycardia, arrhythmias, and potential for increased myocardial oxygen demand.

iii. **Milrinone:**

1. **Mechanism of Action:** Inhibits phosphodiesterase-3, leading to increased cAMP and enhanced myocardial contractility and vasodilation.
2. **Use:** Used in acute heart failure and for short-term management in severe heart failure.
3. **Adverse Effects:** Hypotension, arrhythmias, and thrombocytopenia.

8. Hydralazine and Nitrates

Hydralazine and nitrates are used in combination to manage heart failure, particularly in patients who cannot tolerate ACE inhibitors or ARBs.

a. **Examples:** Hydralazine, Isosorbide Dinitrate.
b. **Mechanism of Action:** Hydralazine causes direct arterial vasodilation, reducing afterload, while nitrates primarily reduce preload by dilating veins.
c. **Use:** Used for heart failure with reduced ejection fraction (HFrEF), particularly in African American patients and those with contraindications to other therapies.
d. **Adverse Effects:** Hydralazine can cause headache, dizziness, and hypotension. Nitrates can cause headache, hypotension, and tolerance with prolonged use.

Clinical Considerations

a. **Personalized Therapy:** Treatment should be tailored to individual patient needs, considering comorbid conditions, the severity of heart failure, and patient response to medications.
b. **Monitoring:** Regular monitoring of renal function, electrolytes, and blood pressure is important, especially when using diuretics, ACE inhibitors, and MRAs.

c. **Adherence:** Ensuring patient adherence to prescribed medications and lifestyle modifications is crucial for effective management of heart failure.

CHAPTER – 5

ANTI – HYPERLIPIDEMIC DRUGS

Mrs. Neelam Singh

Assistant Professor, Rajiv Gandhi Institute of Pharmacy, Faculty of Pharmaceutical Science & Technology, AKS University Satna, (M.P.)

ABSTRACT:

Anti-hyperlipidemic drugs are medications designed to lower lipid levels in the blood, particularly cholesterol and triglycerides, to reduce the risk of cardiovascular diseases such as heart attack, stroke, and atherosclerosis. These drugs work through various mechanisms to reduce the production of lipids, enhance their removal, or inhibit their absorption from the digestive tract. Statins, such as atorvastatin and simvastatin, are the most commonly prescribed anti-hyperlipidemic drugs. They inhibit HMG-CoA reductase, an enzyme involved in cholesterol synthesis in the liver, effectively lowering LDL cholesterol levels. Other classes include fibrates like gemfibrozil and fenofibrate, which primarily reduce triglyceride levels and can increase HDL cholesterol. Bile acid sequestrants, such as cholestyramine and colesevelam, bind bile acids in the intestines, preventing their reabsorption and prompting the liver to use more cholesterol to produce bile acids, thereby reducing blood cholesterol levels. Ezetimibe, a cholesterol absorption inhibitor, blocks the absorption of cholesterol from the small intestine, complementing the action of statins. PCSK9 inhibitors, including evolocumab and alirocumab, are newer agents that enhance the liver's ability to remove LDL cholesterol from the blood. Niacin, also known as vitamin B3, can reduce LDL cholesterol and triglycerides while raising HDL cholesterol. The choice of anti-hyperlipidemic therapy depends on the patient's lipid profile, risk factors, and tolerance to medications. By effectively managing blood lipid levels, anti-hyperlipidemic drugs play a crucial role in preventing cardiovascular events and promoting overall heart health.

Introduction:

Lipid-lowering agents are a critical component in managing cardiovascular disease, particularly in reducing the risk of atherosclerosis and related complications like myocardial infarction and stroke. These medications work by various mechanisms to lower levels of lipids (fats) in the blood, such as cholesterol and triglycerides. Here's a detailed overview of the different classes of lipid-lowering agents:

1. Statins (HMG-CoA Reductase Inhibitors)

Statins are the first-line treatment for lowering low-density lipoprotein cholesterol (LDL-C) and have been shown to reduce cardiovascular events.

a. **Examples:** Atorvastatin, Simvastatin, Rosuvastatin, Pravastatin, Lovastatin.
b. **Mechanism of Action:** Inhibit HMG-CoA reductase, an enzyme crucial in the biosynthesis of cholesterol in the liver. This leads to decreased production of cholesterol and increased uptake of LDL-C from the bloodstream.
c. **Use:** Primarily used to lower LDL-C levels and reduce the risk of cardiovascular events, including heart attack and stroke.
d. **Adverse Effects:** Common side effects include myopathy, rhabdomyolysis, hepatotoxicity, and gastrointestinal disturbances. Rarely, they may cause cognitive impairment or type 2 diabetes.

2. Non-Statin LDL-C Lowering Agents

These agents are used when statins are not sufficient or are contraindicated.

a. **Ezetimibe:**
    i. **Mechanism of Action:** Inhibits the intestinal absorption of cholesterol, leading to reduced LDL-C levels. It acts on the Niemann-Pick C1-like 1 (NPC1L1) transporter in the intestinal brush border.

ii. **Use:** Often used in combination with statins to further reduce LDL-C levels, or as monotherapy in statin-intolerant patients.

iii. **Adverse Effects:** Generally well-tolerated but may include gastrointestinal symptoms and, rarely, liver enzyme elevations.

b. **Bempedoic Acid:**

i. **Mechanism of Action:** Inhibits ATP-citrate lyase, an enzyme involved in cholesterol synthesis upstream of HMG-CoA reductase. This leads to reduced cholesterol levels and increased LDL-C clearance.

ii. **Use:** Used as an adjunct to diet and maximally tolerated statin therapy or alone when statins are not appropriate.

iii. **Adverse Effects:** Potential for muscle-related symptoms, liver enzyme elevation, and gout.

3. PCSK9 Inhibitors

PCSK9 inhibitors are a newer class of drugs that significantly lower LDL-C levels.

a. **Examples:** Alirocumab, Evolocumab.

b. **Mechanism of Action:** Inhibit proprotein convertase subtilisin/kexin type 9 (PCSK9), which increases the availability of LDL receptors on hepatocytes, leading to enhanced clearance of LDL-C from the blood.

c. **Use:** Used in patients with familial hypercholesterolemia, statin intolerance, or in addition to statins when LDL-C goals are not met.

d. **Adverse Effects:** Generally well-tolerated; potential side effects include injection site reactions, flu-like symptoms, and, rarely, neurocognitive effects.

4. Fibrates

Fibrates primarily target triglyceride levels and have modest effects on LDL-C and HDL-C levels.

a. **Examples:** Fenofibrate, Gemfibrozil, Bezafibrate.

b. **Mechanism of Action:** Activate peroxisome proliferator-activated receptor-alpha (PPAR-alpha), leading to increased fatty acid oxidation and reduced triglyceride levels. They also increase HDL-C levels.
c. **Use:** Primarily used for managing high triglyceride levels and in some cases for increasing HDL-C levels.
d. **Adverse Effects:** May include gastrointestinal symptoms, myopathy, rhabdomyolysis (especially when used with statins), and liver enzyme abnormalities.

5. Niacin (Nicotinic Acid)

Niacin, or vitamin B3, has lipid-altering effects and is used less frequently due to side effects.

a. **Mechanism of Action:** Reduces the production of very-low-density lipoprotein (VLDL) in the liver, which leads to a reduction in LDL-C and triglycerides and an increase in HDL-C levels.
b. **Use:** Used to increase HDL-C levels and to lower triglycerides.
c. **Adverse Effects:** Common side effects include flushing, itching, and gastrointestinal discomfort. Long-term use may lead to hepatotoxicity and glucose intolerance.

6. Omega-3 Fatty Acids

Omega-3 fatty acids are used primarily to lower triglyceride levels.

a. **Examples:** Eicosapentaenoic acid (EPA), Docosahexaenoic acid (DHA), and prescription formulations such as EPA (Vascepa).
b. **Mechanism of Action:** Reduce hepatic triglyceride synthesis and increase fatty acid oxidation, leading to lower triglyceride levels.
c. **Use:** Used to manage elevated triglycerides and may have additional cardiovascular benefits.
d. **Adverse Effects:** May include gastrointestinal symptoms such as nausea and diarrhea, and rarely, bleeding complications.

Clinical Considerations

a. **Individualized Therapy:** Choice of lipid-lowering medication depends on the patient's lipid profile, presence of cardiovascular disease, and tolerability of the medication.
b. **Monitoring:** Regular monitoring of lipid levels, liver function tests, and muscle symptoms (with statins) is important to assess efficacy and detect side effects.
c. **Adherence:** Ensuring patient adherence to therapy is crucial for achieving optimal lipid control and reducing cardiovascular risk.

CHAPTER – 6

DRUG USED IN THE THERAPY OF SHOCK

Mr. Abu Tahir

Assistant Professor, Rajiv Gandhi Institute of Pharmacy, Faculty of Pharmaceutical Science & Technology, AKS University Satna, (M.P.)

ABSTRACT:

Drugs used in the therapy of shock are essential for stabilizing patients and improving outcomes in this critical condition, characterized by inadequate blood flow and oxygen delivery to tissues. Various types of shock, including hypovolemic, cardiogenic, distributive, and obstructive shock, require specific pharmacological interventions tailored to their underlying causes. Vasopressors, such as norepinephrine and dopamine, are commonly used to increase vascular tone and elevate blood pressure in patients with distributive shock, like septic shock. These drugs act on alpha-adrenergic receptors to induce vasoconstriction, thereby improving perfusion to vital organs. Inotropes like dobutamine and milrinone are crucial for managing cardiogenic shock, where they enhance cardiac contractility and improve cardiac output. Fluids and blood products are often administered in hypovolemic shock to restore circulating volume and improve tissue perfusion. Corticosteroids, such as hydrocortisone, may be used in septic shock to modulate the inflammatory response and improve vascular responsiveness to vasopressors. Additionally, antibiotics are essential in septic shock to eradicate the underlying infection, while antithrombotic agents may be used in obstructive shock to dissolve clots and restore blood flow. The choice and combination of these drugs depend on the type of shock, the patient's clinical status, and the response to initial treatment. Effective management of shock involves not only pharmacotherapy but also rapid identification and treatment of the underlying cause, along with supportive measures to stabilize the patient and prevent organ failure.

Introduction:

Shock is a life-threatening condition characterized by inadequate blood flow and oxygen delivery to tissues and organs, leading to cellular dysfunction and potential organ failure. It can result from various causes, including severe blood loss, heart failure, infections, and blockages in the blood vessels. The treatment of shock is aimed at restoring adequate perfusion and oxygenation, stabilizing the patient, and addressing the underlying cause. Pharmacological intervention plays a critical role in the management of shock, with different classes of drugs used to achieve these therapeutic goals.

Classification of Drugs Used in the Therapy of Shock

1. **Vasopressors**
2. **Inotropes**
3. **Fluids and Blood Products**
4. **Corticosteroids**
5. **Antibiotics**
6. **Antithrombotic Agents**
7. **Vasodilators**

Classification with Examples and Discussion

1. **Vasopressors**
   - **Examples**: Norepinephrine, Dopamine, Epinephrine, Vasopressin
   - **Mechanism of Action**: Vasopressors increase vascular tone by stimulating alpha-adrenergic receptors, leading to vasoconstriction and an increase in blood pressure. They are essential in treating distributive shock, such as septic shock, where vasodilation and low blood pressure are predominant.
   - **Clinical Use**: Norepinephrine is commonly used as a first-line agent in septic shock, while dopamine and epinephrine may be used in other types of shock or when norepinephrine is insufficient.

2. **Inotropes**
   - **Examples**: Dobutamine, Milrinone, Dopamine
   - **Mechanism of Action**: Inotropes enhance cardiac contractility and increase cardiac output by stimulating beta-adrenergic receptors. They are crucial in managing cardiogenic shock, where the heart's pumping ability is compromised.
   - **Clinical Use**: Dobutamine is often used in acute heart failure and cardiogenic shock to improve myocardial contractility and support cardiac output.
3. **Fluids and Blood Products**
   - **Examples**: Crystalloids (Normal Saline, Lactated Ringer's), Colloids (Albumin), Blood Transfusions
   - **Mechanism of Action**: Fluids increase intravascular volume, improving tissue perfusion and oxygen delivery. Blood products are used to replace lost blood and improve oxygen-carrying capacity.
   - **Clinical Use**: Crystalloids are the first-line treatment for hypovolemic shock, while blood transfusions are necessary for significant blood loss.
4. **Corticosteroids**
   - **Examples**: Hydrocortisone, Prednisone
   - **Mechanism of Action**: Corticosteroids modulate the inflammatory response and enhance vascular responsiveness to vasopressors.
   - **Clinical Use**: Hydrocortisone is used in septic shock, particularly in patients with adrenal insufficiency or those who do not respond adequately to vasopressors alone.
5. **Antibiotics**
   - **Examples**: Broad-spectrum antibiotics (Piperacillin-Tazobactam, Vancomycin)

- **Mechanism of Action**: Antibiotics eliminate the underlying infection causing septic shock.
- **Clinical Use**: Prompt administration of broad-spectrum antibiotics is critical in septic shock to control the source of infection.

6. **Antithrombotic Agents**
   - **Examples**: Heparin, Alteplase
   - **Mechanism of Action**: Antithrombotic agents dissolve clots and prevent further thrombus formation.
   - **Clinical Use**: In obstructive shock caused by conditions like pulmonary embolism, antithrombotic agents are used to restore blood flow.
7. **Vasodilators**
   - **Examples**: Nitroprusside, Nitroglycerin
   - **Mechanism of Action**: Vasodilators reduce afterload and preload by dilating blood vessels, which can be beneficial in certain types of shock.
   - **Clinical Use**: In cardiogenic shock with high systemic vascular resistance, vasodilators may be used to improve cardiac output and reduce myocardial oxygen demand.

Norepinephrine

- **Pharmacological Action**: Vasopressor and cardiac stimulant.
- **Mechanism of Action**: Stimulates alpha-adrenergic receptors causing vasoconstriction and beta-1 adrenergic receptors increasing cardiac contractility and heart rate.
- **Adverse Effects**: Hypertension, arrhythmias, peripheral ischemia, bradycardia, anxiety, headache.
- **Therapeutic Application**: First-line treatment for septic shock, cardiogenic shock, and other distributive shock states to increase blood pressure and perfusion.

Dopamine

- **Pharmacological Action**: Dose-dependent inotrope and vasopressor.
- **Mechanism of Action**: Low doses stimulate dopaminergic receptors causing renal vasodilation; moderate doses stimulate beta-1 adrenergic receptors increasing cardiac contractility; high doses stimulate alpha-adrenergic receptors causing vasoconstriction.
- **Adverse Effects**: Tachycardia, arrhythmias, hypertension, vasoconstriction, nausea, vomiting.
- **Therapeutic Application**: Used in shock states to support blood pressure and cardiac output, especially in cases of cardiogenic and septic shock.

Epinephrine

- **Pharmacological Action**: Potent vasopressor, inotrope, and bronchodilator.
- **Mechanism of Action**: Stimulates alpha, beta-1, and beta-2 adrenergic receptors, causing vasoconstriction, increased cardiac output, and bronchodilation.
- **Adverse Effects**: Tachycardia, arrhythmias, hypertension, anxiety, headache, tremor.
- **Therapeutic Application**: Used in anaphylactic shock, cardiac arrest, and severe asthma attacks; also used as a secondary agent in septic shock.

Vasopressin

- **Pharmacological Action**: Vasoconstrictor and antidiuretic hormone.
- **Mechanism of Action**: Acts on V1 receptors in vascular smooth muscle causing vasoconstriction, and V2 receptors in kidneys promoting water reabsorption.
- **Adverse Effects**: Hypertension, decreased cardiac output, ischemia, water retention, hyponatremia.

- **Therapeutic Application**: Adjunct to catecholamine vasopressors in septic shock to increase blood pressure and reduce catecholamine requirements.

Dobutamine

- **Pharmacological Action**: Inotropic agent.
- **Mechanism of Action**: Stimulates beta-1 adrenergic receptors, increasing cardiac contractility and stroke volume with minimal effects on heart rate and vascular resistance.
- **Adverse Effects**: Tachycardia, arrhythmias, hypertension, headache, nausea.
- **Therapeutic Application**: Used in acute heart failure and cardiogenic shock to improve cardiac output and tissue perfusion.

Milrinone

- **Pharmacological Action**: Inotropic and vasodilator agent.
- **Mechanism of Action**: Inhibits phosphodiesterase-3, increasing cyclic AMP levels leading to enhanced cardiac contractility and vasodilation.
- **Adverse Effects**: Hypotension, arrhythmias, headache, thrombocytopenia.
- **Therapeutic Application**: Used in acute decompensated heart failure and cardiogenic shock to improve cardiac output and reduce vascular resistance.

Hydrocortisone

- **Pharmacological Action**: Anti-inflammatory and immunosuppressive corticosteroid.
- **Mechanism of Action**: Modulates gene expression to reduce production of inflammatory mediators and enhance vascular responsiveness to catecholamines.
- **Adverse Effects**: Hyperglycemia, immunosuppression, hypertension, fluid retention, gastrointestinal bleeding.

- **Therapeutic Application**: Used in septic shock, particularly in patients with adrenal insufficiency or those who do not adequately respond to vasopressors alone.

Prednisone

- **Pharmacological Action**: Anti-inflammatory and immunosuppressive corticosteroid.
- **Mechanism of Action**: Modulates gene expression to reduce production of inflammatory mediators.
- **Adverse Effects**: Hyperglycemia, osteoporosis, hypertension, fluid retention, increased risk of infection.
- **Therapeutic Application**: Used for chronic inflammatory and autoimmune conditions, less commonly in acute shock states.

Nitroprusside

- **Pharmacological Action**: Potent vasodilator.
- **Mechanism of Action**: Releases nitric oxide, causing direct relaxation of vascular smooth muscle and reducing both preload and afterload.
- **Adverse Effects**: Hypotension, cyanide toxicity, headache, dizziness, nausea.
- **Therapeutic Application**: Used in hypertensive emergencies and acute heart failure to rapidly lower blood pressure and decrease cardiac workload.

Nitroglycerin

- **Pharmacological Action**: Vasodilator.
- **Mechanism of Action**: Increases availability of nitric oxide, primarily causing venodilation and reducing myocardial oxygen demand.
- **Adverse Effects**: Headache, hypotension, dizziness, reflex tachycardia.
- **Therapeutic Application**: Used in acute coronary syndromes, angina pectoris, and heart failure to relieve ischemic pain and reduce cardiac workload.

CHAPTER – 7

HEMATINIC

Mr. Ashutosh Jain

Assistant Professor, Rajiv Gandhi Institute of Pharmacy, Faculty of Pharmaceutical Science & Technology, AKS University Satna, (M.P.)

ABSTRACT:

Hematinics are a class of medications and nutrients that are essential for the formation of blood components, particularly hemoglobin, and are used to treat or prevent anemia. Anemia is a condition characterized by a deficiency in the number or quality of red blood cells, which impairs the blood's ability to carry oxygen to the body's tissues. Common causes of anemia include iron deficiency, vitamin B12 deficiency, and folate deficiency. Hematinics work by supplying the necessary raw materials required for red blood cell production and proper hemoglobin function. Iron supplements, such as ferrous sulfate and ferrous gluconate, are the most widely used hematinics for treating iron-deficiency anemia. These supplements replenish iron stores in the body, allowing for the synthesis of hemoglobin. Vitamin B12 supplements, available as cyanocobalamin or hydroxocobalamin, are essential for the treatment of pernicious anemia and other forms of vitamin B12 deficiency. Folate supplements, often given as folic acid, are crucial for DNA synthesis and repair, particularly in rapidly dividing cells like those in the bone marrow. Hematinics can be administered orally or, in cases of severe deficiency or malabsorption, intravenously. They play a critical role in improving symptoms of anemia, such as fatigue, weakness, and pallor, and in preventing complications associated with chronic anemia. Effective use of hematinics requires accurate diagnosis of the underlying cause of anemia and appropriate dosing to avoid potential side effects like gastrointestinal discomfort from iron supplements. By supporting the production of healthy red blood cells, hematinics contribute significantly to overall health and well-being.

Introduction:

Hematinics are substances used to improve the quality and quantity of blood by increasing the hemoglobin content and the number of erythrocytes. They are primarily used to treat different forms of anemia, where there is a deficiency in the production or function of red blood cells. The main types of hematinics include iron supplements, vitamin B12, and folic acid, each addressing specific deficiencies that lead to anemia.

Classification of Hematinics

1. **Iron Supplements**
   - Ferrous sulfate
   - Ferrous gluconate
   - Iron dextran
2. **Vitamin B12 Supplements**
   - Cyanocobalamin
   - Hydroxocobalamin
3. **Folic Acid Supplements**
   - Folic acid
   - Folinic acid (Leucovorin)

1. Iron Supplements

Ferrous Sulfate, Ferrous Gluconate, Iron Dextran

Mechanism of Action: Iron supplements replenish body iron stores, necessary for hemoglobin production and red blood cell formation. They are absorbed in the small intestine and incorporated into hemoglobin in the bone marrow.

Adverse Effects: Gastrointestinal disturbances (nausea, constipation, diarrhea), dark stools, stomach pain, and, with parenteral forms like iron dextran, potential allergic reactions.
Contraindications: Hemochromatosis, hemosiderosis, peptic ulcer disease, inflammatory bowel disease, known hypersensitivity to iron preparations.
Therapeutic Uses: Treatment of iron deficiency anemia due to chronic blood loss, poor dietary intake, or increased demand (e.g., pregnancy).

2. Vitamin B12 Supplements

Cyanocobalamin

Mechanism of Action: Cyanocobalamin is a synthetic form of vitamin B12, essential for DNA synthesis, red blood cell formation, and neurological function. It acts as a coenzyme in the conversion of homocysteine to methionine, which is crucial for methylation reactions, and in the conversion of methylmalonyl-CoA to succinyl-CoA, an important step in energy production from fats and proteins.
Adverse Effects: Cyanocobalamin is generally well-tolerated. Adverse effects are rare but can include allergic reactions such as rash, itching, and anaphylaxis. Other possible side effects include mild diarrhea, headache, and dizziness.
Therapeutic Uses:

- **Treatment of Vitamin B12 Deficiency**: Used in conditions like pernicious anemia, where intrinsic factor deficiency impairs B12 absorption.
- **Megaloblastic Anemia**: Helps correct the anemia caused by B12 deficiency, which leads to improper red blood cell formation.
- **Dietary Deficiency**: Used in individuals with poor dietary intake, such as vegetarians and elderly patients.

- **Neurological Symptoms**: Addresses neurological issues arising from B12 deficiency, such as neuropathy and cognitive disturbances.

Hydroxocobalamin

Mechanism of Action: Hydroxocobalamin is a natural, highly bioavailable form of vitamin B12, functioning similarly to cyanocobalamin. It serves as a coenzyme in critical biochemical processes, including DNA synthesis and the maintenance of myelin, the protective sheath around nerves.

Adverse Effects: Like cyanocobalamin, hydroxocobalamin is typically well-tolerated. Potential adverse effects include allergic reactions, such as skin rash, itching, and, in rare cases, anaphylaxis. Other side effects may include injection site pain, mild diarrhea, and dizziness.

Therapeutic Uses:

- **Vitamin B12 Deficiency**: More effective in maintaining B12 levels due to its longer half-life and better retention in the body compared to cyanocobalamin.
- **Pernicious Anemia**: Used to treat this condition caused by the lack of intrinsic factor necessary for B12 absorption.
- **Detoxification**: Hydroxocobalamin is used as an antidote for cyanide poisoning because it binds cyanide ions to form cyanocobalamin, which can be excreted by the body.
- **Optic Neuropathy**: Effective in treating Leber's optic neuropathy, a genetic disorder affecting vision due to mitochondrial dysfunction.

3. Folic Acid Supplements

Folic Acid

Mechanism of Action: Folic acid (vitamin B9) is a crucial nutrient involved in DNA synthesis, repair, and methylation, as well as amino acid metabolism. In the body, folic acid is converted into its active form, tetrahydrofolate (THF), which acts as a coenzyme in various one-carbon transfer reactions necessary for the synthesis of purines and thymidylate, components of DNA.

Adverse Effects: Folic acid is generally well-tolerated with minimal side effects. In rare cases, it may cause allergic reactions, gastrointestinal disturbances such as nausea and bloating, and a potential masking of vitamin B12 deficiency symptoms, which can lead to neurological damage if not addressed.

Therapeutic Uses:

- **Treatment of Folate Deficiency Anemia**: Folate deficiency can result from poor dietary intake, malabsorption, increased demand during pregnancy, and chronic hemolytic anemias.
- **Prevention of Neural Tube Defects**: Supplementation in pregnant women to prevent birth defects such as spina bifida.
- **Support in Certain Chronic Conditions**: Used in patients with chronic alcohol consumption, inflammatory bowel disease, and certain anemias.

Folinic Acid (Leucovorin)

Mechanism of Action: Folinic acid, also known as leucovorin, is the active form of folic acid that bypasses the need for dihydrofolate reductase for activation. It is directly converted into tetrahydrofolate, participating in the same one-carbon transfer reactions as folic acid. Leucovorin enhances the effects of folate by supplying a readily usable form for DNA synthesis and repair.

Adverse Effects: Folinic acid is typically well-tolerated, but it can occasionally cause allergic reactions, gastrointestinal disturbances, and rare cases of seizures in predisposed individuals.

Therapeutic Uses:

- **Methotrexate Toxicity**: Used as a "rescue" therapy to reduce the toxic effects of high-dose methotrexate in cancer treatment by providing a source of folate that is not inhibited by methotrexate.
- **Megaloblastic Anemia**: Treats anemia due to folate deficiency, particularly when rapid repletion of active folate is necessary.
- **Chemotherapy Adjunct**: Enhances the effectiveness of 5-fluorouracil (5-FU) in colorectal cancer treatment by stabilizing the binding of 5-FU to thymidylate synthase.

CHAPTER – 8

PHARMACOLOGY OF DRUGS ACTING ON CARDIO VASCULAR SYSTEM – II

Ms. Shikha Singh

Assistant Professor, Rajiv Gandhi Institute of Pharmacy, Faculty of Pharmaceutical Science & Technology, AKS University Satna, (M.P.)

ABSTRACT:

Coagulants and anticoagulants are essential medications in the management of hemostasis and thrombosis. Coagulants, such as vitamin K, promote blood clotting and are used to treat bleeding disorders by enhancing clot formation. They are often employed in conditions like vitamin K deficiency, liver disease, or during surgical procedures to prevent excessive bleeding. Anticoagulants, like warfarin, heparin, and direct oral anticoagulants (DOACs) such as apixaban, prevent the formation of harmful clots by inhibiting various factors in the coagulation cascade. These drugs are crucial in managing and preventing thromboembolic disorders, such as deep vein thrombosis, pulmonary embolism, and atrial fibrillation. Fibrinolytics, also known as thrombolytics, are medications that dissolve existing blood clots. Drugs like alteplase and streptokinase activate the fibrinolytic pathway, converting plasminogen to plasmin, which breaks down fibrin, the structural component of blood clots. Fibrinolytics are vital in the acute management of conditions like myocardial infarction, ischemic stroke, and massive pulmonary embolism, where rapid clot dissolution can restore blood flow and minimize tissue damage. Plasma volume expanders are fluids used to increase blood volume in patients experiencing hypovolemia due to blood loss, dehydration, or shock. They include crystalloids like saline and colloids like albumin. These expanders help maintain adequate circulation, ensuring that organs receive sufficient oxygen and nutrients. They are crucial in emergency settings, surgeries, and critical care to stabilize patients and support hemodynamic stability. Each of these therapies plays a distinct but complementary role in managing different aspects of blood and fluid balance in clinical practice.

COAGULANTS AND ANTICOAGULANTS

Coagulants:

Coagulants are agents that promote blood clotting. They are typically used to manage conditions where increased bleeding risk is a concern, such as in hemophilia or after certain surgeries. Key coagulants include:

1. **Vitamin K:**
    a. **Mechanism of Action:** Essential for the synthesis of clotting factors II, VII, IX, and X in the liver. Vitamin K is necessary for the gamma-carboxylation of these factors, which is crucial for their activity.
    b. **Use:** Treats and prevents bleeding due to Vitamin K deficiency. Often used to reverse the effects of anticoagulants like warfarin.
    c. **Formulations:** Oral and injectable forms (e.g., Phytonadione).
2. **Prothrombin Complex Concentrates (PCCs):**
    a. **Mechanism of Action:** Contains clotting factors II, VII, IX, and X. Helps in rapid replacement of deficient factors in patients with bleeding disorders.
    b. **Use:** Treatment of bleeding episodes in patients with hemophilia or after anticoagulant overdose. Also used in patients with Vitamin K deficiency.
3. **Recombinant Activated Factor VII (rFVIIa):**
    a. **Mechanism of Action:** Activates the extrinsic pathway of the coagulation cascade, leading to clot formation.
    b. **Use:** Used in the treatment of bleeding in hemophilia patients who have developed inhibitors to standard clotting factors. Can also be used in some cases of trauma or surgical bleeding.

2. Anticoagulants

Anticoagulants are medications used to prevent the formation of blood clots or to treat existing clots. They are crucial in managing and preventing thrombotic disorders, such as deep vein thrombosis (DVT), pulmonary embolism (PE), and stroke. Anticoagulants are classified into several categories:

a. Vitamin K Antagonists

1. **Warfarin:**
   i. **Mechanism of Action:** Inhibits Vitamin K epoxide reductase, reducing the synthesis of Vitamin K-dependent clotting factors (II, VII, IX, and X) and anticoagulant proteins C and S.
   ii. **Use:** Long-term anticoagulation for conditions like atrial fibrillation, mechanical heart valves, and venous thromboembolism.
   iii. **Monitoring:** Requires regular monitoring of the International Normalized Ratio (INR) to ensure therapeutic levels.

b. Direct Oral Anticoagulants (DOACs)

1. **Direct Thrombin Inhibitors:**
   i. **Examples:** Dabigatran.
   ii. **Mechanism of Action:** Directly inhibits thrombin, preventing the conversion of fibrinogen to fibrin.
   iii. **Use:** Used in atrial fibrillation, DVT, and PE. No routine monitoring required.
2. **Direct Factor Xa Inhibitors:**
   i. **Examples:** Rivaroxaban, Apixaban, Edoxaban.
   ii. **Mechanism of Action:** Directly inhibits Factor Xa, which is essential for the conversion of prothrombin to thrombin.
   iii. **Use:** Used for the prevention and treatment of DVT, PE, and stroke in atrial fibrillation. No routine monitoring required.

c. Heparins

1. **Unfractionated Heparin (UFH):**

i. **Mechanism of Action:** Binds to antithrombin III, accelerating the inhibition of thrombin and Factor Xa.

ii. **Use:** Acute anticoagulation in settings like myocardial infarction, DVT, and PE. Requires monitoring of activated partial thromboplastin time (aPTT).

2. **Low Molecular Weight Heparins (LMWHs):**

   i. **Examples:** Enoxaparin, Dalteparin.

   ii. **Mechanism of Action:** Inhibit Factor Xa more selectively than UFH. Have a more predictable dose-response relationship.

   iii. **Use:** Used for the treatment and prevention of DVT and PE. Monitoring is less frequent compared to UFH.

d. Fondaparinux

1. **Mechanism of Action:** Synthetic pentasaccharide that selectively inhibits Factor Xa via antithrombin III.
2. **Use:** Used for the prevention and treatment of DVT and PE. No routine monitoring required.

Clinical Considerations

1. **Bleeding Risks:** All anticoagulants increase the risk of bleeding. Monitoring and dose adjustments are crucial to minimize this risk.
2. **Reversal Agents:** Specific antidotes are available for some anticoagulants (e.g., Vitamin K for warfarin, and andexanet alfa for Factor Xa inhibitors).
3. **Drug Interactions:** Anticoagulants can interact with other medications, affecting their efficacy and safety.

FIBRINOLYTICS

Fibrinolytics, also known as thrombolytics, are a class of drugs used to dissolve blood clots that have formed in blood vessels. They play a crucial role in the acute management of conditions like myocardial infarction (heart attack), pulmonary embolism, and ischemic stroke. Here's a detailed overview of fibrinolytics:

1. Mechanism of Action

Fibrinolytics work by activating the fibrinolytic system, which is responsible for breaking down fibrin, a protein that stabilizes blood clots. They do this by converting plasminogen, a precursor enzyme present in the blood, into plasmin, the active enzyme that degrades fibrin and dissolves clots.

2. Types of Fibrinolytics

Fibrinolytics can be categorized into different classes based on their mechanism of action and their source:

a. Tissue Plasminogen Activators (tPAs)

These are the most commonly used fibrinolytics and are engineered to specifically target fibrin-bound plasminogen, minimizing systemic activation of plasminogen and thus reducing the risk of bleeding.

1. **Alteplase (rtPA):**
   i. **Mechanism of Action:** Recombinant tissue plasminogen activator (rtPA) that binds to fibrin in a thrombus and converts plasminogen to plasmin, leading to clot dissolution.
   ii. **Use:** Primarily used for acute myocardial infarction, ischemic stroke, and pulmonary embolism. The treatment window is typically within 3-4.5 hours for stroke and up to 12 hours for myocardial infarction.
   iii. **Administration:** Intravenous (IV) infusion.
2. **Reteplase:**
   i. **Mechanism of Action:** A modified form of rtPA with a longer half-life and faster onset of action compared to alteplase. It also acts specifically on fibrin-bound plasminogen.
   ii. **Use:** Used for acute myocardial infarction. Given as a bolus injection followed by a second bolus.

iii. **Administration:** IV bolus.

3. **Tenecteplase:**
   i. **Mechanism of Action:** A genetically modified form of rtPA with increased fibrin specificity and a longer half-life. Allows for a single bolus dose administration.
   ii. **Use:** Used for acute myocardial infarction.
   iii. **Administration:** Single IV bolus injection.

b. Streptokinase

1. **Mechanism of Action:** A bacterial protein that activates plasminogen to plasmin throughout the bloodstream, not just at the site of the clot. This systemic activation can lead to a higher risk of bleeding complications.
2. **Use:** Used for myocardial infarction, pulmonary embolism, and deep vein thrombosis. Less commonly used today due to the availability of more selective tPAs.
3. **Administration:** IV infusion.

c. Urokinase

1. **Mechanism of Action:** A naturally occurring enzyme that converts plasminogen to plasmin, similar to streptokinase but with a more selective action.
2. **Use:** Used for pulmonary embolism and to clear occluded catheters.
3. **Administration:** IV infusion.

3. Clinical Uses

a. **Acute Myocardial Infarction (AMI):** Fibrinolytics are used to dissolve the thrombus blocking the coronary artery, restoring blood flow to the heart muscle. This treatment is most effective when administered within the first few hours of symptom onset.
b. **Ischemic Stroke:** In cases of ischemic stroke, fibrinolytics help to dissolve the clot obstructing blood flow to the brain, which can

significantly reduce disability if administered within the recommended time window (typically within 3-4.5 hours of symptom onset).

c. **Pulmonary Embolism (PE):** For massive PE, fibrinolytics can dissolve clots in the pulmonary arteries, improving hemodynamic stability and oxygenation.

4. Adverse Effects

a. **Bleeding Complications:** The most serious adverse effect of fibrinolytics is bleeding, including intracranial hemorrhage. Patients need careful monitoring for signs of bleeding.

b. **Allergic Reactions:** Some patients may experience allergic reactions, especially with streptokinase, which can cause anaphylaxis in rare cases.

5. Contraindications

Fibrinolytics are contraindicated in certain conditions due to the high risk of bleeding:

a. **Recent Surgery or Trauma:** Increases the risk of bleeding from surgical sites.

b. **Active Bleeding Disorders:** Such as peptic ulcer disease or recent gastrointestinal bleeding.

c. **Severe Hypertension:** Uncontrolled high blood pressure can increase the risk of hemorrhagic complications.

d. **History of Intracranial Hemorrhage:** Previous bleeding in the brain increases the risk of recurrent bleeding.

6. Monitoring and Management

a. **Bleeding Risk:** Continuous monitoring for signs of bleeding, especially in high-risk areas like the brain.

b. **Reversal:** There is no specific reversal agent for fibrinolytics, but supportive care and blood transfusions can be used to manage bleeding complications.

PLASMA VOLUME EXPANDERS

Anti-platelet drugs are crucial in preventing and treating cardiovascular diseases by inhibiting platelet aggregation and thrombus formation. They are commonly used in conditions such as acute coronary syndrome (ACS), stroke, and peripheral artery disease (PAD). Here's a detailed look at the various anti-platelet drugs:

1. Mechanism of Action

Anti-platelet drugs work by interfering with the platelet activation and aggregation processes. Platelets play a key role in the formation of blood clots by adhering to vascular injury sites and aggregating to form a thrombus. These drugs inhibit different pathways involved in platelet activation:

a. **Inhibition of ADP receptors:** Prevents platelet activation and aggregation.
b. **Inhibition of cyclooxygenase (COX):** Reduces thromboxane A2 production, which is a potent platelet aggregator.
c. **Inhibition of glycoprotein IIb/IIIa receptors:** Prevents platelet aggregation by blocking the binding of fibrinogen and other adhesive molecules.

2. Classes of Anti-platelet Drugs

a. Aspirin (Acetylsalicylic Acid)

1. **Mechanism of Action:** Inhibits cyclooxygenase-1 (COX-1), which reduces the production of thromboxane A2, a potent platelet aggregator and vasoconstrictor.
2. **Use:** Widely used for the prevention of cardiovascular events such as myocardial infarction, stroke, and in patients with peripheral artery disease. Also used in combination with other anti-platelet agents in certain conditions (e.g., dual anti-platelet therapy after stent placement).
3. **Administration:** Oral, typically in low doses (e.g., 75-325 mg daily).

4. **Adverse Effects:** Gastrointestinal bleeding, ulceration, and allergic reactions.

b. ADP Receptor Inhibitors

These drugs block the P2Y12 receptor on platelets, which is activated by adenosine diphosphate (ADP) and leads to platelet aggregation.

1. **Clopidogrel:**
   i. **Mechanism of Action:** Irreversibly inhibits the P2Y12 receptor, preventing ADP-induced platelet activation and aggregation.
   ii. **Use:** Used in the prevention of atherothrombotic events in patients with acute coronary syndrome, stroke, and peripheral artery disease. Often used in combination with aspirin (dual anti-platelet therapy).
   iii. **Administration:** Oral, typically 75 mg daily.
   iv. **Adverse Effects:** Bleeding, gastrointestinal upset, and rare cases of thrombotic thrombocytopenic purpura (TTP).
2. **Prasugrel:**
   i. **Mechanism of Action:** Irreversibly inhibits the P2Y12 receptor with a more rapid onset and greater potency than clopidogrel.
   ii. **Use:** Used in patients with acute coronary syndrome undergoing percutaneous coronary intervention (PCI). Provides more consistent platelet inhibition compared to clopidogrel.
   iii. **Administration:** Oral, typically 10 mg daily.
   iv. **Adverse Effects:** Higher risk of bleeding compared to clopidogrel, especially in the elderly or those with a history of stroke.
3. **Ticagrelor:**
   i. **Mechanism of Action:** Reversibly inhibits the P2Y12 receptor, leading to rapid and reversible platelet inhibition.

ii. **Use:** Used for the prevention of atherothrombotic events in acute coronary syndrome. Provides faster and more potent platelet inhibition than clopidogrel.
iii. **Administration:** Oral, typically 90 mg twice daily.
iv. **Adverse Effects:** Bleeding, dyspnea, and rare cases of bradycardia.

4. **Cangrelor:**
   i. **Mechanism of Action:** Reversible P2Y12 receptor antagonist administered intravenously.
   ii. **Use:** Used for patients undergoing PCI when rapid onset and offset of platelet inhibition is desired.
   iii. **Administration:** Intravenous infusion.
   iv. **Adverse Effects:** Bleeding, including the risk of significant bleeding complications.

c. Glycoprotein IIb/IIIa Receptor Inhibitors

These drugs inhibit the glycoprotein IIb/IIIa receptor on platelets, which is crucial for platelet aggregation by binding to fibrinogen and other adhesive molecules.

1. **Abciximab:**
   i. **Mechanism of Action:** Monoclonal antibody that binds to the glycoprotein IIb/IIIa receptor, preventing platelet aggregation.
   ii. **Use:** Used during PCI to prevent platelet aggregation and reduce the risk of cardiac events.
   iii. **Administration:** Intravenous infusion.
   iv. **Adverse Effects:** Major bleeding, thrombocytopenia, and allergic reactions.
2. **Eptifibatide:**
   i. **Mechanism of Action:** Cyclic peptide that reversibly binds to the glycoprotein IIb/IIIa receptor.

ii. **Use:** Used for patients with acute coronary syndrome and those undergoing PCI.
iii. **Administration:** Intravenous infusion.
iv. **Adverse Effects:** Bleeding, thrombocytopenia.

3. **Tirofiban:**
    i. **Mechanism of Action:** Non-peptide small molecule that reversibly inhibits the glycoprotein IIb/IIIa receptor.
    ii. **Use:** Used for acute coronary syndrome and PCI.
    iii. **Administration:** Intravenous infusion.
    iv. **Adverse Effects:** Bleeding, thrombocytopenia.

d. Other Anti-platelet Agents

1. **Dipyridamole:**
    i. **Mechanism of Action:** Inhibits platelet aggregation by increasing the availability of adenosine, which inhibits platelet activation. Also has vasodilatory effects.
    ii. **Use:** Often used in combination with aspirin for secondary prevention of stroke. Can also be used for cardiac stress testing.
    iii. **Administration:** Oral, typically in combination with aspirin (e.g., Aggrenox).
    iv. **Adverse Effects:** Headache, gastrointestinal symptoms, and bleeding.

2. **Vorapaxar:**
    i. **Mechanism of Action:** Protease-activated receptor-1 (PAR-1) antagonist, which inhibits thrombin-induced platelet activation.
    ii. **Use:** Used for the prevention of cardiovascular events in patients with a history of myocardial infarction or peripheral artery disease.
    iii. **Administration:** Oral, typically 2.08 mg daily.
    iv. **Adverse Effects:** Bleeding, including intracranial hemorrhage.

3. Clinical Considerations

a. **Combination Therapy:** Anti-platelet drugs are often used in combination to achieve a synergistic effect, such as aspirin with clopidogrel or another ADP receptor inhibitor. Dual anti-platelet therapy is particularly important in acute coronary syndrome and post-stent implantation.

b. **Bleeding Risk:** All anti-platelet drugs increase the risk of bleeding, which can be serious. Patients should be monitored closely for signs of bleeding.

c. **Discontinuation:** Some anti-platelet drugs, like clopidogrel and prasugrel, should be discontinued prior to surgery to reduce the risk of bleeding complications.

CHAPTER – 9

ANTI – PLATELET DRUGS

Mrs. Saba Ruksaar

Assistant Professor, Rajiv Gandhi Institute of Pharmacy, Faculty of Pharmaceutical Science & Technology, AKS University Satna, (M.P.)

ABSTRACT:

Anti-platelet drugs are a critical class of medications used to prevent blood clots by inhibiting platelet aggregation, a key step in thrombus formation. These drugs are particularly important in the prevention and treatment of cardiovascular diseases such as myocardial infarction, stroke, and peripheral artery disease. The primary mechanism of action involves the inhibition of enzymes or receptors involved in platelet activation and aggregation. Aspirin, one of the most widely used anti-platelet agents, irreversibly inhibits the enzyme cyclooxygenase-1 (COX-1), which is essential for the synthesis of thromboxane A2, a potent promoter of platelet aggregation. By blocking this pathway, aspirin reduces the ability of platelets to clump together and form clots. Clopidogrel, another commonly used anti-platelet drug, works by inhibiting the P2Y12 receptor on the platelet surface, which is involved in the activation of platelets by adenosine diphosphate (ADP). This inhibition prevents the activation of the glycoprotein IIb/IIIa complex, crucial for platelet aggregation. Prasugrel and ticagrelor are newer agents in the same class with similar mechanisms but different pharmacokinetic properties. Glycoprotein IIb/IIIa inhibitors, such as abciximab, eptifibatide, and tirofiban, directly block the glycoprotein IIb/IIIa receptor on the platelet surface, preventing fibrinogen binding and subsequent platelet aggregation. These drugs are often used during percutaneous coronary interventions (PCI) to prevent acute thrombotic events. Dipyridamole, another anti-platelet drug, inhibits the phosphodiesterase enzyme, leading to increased levels of cyclic AMP within platelets, which in turn reduces platelet aggregation. It is often used in combination with aspirin for stroke prevention. While anti-platelet drugs are highly effective in reducing the risk of thrombotic events, they also carry the risk of bleeding, including gastrointestinal bleeding and hemorrhagic stroke. Therefore, their use requires careful consideration of the balance between the benefits of clot prevention and the risks of bleeding. Patients on anti-platelet therapy need regular monitoring and sometimes adjustments in dosage or combinations with other medications to optimize their therapeutic outcomes and minimize adverse effects. These drugs have revolutionized the management of cardiovascular diseases, significantly improving patient survival and quality of life.

ANTI-PLATELET DRUGS

Anti-platelet drugs are crucial in preventing and treating cardiovascular diseases by inhibiting platelet aggregation and thrombus formation. They are commonly used in conditions such as acute coronary syndrome (ACS), stroke, and peripheral artery disease (PAD). Here's a detailed look at the various anti-platelet drugs:

1. Mechanism of Action

Anti-platelet drugs work by interfering with the platelet activation and aggregation processes. Platelets play a key role in the formation of blood clots by adhering to vascular injury sites and aggregating to form a thrombus. These drugs inhibit different pathways involved in platelet activation:

a. **Inhibition of ADP receptors:** Prevents platelet activation and aggregation.

b. **Inhibition of cyclooxygenase (COX):** Reduces thromboxane A2 production, which is a potent platelet aggregator.

c. **Inhibition of glycoprotein IIb/IIIa receptors:** Prevents platelet aggregation by blocking the binding of fibrinogen and other adhesive molecules.

2. Classes of Anti-platelet Drugs

a. Aspirin (Acetylsalicylic Acid)

1. **Mechanism of Action:** Inhibits cyclooxygenase-1 (COX-1), which reduces the production of thromboxane A2, a potent platelet aggregator and vasoconstrictor.
2. **Use:** Widely used for the prevention of cardiovascular events such as myocardial infarction, stroke, and in patients with peripheral artery disease. Also used in combination with other anti-platelet agents in certain conditions (e.g., dual anti-platelet therapy after stent placement).
3. **Administration:** Oral, typically in low doses (e.g., 75-325 mg daily).
4. **Adverse Effects:** Gastrointestinal bleeding, ulceration, and allergic reactions.

b. ADP Receptor Inhibitors

These drugs block the P2Y12 receptor on platelets, which is activated by adenosine diphosphate (ADP) and leads to platelet aggregation.

1. **Clopidogrel:**
   i. **Mechanism of Action:** Irreversibly inhibits the P2Y12 receptor, preventing ADP-induced platelet activation and aggregation.
   ii. **Use:** Used in the prevention of atherothrombotic events in patients with acute coronary syndrome, stroke, and peripheral artery disease. Often used in combination with aspirin (dual anti-platelet therapy).
   iii. **Administration:** Oral, typically 75 mg daily.
   iv. **Adverse Effects:** Bleeding, gastrointestinal upset, and rare cases of thrombotic thrombocytopenic purpura (TTP).
2. **Prasugrel:**
   i. **Mechanism of Action:** Irreversibly inhibits the P2Y12 receptor with a more rapid onset and greater potency than clopidogrel.
   ii. **Use:** Used in patients with acute coronary syndrome undergoing percutaneous coronary intervention (PCI). Provides more consistent platelet inhibition compared to clopidogrel.

iii. **Administration:** Oral, typically 10 mg daily.
iv. **Adverse Effects:** Higher risk of bleeding compared to clopidogrel, especially in the elderly or those with a history of stroke.

3. **Ticagrelor:**
   i. **Mechanism of Action:** Reversibly inhibits the P2Y12 receptor, leading to rapid and reversible platelet inhibition.
   ii. **Use:** Used for the prevention of atherothrombotic events in acute coronary syndrome. Provides faster and more potent platelet inhibition than clopidogrel.
   iii. **Administration:** Oral, typically 90 mg twice daily.
   iv. **Adverse Effects:** Bleeding, dyspnea, and rare cases of bradycardia.
4. **Cangrelor:**
   i. **Mechanism of Action:** Reversible P2Y12 receptor antagonist administered intravenously.
   ii. **Use:** Used for patients undergoing PCI when rapid onset and offset of platelet inhibition is desired.
   iii. **Administration:** Intravenous infusion.
   iv. **Adverse Effects:** Bleeding, including the risk of significant bleeding complications.

c. Glycoprotein IIb/IIIa Receptor Inhibitors

These drugs inhibit the glycoprotein IIb/IIIa receptor on platelets, which is crucial for platelet aggregation by binding to fibrinogen and other adhesive molecules.

1. **Abciximab:**
   i. **Mechanism of Action:** Monoclonal antibody that binds to the glycoprotein IIb/IIIa receptor, preventing platelet aggregation.
   ii. **Use:** Used during PCI to prevent platelet aggregation and reduce the risk of cardiac events.
   iii. **Administration:** Intravenous infusion.

iv. **Adverse Effects:** Major bleeding, thrombocytopenia, and allergic reactions.

2. **Eptifibatide:**

   i. **Mechanism of Action:** Cyclic peptide that reversibly binds to the glycoprotein IIb/IIIa receptor.

   ii. **Use:** Used for patients with acute coronary syndrome and those undergoing PCI.

   iii. **Administration:** Intravenous infusion.

   iv. **Adverse Effects:** Bleeding, thrombocytopenia.

3. **Tirofiban:**

   i. **Mechanism of Action:** Non-peptide small molecule that reversibly inhibits the glycoprotein IIb/IIIa receptor.

   ii. **Use:** Used for acute coronary syndrome and PCI.

   iii. **Administration:** Intravenous infusion.

   iv. **Adverse Effects:** Bleeding, thrombocytopenia.

d. Other Anti-platelet Agents

1. **Dipyridamole:**

   i. **Mechanism of Action:** Inhibits platelet aggregation by increasing the availability of adenosine, which inhibits platelet activation. Also has vasodilatory effects.

   ii. **Use:** Often used in combination with aspirin for secondary prevention of stroke. Can also be used for cardiac stress testing.

   iii. **Administration:** Oral, typically in combination with aspirin (e.g., Aggrenox).

   iv. **Adverse Effects:** Headache, gastrointestinal symptoms, and bleeding.

2. **Vorapaxar:**

   i. **Mechanism of Action:** Protease-activated receptor-1 (PAR-1) antagonist, which inhibits thrombin-induced platelet activation.

ii. **Use:** Used for the prevention of cardiovascular events in patients with a history of myocardial infarction or peripheral artery disease.

iii. **Administration:** Oral, typically 2.08 mg daily.

iv. **Adverse Effects:** Bleeding, including intracranial hemorrhage.

3. Clinical Considerations

a. **Combination Therapy:** Anti-platelet drugs are often used in combination to achieve a synergistic effect, such as aspirin with clopidogrel or another ADP receptor inhibitor. Dual anti-platelet therapy is particularly important in acute coronary syndrome and post-stent implantation.

b. **Bleeding Risk:** All anti-platelet drugs increase the risk of bleeding, which can be serious. Patients should be monitored closely for signs of bleeding.

c. **Discontinuation:** Some anti-platelet drugs, like clopidogrel and prasugrel, should be discontinued prior to surgery to reduce the risk of bleeding complications.

Anti-platelet drugs are essential for managing and preventing cardiovascular events, particularly those related to thrombosis. Understanding their mechanisms, uses, and potential side effects is crucial for optimizing patient outcomes in cardiovascular care.

CHAPTER – 10

PHARMACOLOGY OF DRUGS ACTING ON URINARY SYSTEM

Dr. Surya Prakash Gupta

Professor & Director, Rajiv Gandhi Institute of Pharmacy, Faculty of Pharmaceutical Science & Technology, AKS University, Satna (M.P.)

ABSTRACT:

Drugs acting on the urinary system are essential for managing various conditions affecting the kidneys, bladder, and urethra. Diuretics, such as furosemide, hydrochlorothiazide, and spironolactone, are among the most commonly used urinary system drugs. They increase urine output by promoting the excretion of sodium and water, making them vital in treating hypertension, heart failure, and edema. Anticholinergics, like oxybutynin and tolterodine, are used to manage overactive bladder by relaxing the bladder muscles and reducing urinary frequency and urgency. Alpha-blockers, such as tamsulosin, are used to improve urine flow in men with benign prostatic hyperplasia (BPH) by relaxing the smooth muscles in the prostate and bladder neck. Antibiotics like nitrofurantoin and ciprofloxacin are essential in treating urinary tract infections (UTIs) by targeting the bacterial pathogens responsible for these infections. Potassium citrate is used to prevent the formation of kidney stones by alkalizing the urine and reducing the crystallization of stone-forming salts. Each class of these drugs has specific mechanisms of action, therapeutic applications, and potential side effects, requiring careful selection and monitoring by healthcare providers to ensure effective and safe treatment of urinary system disorders. By targeting various aspects of renal and urinary physiology, these medications play crucial roles in maintaining urinary health and managing diseases.

INTRODUCTION:

Pharmacology of drugs acting on the urinary system focuses on medications that influence the function of the kidneys, bladder, and other parts of the urinary tract. These drugs can be broadly categorized based on their therapeutic effects and the conditions they treat. Here's an introduction to the key classes and their functions:

1. Diuretics

Function: Diuretics increase urine production, which helps to reduce fluid retention and lower blood pressure.

a. **Thiazide Diuretics**:
   i. **Examples:** Hydrochlorothiazide, Chlorthalidone.
   ii. **Mechanism:** Inhibit sodium reabsorption in the distal convoluted tubule of the nephron.
   iii. **Uses:** Hypertension, edema.

b. **Loop Diuretics**:
   i. **Examples:** Furosemide, Bumetanide.
   ii. **Mechanism:** Inhibit sodium reabsorption in the ascending loop of Henle.
   iii. **Uses:** Edema, heart failure, hypertension.

c. **Potassium-Sparing Diuretics**:
   i. **Examples:** Spironolactone, Eplerenone, Amiloride.
   ii. **Mechanism:** Inhibit sodium reabsorption in the distal nephron while sparing potassium.
   iii. **Uses:** Hypertension, heart failure, hypokalemia prevention.

2. Antidiuretics

Function: Antidiuretics reduce urine production and are used to treat conditions such as diabetes insipidus.

a. **Desmopressin**:
   i. **Mechanism:** Mimics antidiuretic hormone (ADH), enhancing water reabsorption in the kidneys.
   ii. **Uses:** Diabetes insipidus, nocturnal enuresis.

3. Urological Agents

Function: These drugs are used to manage conditions affecting the urinary tract and bladder.

a. **Alpha-Blockers**:
    i. **Examples:** Tamsulosin, Alfuzosin.
    ii. **Mechanism:** Relax smooth muscle in the prostate and bladder neck.
    iii. **Uses:** Benign prostatic hyperplasia (BPH), urinary obstruction.
b. **5-Alpha-Reductase Inhibitors**:
    i. **Examples:** Finasteride, Dutasteride.
    ii. **Mechanism:** Inhibit the enzyme that converts testosterone to dihydrotestosterone (DHT), reducing prostate size.
    iii. **Uses:** BPH.
c. **Bladder Antispasmodics**:
    i. **Examples:** Oxybutynin, Tolterodine.
    ii. **Mechanism:** Relax bladder smooth muscle and reduce spasms.
    iii. **Uses:** Overactive bladder, urge incontinence.

4. Phosphodiesterase Inhibitors

Function: These drugs can also affect urinary function by influencing smooth muscle relaxation.

a. **Examples:** Sildenafil, Tadalafil.
b. **Mechanism:** Inhibit phosphodiesterase type 5 (PDE5), leading to increased levels of cyclic GMP and smooth muscle relaxation.
c. **Uses:** Erectile dysfunction, and sometimes used off-label for other urological conditions.

5. Others

a. **Urinary Tract Analgesics**:
    i. **Examples:** Phenazopyridine.

ii. **Mechanism:** Provides symptomatic relief of pain and discomfort in the urinary tract.

iii. **Uses:** Urinary tract infections, urinary tract irritation.

b. **Urinary Acidifiers/Alkalinizers**:

i. **Examples:** Sodium bicarbonate, ammonium chloride.

ii. **Mechanism:** Modify urine pH to prevent or treat urinary stone formation.

iii. **Uses:** Preventing urinary stones, managing systemic alkalosis or acidosis.

Clinical Considerations

a. **Adverse Effects:** Diuretics can cause electrolyte imbalances, dehydration, and hypotension. Antidiuretics may lead to fluid overload if not properly dosed. Urological agents may have side effects related to their impact on smooth muscle or hormonal pathways.

b. **Drug Interactions:** Many drugs affecting the urinary system can interact with other medications, so careful management and monitoring are required.

DIURETICS

Diuretics are a crucial class of drugs in the pharmacology of the urinary system, primarily used to increase urine output. They are effective in treating conditions related to fluid overload, such as hypertension, heart failure, and edema. Here's a detailed look at the various types of diuretics, their mechanisms, uses, and key considerations:

1. Thiazide Diuretics

Examples:

a. Hydrochlorothiazide

b. Chlorthalidone

c. Indapamide

d. Metolazone

Mechanism of Action:

a. Thiazide diuretics act on the distal convoluted tubule of the nephron.
b. They inhibit the Na+/Cl- cotransporter, reducing sodium and chloride reabsorption.
c. This action results in increased excretion of sodium and chloride, along with water.

Uses:

a. **Hypertension:** Thiazides are often used as first-line treatment for high blood pressure.
b. **Edema:** They are used to manage edema associated with heart failure, liver cirrhosis, or kidney disorders.
c. **Kidney Stones:** They help in reducing calcium excretion, which can prevent calcium-based kidney stones.

Adverse Effects:

a. **Electrolyte Imbalances:** Hypokalemia (low potassium), hyponatremia (low sodium), hypomagnesemia (low magnesium).
b. **Metabolic Effects:** Hyperglycemia, hyperlipidemia.
c. **Allergic Reactions:** Rare, but may include rash or photosensitivity.

Clinical Considerations:

a. Monitor electrolyte levels regularly.
b. May require potassium supplementation or combination with potassium-sparing diuretics to prevent hypokalemia.

2. Loop Diuretics

Examples:

a. Furosemide
b. Bumetanide
c. Torsemide
d. Ethacrynic Acid

Mechanism of Action:

a. Loop diuretics act on the thick ascending limb of the loop of Henle.
b. They inhibit the $Na^+/K^+/2Cl^-$ cotransporter, leading to decreased reabsorption of sodium, potassium, and chloride.
c. This results in a significant increase in urine output and excretion of electrolytes.

Uses:

a. **Edema:** Used for acute and chronic conditions such as heart failure, renal impairment, and liver cirrhosis.
b. **Hypertension:** Used in resistant cases or when more potent diuretics are needed.
c. **Hypercalcemia:** Loop diuretics can help in conditions with elevated calcium levels.

Adverse Effects:

a. **Electrolyte Imbalances:** Hypokalemia, hypomagnesemia, hypocalcemia.
b. **Dehydration:** Risk of volume depletion and hypotension.
c. **Ototoxicity:** Risk of hearing impairment with high doses or rapid intravenous administration.

Clinical Considerations:

a. Monitor renal function and electrolytes frequently.
b. Adjust doses in patients with renal impairment.

3. Potassium-Sparing Diuretics

Examples:

a. Spironolactone
b. Eplerenone
c. Amiloride
d. Triamterene

Mechanism of Action:

a. **Aldosterone Antagonists (e.g., Spironolactone, Eplerenone):** Block the effects of aldosterone in the distal convoluted tubule and collecting duct, leading to decreased sodium reabsorption and potassium retention.

b. **Epithelial Sodium Channel Blockers (e.g., Amiloride, Triamterene):** Directly block sodium channels in the distal nephron, reducing sodium reabsorption and preventing potassium loss.

Uses:

a. **Hypertension:** Often used in combination with other diuretics to prevent hypokalemia.

b. **Heart Failure:** Reduce symptoms of heart failure and improve survival.

c. **Primary Hyperaldosteronism:** Treat conditions with excessive aldosterone production.

Adverse Effects:

a. **Hyperkalemia:** Elevated potassium levels, especially when used with other potassium-sparing agents or in renal impairment.

b. **Gynecomastia:** Particularly with spironolactone, due to its anti-androgenic effects.

Clinical Considerations:

a. Regularly monitor potassium levels and renal function.

b. Caution when used with other drugs that increase potassium levels.

4. Osmotic Diuretics

Examples:

a. Mannitol

b. Urea

Mechanism of Action:

a. Osmotic diuretics work by increasing the osmolarity of the glomerular filtrate.

b. They prevent reabsorption of water and electrolytes by creating an osmotic gradient that pulls water into the renal tubules.

Uses:

a. **Acute Renal Failure:** Helps to maintain urine flow and prevent acute renal failure.

b. **Intracranial Pressure Reduction:** Used to reduce intracranial pressure in conditions like traumatic brain injury.

Adverse Effects:

a. **Dehydration:** Risk of severe fluid and electrolyte imbalances.

b. **Electrolyte Imbalances:** Changes in sodium, potassium, and other electrolytes.

Clinical Considerations:

a. Administer in a controlled setting with close monitoring of fluid and electrolytes.

b. Avoid in patients with renal failure or severe dehydration.

General Considerations for Diuretics:

a. **Monitoring:** Regular monitoring of electrolytes, renal function, and blood pressure is crucial.

b. **Patient Education:** Educate patients about signs of electrolyte imbalances and the importance of adhering to prescribed dosages.

c. **Drug Interactions:** Be aware of interactions with other medications, particularly those affecting electrolytes or renal function.

ANTI-DIURETICS

Anti-diuretics, or antidiuretic agents, are used to reduce urine output and manage conditions related to excessive urine production. These drugs are particularly important in treating conditions like diabetes insipidus and nocturnal enuresis. Here's a detailed look at antidiuretics, their mechanisms, uses, and considerations:

1. Vasopressin (ADH) Analogues

Examples:

a. **Desmopressin** (DDAVP)
b. **Vasopressin** (Pitressin)

Mechanism of Action:

a. **Desmopressin:** Acts as a synthetic analog of antidiuretic hormone (ADH) or vasopressin. It binds to V2 receptors in the renal collecting ducts, enhancing water reabsorption and reducing urine volume.
b. **Vasopressin:** A naturally occurring hormone that also acts on V1 receptors to induce vasoconstriction and V2 receptors in the kidneys to promote water reabsorption.

Uses:

a. **Diabetes Insipidus:** Desmopressin is primarily used for central diabetes insipidus, where there is insufficient production of ADH. It helps to concentrate urine and reduce excessive urination.
b. **Nocturnal Enuresis:** Desmopressin can be used to manage bedwetting in children, as it decreases nocturnal urine production.
c. **Coagulation Disorders:** Vasopressin and Desmopressin are sometimes used to manage bleeding disorders like hemophilia A and von Willebrand disease by stimulating the release of von Willebrand factor and factor VIII.

Adverse Effects:

a. **Water Retention:** Can lead to hyponatremia (low sodium levels) due to excessive water reabsorption.
b. **Headache:** May occur as a side effect.
c. **Nausea and Abdominal Cramping:** Some patients may experience gastrointestinal symptoms.

Clinical Considerations:

a. **Dosage:** Must be carefully adjusted based on the patient's response and monitoring of fluid status and electrolytes.

b. **Monitoring:** Regular monitoring of electrolytes, especially sodium levels, is essential to avoid water intoxication.

2. Non-vasopressin Agents

Examples:

a. **Lithium Carbonate** (though not typically an antidiuretic, it is used to treat conditions where antidiuretics are ineffective due to its effects on the kidneys)

Mechanism of Action:

a. **Lithium:** Although primarily a mood stabilizer, lithium is used in cases where diabetes insipidus is resistant to standard treatment. It can be used to manage certain conditions related to antidiuretic therapy.

Uses:

a. **Bipolar Disorder:** Lithium is primarily used as a mood stabilizer in bipolar disorder but can affect kidney function and urine output.

Adverse Effects:

a. **Renal Impairment:** Long-term use can lead to nephrotoxicity and impaired kidney function.

b. **Electrolyte Imbalances:** Lithium can affect sodium and fluid balance, leading to potential complications.

Clinical Considerations:

a. **Monitoring:** Regular kidney function tests and monitoring of lithium levels are important to prevent toxicity.

General Considerations for Antidiuretics

1. **Indication:** Ensure the correct diagnosis of conditions such as central or nephrogenic diabetes insipidus before initiating treatment with antidiuretics.
2. **Dosage and Administration:** Dosage must be individualized based on patient response and specific condition. For example, desmopressin can

be administered intranasally, orally, or intravenously, depending on the clinical scenario.

3. **Hydration Status:** Monitor the patient's hydration status closely to avoid complications from fluid overload or dehydration.
4. **Patient Education:** Educate patients about the potential side effects and the importance of adhering to prescribed doses and monitoring schedules.
5. **Drug Interactions:** Be aware of potential interactions with other medications that might affect fluid balance or electrolyte levels.

CLASSIFICATION:

The pharmacology of drugs acting on the urinary system can be classified into several major categories based on their mechanisms of action and therapeutic uses. Here's a comprehensive classification along with examples for each category:

1. Diuretics

Function: Increase urine production and are used to manage fluid overload, hypertension, and other conditions.

a. Thiazide Diuretics

i. **Examples:** Hydrochlorothiazide, Chlorthalidone, Indapamide.
ii. **Mechanism:** Inhibit sodium and chloride reabsorption in the distal convoluted tubule.

b. Loop Diuretics

i. **Examples:** Furosemide, Bumetanide, Torsemide, Ethacrynic Acid.
ii. **Mechanism:** Inhibit sodium, potassium, and chloride reabsorption in the thick ascending limb of the loop of Henle.

c. Potassium-Sparing Diuretics

a. **Examples:** Spironolactone, Eplerenone, Amiloride, Triamterene.
b. **Mechanism:**

i. **Aldosterone Antagonists (e.g., Spironolactone, Eplerenone):** Block aldosterone receptors in the distal nephron, reducing sodium reabsorption and potassium excretion.
ii. **Epithelial Sodium Channel Blockers (e.g., Amiloride, Triamterene):** Directly block sodium channels in the distal nephron.

d. Osmotic Diuretics

i. **Examples:** Mannitol, Urea.
ii. **Mechanism:** Increase the osmolarity of the filtrate, preventing water reabsorption in the renal tubules.

2. Antidiuretics

Function: Decrease urine output and are used to treat conditions like diabetes insipidus.

a. Vasopressin Analogues

i. **Examples:** Desmopressin (DDAVP), Vasopressin.
ii. **Mechanism:** Mimic the effects of antidiuretic hormone (ADH) by acting on V2 receptors in the renal collecting ducts to enhance water reabsorption.

3. Urological Agents

Function: Manage symptoms related to urinary tract and bladder conditions.

a. Alpha-Blockers

i. **Examples:** Tamsulosin, Alfuzosin.
ii. **Mechanism:** Relax smooth muscle in the prostate and bladder neck, improving urine flow in benign prostatic hyperplasia (BPH).

b. 5-Alpha-Reductase Inhibitors

i. **Examples:** Finasteride, Dutasteride.
ii. **Mechanism:** Inhibit the enzyme that converts testosterone to dihydrotestosterone (DHT), reducing prostate size.

c. Bladder Antispasmodics

i. **Examples:** Oxybutynin, Tolterodine.

ii. **Mechanism:** Reduce bladder muscle spasms and overactivity.

4. Urinary Tract Analgesics

Function: Provide symptomatic relief from pain and discomfort in the urinary tract.

Examples: Phenazopyridine.

i. **Mechanism:** Acts as a local analgesic on the urinary tract mucosa.

5. Urinary Acidifiers/Alkalinizers

Function: Modify urine pH to prevent or treat urinary stone formation and manage systemic acid-base imbalances.

a. Urinary Acidifiers

i. **Examples:** Methenamine mandelate, Cranberry supplements.

ii. **Mechanism:** Acidify the urine to prevent the formation of certain types of urinary stones.

b. Urinary Alkalinizers

i. **Examples:** Sodium bicarbonate, Potassium citrate.

ii. **Mechanism:** Alkalinize the urine to dissolve or prevent the formation of uric acid and cystine stones.

6. Other Agents

a. Phosphodiesterase Inhibitors

i. **Examples:** Sildenafil, Tadalafil.

ii. **Mechanism:** Inhibit phosphodiesterase type 5 (PDE5), leading to smooth muscle relaxation and increased blood flow in the penile tissues, used in erectile dysfunction but sometimes used off-label for urological conditions.

b. Anticholinergic Agents

i. **Examples:** Solifenacin, Darifenacin.

ii. **Mechanism:** Block the action of acetylcholine in the bladder, reducing bladder contractions and symptoms of overactive bladder.

Each class of drugs plays a specific role in managing urinary system conditions and must be used based on individual patient needs and conditions.

A. Hydrochlorothiazide:

Class: Thiazide Diuretic

Mechanism of Action:

a. **Site of Action:** Acts on the distal convoluted tubule of the nephron.
b. **Mechanism:** Hydrochlorothiazide inhibits the Na+/Cl- cotransporter in the distal convoluted tubule, leading to decreased reabsorption of sodium and chloride ions. This results in increased excretion of sodium, chloride, and water, thereby increasing urine output.

Pharmacokinetics:

a. **Absorption:** Well absorbed orally.
b. **Distribution:** Widely distributed in body tissues, including the kidneys.
c. **Metabolism:** Minimal metabolism; primarily excreted unchanged in the urine.
d. **Excretion:** Excreted mainly by the kidneys.

Uses:

a. **Hypertension:** Often used as a first-line treatment for high blood pressure, either alone or in combination with other antihypertensives.
b. **Edema:** Used to manage fluid retention associated with heart failure, liver cirrhosis, or kidney disorders.
c. **Kidney Stones:** Can help in preventing calcium-based kidney stones by reducing calcium excretion.

Adverse Effects:

a. **Electrolyte Imbalances:** Hypokalemia (low potassium), hyponatremia (low sodium), hypomagnesemia (low magnesium).

b. **Metabolic Effects:** Hyperglycemia, hyperlipidemia, and hyperuricemia (which can exacerbate gout).
c. **Gastrointestinal:** Nausea, vomiting, and anorexia.
d. **Allergic Reactions:** Rare but may include rash or photosensitivity.

Clinical Considerations:

a. **Monitoring:** Regular monitoring of electrolytes and renal function is essential to detect and manage potential imbalances.
b. **Combination Therapy:** Often used in combination with other antihypertensives or diuretics to enhance therapeutic effects and reduce the risk of hypokalemia.

B. Chlorthalidone:

Class: Thiazide-Like Diuretic

Mechanism of Action:

a. **Site of Action:** Acts on the distal convoluted tubule of the nephron.
b. **Mechanism:** Chlorthalidone inhibits the Na+/Cl- cotransporter in the distal convoluted tubule, similar to hydrochlorothiazide. This inhibition results in decreased reabsorption of sodium and chloride, leading to increased excretion of these ions and water.

Pharmacokinetics:

a. **Absorption:** Well absorbed orally, with peak plasma concentrations occurring within 6-12 hours.
b. **Distribution:** Extensively bound to plasma proteins and widely distributed in body tissues.
c. **Metabolism:** Minimal metabolism; primarily excreted unchanged in the urine.
d. **Excretion:** Excreted mainly by the kidneys; has a longer half-life compared to hydrochlorothiazide.

Uses:

a. **Hypertension:** Effective in managing high blood pressure; often used in chronic hypertension management.
b. **Edema:** Used for fluid retention in conditions such as heart failure and chronic kidney disease.
c. **Hypertension in Diabetes:** It may be preferred over other diuretics in diabetic patients due to a lower risk of adverse effects on glucose metabolism.

Adverse Effects:

a. **Electrolyte Imbalances:** Hypokalemia, hypomagnesemia, and hyponatremia.
b. **Metabolic Effects:** Hyperglycemia, hyperlipidemia, and hyperuricemia.
c. **Gastrointestinal:** Nausea, vomiting, and anorexia.
d. **Other Effects:** Dizziness, fatigue, and occasional allergic reactions.

Clinical Considerations:

a. **Monitoring:** Regular monitoring of electrolytes and renal function is crucial to manage potential imbalances and assess efficacy.
b. **Long Half-Life:** Due to its longer half-life, chlorthalidone often provides a more sustained diuretic effect compared to hydrochlorothiazide.

Comparison of Hydrochlorothiazide and Chlorthalidone

1. **Duration of Action:** Chlorthalidone has a longer duration of action compared to hydrochlorothiazide, which can affect dosing frequency and clinical choice.
2. **Effectiveness:** Both are effective in lowering blood pressure and managing edema, but chlorthalidone's longer half-life may offer better 24-hour blood pressure control.

3. **Side Effects:** Both drugs have similar side effects related to electrolyte imbalances and metabolic effects, but the overall side effect profile can vary based on individual patient response and long-term use.

C. **Indapamide:**

Class: Thiazide-Like Diuretic

Mechanism of Action:

a. **Site of Action:** Acts on the distal convoluted tubule of the nephron.
b. **Mechanism:** Indapamide inhibits the Na+/Cl- cotransporter in the distal convoluted tubule, reducing sodium and chloride reabsorption. This leads to increased excretion of sodium, chloride, and water, resulting in a diuretic effect.

Pharmacokinetics:

a. **Absorption:** Well absorbed from the gastrointestinal tract, with peak plasma concentrations typically occurring 1-2 hours after oral administration.
b. **Distribution:** Widely distributed in body tissues, including the kidneys. It has a high protein binding rate.
c. **Metabolism:** Metabolized in the liver to inactive metabolites.
d. **Excretion:** Primarily excreted in the urine; has a half-life that allows for once-daily dosing.

Uses:

a. **Hypertension:** Used to manage high blood pressure, often as a first-line treatment or in combination with other antihypertensives.
b. **Edema:** Can be used to manage fluid retention associated with heart failure, chronic kidney disease, and liver cirrhosis.

Adverse Effects:

a. **Electrolyte Imbalances:** Hypokalemia (low potassium), hypomagnesemia (low magnesium), hyponatremia (low sodium).
b. **Metabolic Effects:** Hyperglycemia, hyperlipidemia.

c. **Gastrointestinal:** Nausea, vomiting, and anorexia.

d. **Allergic Reactions:** Rash and other allergic reactions can occur, though they are relatively rare.

Clinical Considerations:

a. **Monitoring:** Regular monitoring of electrolytes and renal function is important to manage potential imbalances and to ensure efficacy.

b. **Combination Therapy:** Often used in combination with other antihypertensive agents for better control of blood pressure.

D. Furosemide:

Class: Loop Diuretic

Mechanism of Action:

a. **Site of Action:** Acts on the thick ascending limb of the loop of Henle in the nephron.

b. **Mechanism:** Furosemide inhibits the Na+/K+/2Cl- cotransporter in the thick ascending limb of the loop of Henle. This inhibition prevents the reabsorption of sodium, potassium, and chloride, leading to a significant increase in the excretion of these ions and water, and thus a potent diuretic effect.

Pharmacokinetics:

a. **Absorption:** Well absorbed orally; onset of action is typically within 30 minutes to 1 hour when taken orally.

b. **Distribution:** Extensively bound to plasma proteins and distributed widely in body tissues.

c. **Metabolism:** Minimal hepatic metabolism; primarily excreted unchanged in the urine.

d. **Excretion:** Excreted predominantly by the kidneys; has a short half-life (about 1-2 hours), which may necessitate multiple daily doses.

Uses:

a. **Edema:** Used for the management of edema associated with heart failure, liver cirrhosis, chronic kidney disease, and pulmonary edema.
b. **Hypertension:** Can be used in resistant cases of hypertension, often in combination with other antihypertensives.
c. **Hypercalcemia:** Used to promote calcium excretion in cases of hypercalcemia.

Adverse Effects:

a. **Electrolyte Imbalances:** Hypokalemia, hypomagnesemia, hypocalcemia, and metabolic alkalosis.
b. **Dehydration:** Risk of volume depletion and hypotension.
c. **Ototoxicity:** Risk of hearing impairment, particularly with high doses or rapid intravenous administration.
d. **Renal Function:** Can potentially worsen renal function in susceptible individuals.

Clinical Considerations:

a. **Monitoring:** Close monitoring of electrolytes, renal function, and blood pressure is essential to avoid adverse effects and ensure therapeutic efficacy.
b. **Dosing:** Dosage may need to be adjusted based on the severity of the condition and the patient's response, and due to its potent diuretic effect, careful management is necessary to avoid dehydration and electrolyte imbalances.

Comparison of Indapamide and Furosemide

1. **Site of Action:**
    a. **Indapamide:** Distal convoluted tubule.
    b. **Furosemide:** Thick ascending limb of the loop of Henle.
2. **Potency and Duration:**

a. **Indapamide:** Generally less potent compared to furosemide; suitable for mild to moderate fluid retention and hypertension. It has a longer duration of action and is often administered once daily.

b. **Furosemide:** Highly potent diuretic; effective for more severe fluid overload and conditions that require a more substantial diuretic effect. It has a shorter half-life and may require multiple doses per day.

3. **Adverse Effects:**

a. **Indapamide:** Risks include hypokalemia, but typically less severe compared to furosemide. Metabolic effects like hyperglycemia and hyperlipidemia are also notable.

b. **Furosemide:** Higher risk of severe electrolyte imbalances and dehydration. Ototoxicity is a unique risk associated with high doses or rapid intravenous administration.

4. **Clinical Use:**

a. **Indapamide:** Preferred for hypertension and mild to moderate edema; often used in combination with other antihypertensive agents.

b. **Furosemide:** Preferred for acute and severe edema, such as in heart failure or pulmonary edema, and in cases of resistance to other diuretics.

E. **Bumetanide:**

Class: Loop Diuretic

Mechanism of Action:

a. **Site of Action:** Acts on the thick ascending limb of the loop of Henle in the nephron.

b. **Mechanism:** Bumetanide inhibits the $Na^+/K^+/2Cl^-$ cotransporter in the thick ascending limb of the loop of Henle. This inhibition prevents reabsorption of sodium, potassium, and chloride, leading to a substantial increase in the excretion of these ions and water.

Pharmacokinetics:

a. **Absorption:** Well absorbed from the gastrointestinal tract; oral bioavailability is approximately 80-90%.
b. **Distribution:** Widely distributed in body tissues and highly protein-bound.
c. **Metabolism:** Minimal hepatic metabolism; primarily excreted unchanged in the urine.
d. **Excretion:** Excreted primarily by the kidneys. The half-life is approximately 1-2 hours, which may necessitate multiple doses per day for sustained effect.

Uses:

a. **Edema:** Used to manage fluid retention in conditions such as heart failure, liver cirrhosis, and renal disease.
b. **Hypertension:** Can be used for cases of resistant hypertension, often in combination with other antihypertensives.
c. **Hypercalcemia:** Helps to manage hypercalcemia by increasing calcium excretion.

Adverse Effects:

a. **Electrolyte Imbalances:** Hypokalemia (low potassium), hypomagnesemia (low magnesium), and metabolic alkalosis.
b. **Dehydration:** Risk of volume depletion and hypotension.
c. **Ototoxicity:** Potential risk of hearing loss, particularly with rapid intravenous administration or high doses.
d. **Renal Function:** May worsen renal function in patients with preexisting renal conditions.

Clinical Considerations:

a. **Monitoring:** Regular monitoring of electrolytes, renal function, and blood pressure is crucial to avoid complications and ensure efficacy.
b. **Dosing:** Typically requires careful dosage adjustments based on clinical response and tolerance. Due to its potent effect, dosages should be titrated carefully to avoid dehydration and electrolyte imbalances.

F. Torsemide:

Class: Loop Diuretic

Mechanism of Action:

a. **Site of Action:** Acts on the thick ascending limb of the loop of Henle in the nephron.
b. **Mechanism:** Torsemide inhibits the Na+/K+/2Cl- cotransporter in the thick ascending limb of the loop of Henle, similar to other loop diuretics. This inhibition leads to increased excretion of sodium, potassium, and chloride, along with water.

Pharmacokinetics:

a. **Absorption:** Well absorbed from the gastrointestinal tract with an oral bioavailability of approximately 80-90%.
b. **Distribution:** Extensively bound to plasma proteins and distributed throughout the body.
c. **Metabolism:** Metabolized in the liver to inactive metabolites.
d. **Excretion:** Excreted primarily via the urine. Torsemide has a longer half-life compared to other loop diuretics (approximately 3-4 hours), allowing for once-daily dosing in many cases.

Uses:

a. **Edema:** Effective in managing fluid retention associated with heart failure, chronic kidney disease, and liver cirrhosis.
b. **Hypertension:** Used in the treatment of hypertension, particularly in patients who do not respond adequately to other diuretics.

c. **Heart Failure:** Commonly used in heart failure to reduce fluid overload and improve symptoms.

Adverse Effects:

a. **Electrolyte Imbalances:** Hypokalemia, hypomagnesemia, and metabolic alkalosis.

b. **Dehydration:** Risk of volume depletion and hypotension.

c. **Renal Function:** Can potentially worsen renal function in patients with preexisting kidney conditions.

d. **Gastrointestinal:** Nausea and other gastrointestinal symptoms may occur.

Clinical Considerations:

a. **Monitoring:** Regular monitoring of electrolytes and renal function is essential to manage potential side effects and ensure effective treatment.

b. **Dosing:** Due to its longer half-life, torsemide is often dosed once daily, which can improve patient compliance compared to other loop diuretics.

Comparison of Bumetanide and Torsemide

1. **Potency and Duration:**
    a. **Bumetanide:** More potent on a per-milligram basis compared to many other loop diuretics. Has a shorter half-life (1-2 hours) requiring multiple doses per day.
    b. **Torsemide:** Has a longer half-life (3-4 hours), allowing for once-daily dosing. Generally has a similar or slightly less potent diuretic effect compared to bumetanide.
2. **Adverse Effects:**
    a. **Bumetanide:** Similar risk of electrolyte imbalances and dehydration, with a notable risk of ototoxicity.
    b. **Torsemide:** Similar electrolyte imbalances and dehydration risks, but lower risk of ototoxicity compared to bumetanide.
3. **Clinical Use:**

a. **Bumetanide:** Often used in acute settings or where potent diuretic effects are needed. Useful in managing severe edema and resistant hypertension.
b. **Torsemide:** Preferred for chronic management due to its longer half-life and convenient once-daily dosing. Effective for both hypertension and edema.

J. **Ethacrynic Acid:**

Class: Loop Diuretic

Mechanism of Action:

a. **Site of Action:** Acts on the thick ascending limb of the loop of Henle in the nephron.
b. **Mechanism:** Ethacrynic acid inhibits the Na+/K+/2Cl- cotransporter in the thick ascending limb of the loop of Henle. This inhibition prevents the reabsorption of sodium, potassium, and chloride, leading to significant diuresis (increased urine production) and a reduction in fluid overload.

Pharmacokinetics:

a. **Absorption:** Well absorbed orally; peak plasma concentrations are typically reached within 1-2 hours after oral administration.
b. **Distribution:** Extensively bound to plasma proteins and distributed widely in body tissues.
c. **Metabolism:** Metabolized in the liver to inactive metabolites.
d. **Excretion:** Excreted primarily via the kidneys; has a half-life of about 2-3 hours, which often necessitates multiple doses per day.

Uses:

a. **Edema:** Used for managing fluid retention associated with heart failure, liver cirrhosis, and kidney disorders.
b. **Hypertension:** Can be used in cases of resistant hypertension or when other loop diuretics are ineffective.

c. **Hypercalcemia:** Assists in managing hypercalcemia by increasing calcium excretion.

Adverse Effects:

a. **Electrolyte Imbalances:** Hypokalemia, hypomagnesemia, and metabolic alkalosis.
b. **Dehydration:** Risk of volume depletion, leading to hypotension.
c. **Ototoxicity:** High risk of hearing impairment and tinnitus, particularly with rapid intravenous administration or high doses.
d. **Renal Function:** Can potentially worsen renal function in susceptible individuals.

Clinical Considerations:

a. **Monitoring:** Regular monitoring of electrolytes, renal function, and blood pressure is crucial due to the risk of dehydration and electrolyte imbalances.
b. **Dosing:** Requires careful dosage adjustments to avoid adverse effects, particularly in patients with preexisting renal conditions.

H. Spironolactone:

Class: Potassium-Sparing Diuretic (Aldosterone Antagonist)

Mechanism of Action:

a. **Site of Action:** Acts on the distal convoluted tubule and collecting ducts in the nephron.
b. **Mechanism:** Spironolactone competes with aldosterone for binding to mineralocorticoid receptors in the distal convoluted tubule and collecting ducts. By antagonizing aldosterone, it inhibits sodium reabsorption and reduces potassium excretion, leading to increased potassium retention and sodium and water excretion.

Pharmacokinetics:

a. **Absorption:** Well absorbed from the gastrointestinal tract, but undergoes significant first-pass metabolism in the liver.
b. **Distribution:** Widely distributed in body tissues; highly protein-bound.
c. **Metabolism:** Metabolized in the liver to active metabolites, including canrenone.
d. **Excretion:** Excreted primarily in the urine. The half-life of spironolactone is about 1.4 hours, while its active metabolite canrenone has a longer half-life.

Uses:

a. **Edema:** Used to manage fluid retention associated with heart failure, liver cirrhosis, and nephrotic syndrome.
b. **Hypertension:** Often used in combination with other antihypertensives to manage high blood pressure.
c. **Primary Hyperaldosteronism:** Used to treat conditions caused by excessive aldosterone production.
d. **Acne and Hirsutism:** Used off-label for its anti-androgenic effects in conditions like acne and hirsutism.

Adverse Effects:

a. **Electrolyte Imbalances:** Hyperkalemia (high potassium) is the most notable side effect. Other imbalances include hyponatremia.
b. **Endocrine Effects:** Can cause gynecomastia (breast tissue enlargement in males), menstrual irregularities, and sexual dysfunction.
c. **Gastrointestinal:** Nausea, vomiting, and diarrhea.
d. **Rash:** Can cause skin rashes and allergic reactions.

Clinical Considerations:

a. **Monitoring:** Regular monitoring of serum potassium levels is essential to prevent hyperkalemia. Kidney function should also be monitored regularly.

b. **Combination Therapy:** Often used in combination with other diuretics, such as thiazides or loop diuretics, to counteract hypokalemia and enhance diuretic efficacy.

Comparison of Ethacrynic Acid and Spironolactone

1. **Mechanism of Action:**
    a. **Ethacrynic Acid:** Inhibits the Na+/K+/2Cl- cotransporter in the thick ascending limb of the loop of Henle, leading to potent diuresis.
    b. **Spironolactone:** Antagonizes aldosterone in the distal nephron, leading to potassium retention and sodium and water excretion.
2. **Potency and Duration:**
    a. **Ethacrynic Acid:** Has a strong diuretic effect but requires multiple doses due to its short half-life.
    b. **Spironolactone:** Less potent as a diuretic compared to loop diuretics; typically used for its potassium-sparing properties and as part of combination therapy.
3. **Adverse Effects:**
    a. **Ethacrynic Acid:** High risk of ototoxicity and electrolyte imbalances.
    b. **Spironolactone:** Risk of hyperkalemia and endocrine-related side effects.
4. **Clinical Use:**
    a. **Ethacrynic Acid:** Preferred in acute and severe fluid overload conditions, particularly when other loop diuretics are contraindicated or ineffective.
    b. **Spironolactone:** Preferred for chronic conditions, particularly where potassium-sparing is desirable, and for specific indications like primary hyperaldosteronism and hormonal disorders.

CHAPTER – 11

AUTOCOIDS – I

Mr. Prabhakar Singh Tiwari

Associate Professor, Rajiv Gandhi Institute of Pharmacy, Faculty of Pharmaceutical Science & Technology, AKS University Satna, (M.P.)

ABSTRACT:

Autacoids are locally acting bioactive substances that have hormone-like effects and play key roles in various physiological and pathological processes. They are produced and act locally, with rapid onset and short duration of action. Autacoids include biogenic amines like histamine and serotonin (5-HT), eicosanoids such as prostaglandins and thromboxanes, and peptides like bradykinin. These substances are involved in inflammation, allergy, pain, and vascular homeostasis, mediating responses to injury and stress. Histamine and serotonin (5-HT) are important biogenic amines that regulate numerous physiological functions. Histamine, stored in mast cells and basophils, is released during allergic reactions, causing vasodilation, increased vascular permeability, and bronchoconstriction. Antihistamines, like diphenhydramine (H1 antagonist) and ranitidine (H2 antagonist), are used to treat allergies and acid-peptic diseases. Serotonin, mainly found in the gastrointestinal tract, platelets, and CNS, influences mood, appetite, and vascular tone. Serotonin antagonists, such as ondansetron (5-HT3 antagonist) for nausea and cyproheptadine (5-HT2 antagonist) for migraines, are therapeutic agents that modulate its effects. Prostaglandins are lipid compounds derived from arachidonic acid and produced by almost all tissues. They have diverse functions, including mediating inflammation, pain, fever, and regulating blood flow, gastric protection, and uterine contractions. Specific prostaglandins, like PGE2 and PGI2, act through distinct receptors to exert their effects. Synthetic prostaglandins, such as misoprostol, are used to prevent NSAID-induced gastric ulcers, induce labor, and manage glaucoma. Due to their broad physiological roles, prostaglandins are vital in both normal bodily functions and disease states.Thromboxanes, also derived from arachidonic acid, are primarily produced in platelets and play a crucial role in hemostasis and thrombosis. Thromboxane A2 (TXA2) promotes platelet aggregation and vasoconstriction, essential for blood clot formation. Aspirin, a common thromboxane inhibitor, irreversibly inhibits cyclooxygenase-1 (COX-1), reducing TXA2 production and thereby preventing clot formation. This makes aspirin a key drug in the prevention and treatment of cardiovascular diseases such as myocardial infarction and stroke, highlighting the therapeutic importance of modulating thromboxane activity.

INTRODUCTION:

Autocoids are a diverse group of biologically active substances that are synthesized and act locally within the body. They play crucial roles in various physiological and pathological processes. The term "autocoids" comes from the Greek words "auto" (self) and "coid" (like), implying that these substances act on the cells that produce them or in their immediate vicinity. They can be classified into several categories, each with distinct roles and mechanisms of action.

Types of Autocoids

1. **Histamines**:
    a. **Synthesis and Release**: Histamines are synthesized from histidine by the enzyme histidine decarboxylase. They are stored primarily in mast cells and basophils.
    b. **Action**: Histamines bind to histamine receptors (H1, H2, H3, and H4). H1 receptors are involved in allergic reactions and inflammation, H2 receptors regulate gastric acid secretion, H3 receptors modulate neurotransmitter release, and H4 receptors are involved in immune responses.

c. **Clinical Use**: Antihistamines (H1 antagonists) are used to treat allergic reactions, motion sickness, and insomnia. H2 antagonists are used to treat gastric acid-related conditions like peptic ulcers.

2. **Prostaglandins**:
   a. **Synthesis and Release**: Prostaglandins are synthesized from arachidonic acid via the cyclooxygenase (COX) enzymes (COX-1 and COX-2). They are produced in response to various stimuli and act locally.
   b. **Action**: Prostaglandins influence a wide range of physiological processes including inflammation, pain, fever, and platelet aggregation. They also play roles in the regulation of blood flow, gastrointestinal mucosal protection, and uterine contractions.
   c. **Clinical Use**: Nonsteroidal anti-inflammatory drugs (NSAIDs) and selective COX-2 inhibitors are used to manage pain, inflammation, and fever. Prostaglandin analogs are used to induce labor and manage gastric ulcers.
3. **Leukotrienes**:
   a. **Synthesis and Release**: Leukotrienes are derived from arachidonic acid via the lipoxygenase pathway. They are produced primarily by leukocytes.
   b. **Action**: Leukotrienes are involved in inflammatory responses and play a role in asthma and allergic reactions. They cause bronchoconstriction and increased mucus production.
   c. **Clinical Use**: Leukotriene receptor antagonists are used in the management of asthma and allergic rhinitis.
4. **Bradykinin**:
   a. **Synthesis and Release**: Bradykinin is produced from kininogen by the action of the enzyme kallikrein. It is involved in the kinin-kallikrein system.

b. **Action**: Bradykinin causes vasodilation, increases vascular permeability, and induces pain. It is involved in inflammatory responses and hypotension.
c. **Clinical Use**: Bradykinin-related drugs are not commonly used therapeutically, but ACE inhibitors (which increase bradykinin levels) are used for hypertension and heart failure.

5. **Serotonin (5-HT)**:
    a. **Synthesis and Release**: Serotonin is synthesized from tryptophan and stored in the enterochromaffin cells of the gastrointestinal tract and in platelets.
    b. **Action**: Serotonin regulates mood, appetite, and sleep. It also affects gastrointestinal motility and can induce vasoconstriction.
    c. **Clinical Use**: Serotonin reuptake inhibitors (SSRIs) are used as antidepressants. Other serotonin modulators are used for conditions like migraines and irritable bowel syndrome.
6. **Nitric Oxide (NO)**:
    a. **Synthesis and Release**: Nitric oxide is synthesized from L-arginine by nitric oxide synthase (NOS) enzymes. It is a gaseous signaling molecule.
    b. **Action**: Nitric oxide acts as a vasodilator, influences neurotransmission, and modulates immune responses. It plays a role in regulating blood pressure and penile erection.
    c. **Clinical Use**: Nitric oxide donors and phosphodiesterase type 5 inhibitors (e.g., sildenafil) are used in the treatment of angina and erectile dysfunction.

Related Drugs

1. **Antihistamines**: These include drugs like diphenhydramine (Benadryl), loratadine (Claritin), and ranitidine (Zantac).
2. **NSAIDs**: These include ibuprofen, aspirin, and naproxen.

3. **Leukotriene Receptor Antagonists**: These include montelukast (Singulair).
4. **ACE Inhibitors**: These include enalapril, lisinopril, and ramipril.

HISTAMINE, 5-HT AND THEIR ANTAGONISTS

Histamine:

Histamine is a biogenic amine involved in various physiological processes and pathological conditions. It plays a crucial role in immune responses, gastric acid secretion, and neurotransmission.

Synthesis and Release

1. **Synthesis**: Histamine is synthesized from the amino acid histidine through the decarboxylation reaction catalyzed by the enzyme histidine decarboxylase.
2. **Storage**: Histamine is stored primarily in mast cells and basophils, as well as in enterochromaffin-like cells in the gastric mucosa.
3. **Release**: Histamine is released in response to various stimuli, including allergens, tissue injury, and immune responses.

Receptors and Actions

Histamine acts through four types of receptors, which are G-protein-coupled receptors (GPCRs):

1. **H1 Receptors**:
   a. **Location**: Found in the smooth muscle, endothelium, and central nervous system.
   b. **Effects**: Mediate allergic reactions such as vasodilation, increased vascular permeability, bronchoconstriction, and pruritus. In the central nervous system, they can affect wakefulness and appetite.
2. **H2 Receptors**:
   a. **Location**: Predominantly in the gastric parietal cells.

b. **Effects**: Stimulate gastric acid secretion and pepsin production in the stomach. They also have effects on the cardiovascular system and can influence cardiac rate and force.

3. **H3 Receptors**:
    a. **Location**: Primarily in the central nervous system.
    b. **Effects**: Regulate neurotransmitter release, including histamine, dopamine, and norepinephrine. They have roles in modulating cognition, mood, and appetite.
4. **H4 Receptors**:
    a. **Location**: Found in the bone marrow and various immune cells.
    b. **Effects**: Involved in modulating immune responses and inflammatory processes.

Histamine Antagonists

1. **H1 Antagonists (Antihistamines)**:
    a. **First-Generation**:
        i. **Examples**: Diphenhydramine (Benadryl), Chlorpheniramine, Promethazine.
        ii. **Characteristics**: These can cross the blood-brain barrier, causing sedative effects. They are used to treat allergic reactions, motion sickness, and insomnia.
    b. **Second-Generation**:
        i. **Examples**: Loratadine (Claritin), Cetirizine (Zyrtec), Fexofenadine (Allegra).
        ii. **Characteristics**: These have reduced sedative effects as they are less likely to cross the blood-brain barrier. They are used primarily for allergic rhinitis and chronic urticaria.
2. **H2 Antagonists**:
    a. **Examples**: Ranitidine (Zantac), Famotidine (Pepcid), Cimetidine (Tagamet).

b. **Characteristics**: These are used to reduce gastric acid secretion and treat conditions like peptic ulcers, gastroesophageal reflux disease (GERD), and Zollinger-Ellison syndrome.

Serotonin (5-HT)

Serotonin (5-Hydroxytryptamine, 5-HT) is a biogenic amine involved in regulating mood, appetite, sleep, and gastrointestinal motility.

Synthesis and Release

1. **Synthesis**: Serotonin is synthesized from tryptophan, which is converted into 5-hydroxytryptophan (5-HTP) and then into serotonin by the enzyme aromatic L-amino acid decarboxylase.
2. **Storage**: It is stored in enterochromaffin cells in the gastrointestinal tract and in platelets.
3. **Release**: Serotonin is released in response to various physiological stimuli and acts locally in the gastrointestinal tract and central nervous system.

Receptors and Actions

Serotonin acts through various receptors, classified into several families:

1. **5-HT1 Receptors**:
    a. **Location**: Found in the central nervous system.
    b. **Effects**: These receptors have subtypes (5-HT1A, 5-HT1B, etc.) that influence mood, anxiety, and depression.
2. **5-HT2 Receptors**:
    a. **Location**: Found in various tissues including the central nervous system and smooth muscle.
    b. **Effects**: Involved in regulating mood, cognition, and smooth muscle contraction. Subtypes include 5-HT2A, 5-HT2B, and 5-HT2C.
3. **5-HT3 Receptors**:

a. **Location**: Found in the gastrointestinal tract and central nervous system.
b. **Effects**: These receptors are involved in mediating nausea and vomiting.

4. **5-HT4 Receptors**:
   a. **Location**: Found in the gastrointestinal tract and central nervous system.
   b. **Effects**: These receptors influence gastrointestinal motility and cognition.
5. **5-HT5, 5-HT6, and 5-HT7 Receptors**:
   a. **Location**: Found in various tissues including the central nervous system.
   b. **Effects**: Involved in mood regulation and cognitive functions.

Serotonin Antagonists

1. **5-HT3 Antagonists**:
   a. **Examples**: Ondansetron, Granisetron, Palonosetron.
   b. **Characteristics**: These are primarily used as antiemetics to prevent nausea and vomiting associated with chemotherapy and surgery.
2. **5-HT2A Antagonists**:
   a. **Examples**: Atypical antipsychotics like Clozapine, Olanzapine, and Risperidone.
   b. **Characteristics**: These are used in the treatment of schizophrenia and bipolar disorder due to their effects on mood and cognition.
3. **5-HT1A Agonists**:
   a. **Examples**: Buspirone.
   b. **Characteristics**: Used as an anxiolytic to treat anxiety disorders.
4. **5-HT4 Agonists**:
   a. **Examples**: Tegaserod.

b. **Characteristics**: Used for gastrointestinal motility disorders like irritable bowel syndrome (IBS).

Summary

1. **Histamine**: Plays key roles in allergic reactions, gastric acid secretion, and neurotransmission. Antihistamines are used to counteract its effects.
2. **Serotonin (5-HT)**: Regulates mood, appetite, sleep, and gastrointestinal function. Serotonin receptor modulators are used to treat various conditions including depression, anxiety, and nausea.

PROSTAGLANDINS

Prostaglandins are a group of bioactive lipids that have a wide range of physiological effects in the body. They are synthesized from arachidonic acid, a fatty acid found in cell membranes, through the cyclooxygenase (COX) pathway. Prostaglandins are involved in various processes including inflammation, pain, fever, and regulation of blood flow.

Synthesis and Release

1. **Synthesis**: Prostaglandins are synthesized from arachidonic acid, which is released from cell membrane phospholipids by phospholipase A2. The arachidonic acid is then converted into prostaglandins by the cyclooxygenase (COX) enzymes:
   a. **COX-1**: Constitutively expressed and involved in normal cellular functions and homeostasis.
   b. **COX-2**: Inducible and typically expressed in response to inflammation, growth factors, and cytokines.
2. **Release**: Prostaglandins are produced and released locally at the site of their action. They act in a paracrine or autocrine manner, affecting nearby cells or the cells that produce them.

Types of Prostaglandins and Their Actions

1. **Prostaglandin E2 (PGE2)**:

a. **Effects**: Involved in inflammation, fever, and pain. It promotes vasodilation, increases vascular permeability, and stimulates uterine contractions. It also plays a role in protecting the gastrointestinal mucosa by stimulating mucus secretion and inhibiting gastric acid secretion.
b. **Clinical Use**: PGE2 analogs (e.g., dinoprostone) are used to induce labor and to treat gastric ulcers.

2. **Prostaglandin I2 (PGI2, also known as Prostacyclin)**:
   a. **Effects**: Acts as a potent vasodilator and inhibits platelet aggregation. It is involved in the regulation of blood flow and blood pressure.
   b. **Clinical Use**: PGI2 analogs (e.g., iloprost) are used to treat pulmonary arterial hypertension and to manage conditions where enhanced vasodilation is needed.
3. **Prostaglandin F2α (PGF2α)**:
   a. **Effects**: Stimulates uterine contractions and bronchoconstriction. It is involved in the regulation of reproductive processes and can induce labor.
   b. **Clinical Use**: PGF2α analogs (e.g., carboprost) are used for labor induction and to control postpartum hemorrhage.
4. **Prostaglandin D2 (PGD2)**:
   a. **Effects**: Involved in regulating sleep, causing bronchoconstriction, and modulating immune responses. It plays a role in allergic reactions and inflammation.
   b. **Clinical Use**: PGD2-related drugs are not commonly used clinically but are being studied for their roles in conditions like asthma and allergic diseases.

Clinical Use of Prostaglandin Analogs

1. **Dinoprostone (PGE2 Analog)**:

   a. **Uses**: Induces labor, manages postpartum hemorrhage, and helps in cervical ripening.
   b. **Administration**: Available as a gel or insert for cervical ripening and induction of labor.
2. **Misoprostol (PGE1 Analog)**:
   a. **Uses**: Used for prevention of nonsteroidal anti-inflammatory drug (NSAID)-induced gastric ulcers and as part of medical abortion protocols.
   b. **Administration**: Oral or vaginal tablets.
3. **Iloprost (PGI2 Analog)**:
   a. **Uses**: Used in the treatment of pulmonary arterial hypertension to improve exercise capacity and quality of life.
   b. **Administration**: Inhalation or intravenous infusion.
4. **Carboprost (PGF2α Analog)**:
   a. **Uses**: Controls postpartum hemorrhage by inducing uterine contractions and is used to terminate pregnancies in the second trimester.
   b. **Administration**: Intramuscular injection.
5. **Latanoprost (PGF2α Analog)**:
   a. **Uses**: Used to reduce intraocular pressure in glaucoma.
   b. **Administration**: Ophthalmic drops.

Mechanism of Action of Prostaglandins

Prostaglandins exert their effects by binding to specific G-protein-coupled receptors (GPCRs) on the target cells. These receptors are coupled to various intracellular signaling pathways that regulate cellular responses. The specific effects of prostaglandins depend on the type of receptor activated and the tissue in which they act.

Inhibitors of Prostaglandin Synthesis

1. **Nonsteroidal Anti-Inflammatory Drugs (NSAIDs)**: These drugs inhibit COX enzymes, thereby reducing prostaglandin synthesis. Examples include:
    a. **Aspirin**: Irreversibly inhibits COX-1 and COX-2.
    b. **Ibuprofen and Naproxen**: Reversibly inhibit COX-1 and COX-2.
    c. **Celecoxib**: Selectively inhibits COX-2, reducing inflammation and pain while sparing COX-1 and its protective effects on the gastrointestinal mucosa.

THROMBOXANES

Thromboxanes are a class of eicosanoids derived from arachidonic acid through the cyclooxygenase (COX) pathway. They play a crucial role in hemostasis and thrombus formation. The most well-known thromboxane is **Thromboxane A2 (TXA2)**.

Synthesis and Release

1. **Synthesis**: Thromboxanes are synthesized from arachidonic acid by the enzyme cyclooxygenase (COX) and then converted into thromboxanes by thromboxane synthase. This process primarily occurs in platelets.

$$\text{Arachidonic acid} \xrightarrow{\text{COX}} \text{Prostaglandin H2 (PGH2)} \xrightarrow{\text{Thromboxane synthase}} \text{Thromboxane A2 (TXA2)}$$

2. **Release**: Thromboxanes are released from platelets upon activation or stimulation. They act locally at their site of synthesis, primarily influencing platelet aggregation and vasoconstriction.

Functions of Thromboxanes

1. **Platelet Aggregation**:
    a. **Role**: TXA2 promotes platelet aggregation by stimulating the expression of platelet surface receptors that facilitate the binding of platelets to each other. This aggregation is a crucial step in thrombus (blood clot) formation.

b. **Mechanism**: TXA2 binds to thromboxane receptors (TP receptors) on platelets, leading to increased intracellular calcium levels and activation of platelet aggregation pathways.

2. **Vasoconstriction**:
   a. **Role**: TXA2 induces vasoconstriction, which helps in reducing blood flow and stabilizing the thrombus at the site of injury.
   b. **Mechanism**: TXA2 acts on vascular smooth muscle cells through TP receptors, causing contraction and narrowing of blood vessels.
3. **Regulation of Hemostasis**:
   a. **Role**: TXA2 is involved in the regulation of hemostasis, ensuring proper blood clot formation and prevention of excessive bleeding.
   b. **Mechanism**: By promoting platelet aggregation and vasoconstriction, TXA2 helps in stabilizing the blood clot and preventing further bleeding.

Clinical Relevance and Drugs

1. **Thromboxane Inhibitors**:
   a. **Examples**: There are no specific thromboxane inhibitors widely used in clinical practice. However, drugs that inhibit COX enzymes or affect platelet function can indirectly reduce TXA2 levels.
      i. **Aspirin**: Irreversibly inhibits COX-1, which reduces the synthesis of thromboxane A2 in platelets. This decreases platelet aggregation and is used for the prevention of cardiovascular events, such as heart attacks and strokes.
      ii. **Clopidogrel and Ticagrelor**: These are antiplatelet drugs that inhibit platelet aggregation through mechanisms that may affect TXA2 pathways indirectly.
2. **Thromboxane Receptor Antagonists**:

a. **Examples**: Some experimental or investigational drugs act as thromboxane receptor antagonists, but they are not yet widely used in clinical practice.

    i. **Examples in Research**: Prasugrel and other novel compounds are being studied for their effects on thromboxane receptors and their potential use in managing thrombotic disorders.

Mechanism of Action

1. **Thromboxane A2**: TXA2 binds to thromboxane receptors (TP receptors) on platelets and vascular smooth muscle cells. This binding activates intracellular signaling pathways that lead to:
    a. **Increased Platelet Aggregation**: TXA2 enhances the binding of platelets to each other, promoting clot formation.
    b. **Vasoconstriction**: TXA2 induces contraction of smooth muscle cells, leading to narrowing of blood vessels.

Pathophysiology and Implications

1. **Excessive Thromboxane Production**: Overproduction of thromboxane A2 can lead to excessive platelet aggregation and increased risk of thrombotic events such as heart attacks and strokes.

Inhibition of Thromboxane: Reducing TXA2 production or action can be beneficial in preventing thrombotic disorders and managing conditions such as coronary artery disease and peripheral artery disease

CHAPTER – 12

AUTOCOIDS –II

Ms. Neha Goel

Associate Professor, Rajiv Gandhi Institute of Pharmacy, Faculty of Pharmaceutical Science & Technology, AKS University Satna, (M.P.)

ABSTRACT:

Leukotrienes are eicosanoids derived from arachidonic acid through the lipoxygenase pathway. They play a significant role in the inflammatory response, particularly in conditions like asthma and allergic rhinitis. Leukotrienes cause bronchoconstriction, increase vascular permeability, and attract white blood cells to sites of inflammation. Drugs like montelukast and zafirlukast, which are leukotriene receptor antagonists, are used to manage asthma by preventing leukotriene-induced bronchoconstriction and inflammation, thereby improving respiratory function and reducing symptoms. Angiotensin is a peptide hormone that plays a critical role in the renin-angiotensin-aldosterone system (RAAS), regulating blood pressure and fluid balance. Angiotensin I is converted to the potent vasoconstrictor angiotensin II by the enzyme angiotensin-converting enzyme (ACE). Angiotensin II increases blood pressure by constricting blood vessels and stimulating aldosterone release, leading to sodium and water retention. ACE inhibitors (e.g., lisinopril) and angiotensin II receptor blockers (ARBs, e.g., losartan) are used to treat hypertension, heart failure, and chronic kidney disease by inhibiting these effects. Bradykinin is a peptide that acts as a potent vasodilator, increasing vascular permeability and promoting inflammation. It is involved in the kallikrein-kinin system and plays a role in pain and inflammatory responses. Bradykinin causes the dilation of blood vessels, leading to decreased blood pressure, and can induce symptoms such as coughing and angioedema. ACE inhibitors can increase bradykinin levels, contributing to their blood pressure-lowering effects but also causing side effects like cough. Bradykinin receptor antagonists are being explored for their potential therapeutic uses in conditions involving excessive inflammation and pain. Substance P is a neuropeptide involved in pain transmission and inflammatory processes. It is found in the nervous system and various tissues, where it acts as a neurotransmitter and neuromodulator. Substance P binds to the neurokinin-1 (NK1) receptor, promoting pain perception, vasodilation, and increased vascular permeability. Elevated levels of substance P are associated with conditions like chronic pain, migraines, and inflammatory diseases. NK1 receptor antagonists, such as aprepitant, are used to prevent chemotherapy-induced nausea and vomiting, highlighting the therapeutic potential of targeting substance P pathways in various medical conditions.

LEUKOTRIENES

Leukotrienes are a group of eicosanoids derived from arachidonic acid through the lipoxygenase (LOX) pathway. They play significant roles in inflammatory responses, particularly in allergic and asthma-related conditions. Leukotrienes are produced primarily by leukocytes (white blood cells) and other cells involved in inflammation.

Synthesis and Release

1. **Synthesis**: Leukotrienes are synthesized from arachidonic acid through the lipoxygenase (LOX) pathway. The process involves several steps:
    a. **Release of Arachidonic Acid**: Arachidonic acid is released from cell membrane phospholipids by phospholipase A2.
    b. **Lipoxygenase Conversion**: Arachidonic acid is converted into leukotrienes by lipoxygenase enzymes (e.g., 5-LOX).
    c. **Leukotriene Formation**: The products of lipoxygenase activity are further modified to form various leukotrienes.

$$\text{Arachidonic acid} \xrightarrow{\text{5-LOX}} \text{Leukotriene A4 (LTA4)}$$
$$\text{Leukotriene A4 (LTA4)} \xrightarrow{\text{LTA4 hydrolase}} \text{Leukotriene B4 (LTB4)}$$
$$\text{Leukotriene A4 (LTA4)} \xrightarrow{\text{LTC4 synthase}} \text{Leukotriene C4 (LTC4)}$$
$$\text{Leukotriene C4 (LTC4)} \rightarrow \text{Leukotriene D4 (LTD4)} \rightarrow \text{Leukotriene E4 (LTE4)}$$

2. **Release**: Leukotrienes are released from cells such as mast cells, eosinophils, and neutrophils. They act locally on nearby cells to mediate their effects.

Types of Leukotrienes and Their Actions

1. **Leukotriene B4 (LTB4)**:
    a. **Effects**: Potent chemotactic factor that attracts and activates neutrophils and other leukocytes. It plays a role in amplifying inflammatory responses and promoting tissue damage.
    b. **Mechanism**: Binds to the BLT (leukotriene B4) receptors on neutrophils, leading to increased chemotaxis and activation.
2. **Leukotriene C4 (LTC4), Leukotriene D4 (LTD4), and Leukotriene E4 (LTE4)**:
    a. **Effects**: These leukotrienes are collectively known as cysteinyl leukotrienes. They are involved in bronchoconstriction, increased vascular permeability, and mucus production.
    b. **Mechanism**: Bind to the CystLT (cysteinyl leukotriene) receptors on bronchial smooth muscle and other tissues, leading to bronchoconstriction, increased mucus secretion, and edema.

Clinical Relevance and Drugs

1. **Leukotriene Receptor Antagonists**:
    a. **Examples**: Montelukast (Singulair), Zafirlukast (Accolate), and Pranlukast (Onon).
    b. **Uses**: These drugs block the action of leukotrienes at their receptors and are primarily used to treat asthma and allergic

rhinitis. They help reduce bronchoconstriction, inflammation, and mucus production.

   c. **Mechanism**: By blocking cysteinyl leukotriene receptors, these antagonists reduce the inflammatory response and improve respiratory function in patients with asthma and allergies.

2. **Leukotriene Synthesis Inhibitors**:
   a. **Examples**: Zileuton.
   b. **Uses**: Zileuton inhibits 5-lipoxygenase, the enzyme responsible for the synthesis of leukotrienes. It is used to manage asthma by reducing the production of leukotrienes, thus decreasing inflammation and bronchoconstriction.
   c. **Mechanism**: Inhibits the production of leukotrienes, thereby reducing their levels in the body and mitigating their effects on the respiratory system.

Mechanism of Action

1. **Leukotrienes**: Act through specific G-protein-coupled receptors on target cells. Their actions include:
   a. **LTB4**: Promotes chemotaxis and activation of leukocytes, amplifying the inflammatory response.
   b. **Cysteinyl Leukotrienes (LTC4, LTD4, LTE4)**: Cause bronchoconstriction, increase vascular permeability, and stimulate mucus production, contributing to asthma symptoms and allergic reactions.

Pathophysiology and Implications

1. **Excessive Leukotriene Production**: Overproduction of leukotrienes is associated with inflammatory conditions such as asthma, allergic rhinitis, and certain forms of dermatitis. Elevated levels of cysteinyl leukotrienes contribute to bronchoconstriction and inflammation in asthma.

2. **Inhibition of Leukotrienes**: Reducing leukotriene production or blocking their action can help manage asthma and other inflammatory conditions. Leukotriene receptor antagonists and synthesis inhibitors are valuable in controlling symptoms and improving quality of life for patients with respiratory and allergic conditions.

ANGIOTENSIN

Angiotensin refers to a group of peptides that play a central role in regulating blood pressure, fluid balance, and electrolyte homeostasis. The renin-angiotensin-aldosterone system (RAAS) is a key hormonal system involved in these processes.

Synthesis and Release

1. **Renin**:
    a. **Release**: Renin is an enzyme secreted by the juxtaglomerular cells of the kidneys in response to low blood pressure, low sodium concentration, or sympathetic nervous system activation.
    b. **Function**: Renin catalyzes the conversion of angiotensinogen to angiotensin I.
2. **Angiotensinogen**:
    a. **Source**: A protein produced by the liver and released into the bloodstream.
    b. **Function**: Angiotensinogen is the precursor to angiotensin I.
3. **Angiotensin I**:
    a. **Conversion**: Angiotensin I is converted to angiotensin II by the action of the enzyme angiotensin-converting enzyme (ACE).
4. **Angiotensin II**:
    a. **Synthesis**: Angiotensin II is formed from angiotensin I through the action of ACE.
    b. **Function**: It is the primary active form with potent effects on blood pressure, fluid balance, and electrolyte homeostasis.

5. **Angiotensin III and IV**:
    a. **Synthesis**: These are formed from angiotensin II through the action of various peptidases.
    b. **Function**: They have effects similar to, but generally less potent than, angiotensin II.

Actions of Angiotensin II

1. **Vasoconstriction**:
    a. **Mechanism**: Angiotensin II binds to angiotensin II type 1 receptors (AT1 receptors) on vascular smooth muscle cells, causing vasoconstriction and increasing blood pressure.
    b. **Effect**: Increases systemic vascular resistance, contributing to elevated blood pressure.
2. **Aldosterone Secretion**:
    a. **Mechanism**: Angiotensin II stimulates the adrenal cortex to release aldosterone.
    b. **Effect**: Aldosterone promotes sodium and water reabsorption in the kidneys, increasing blood volume and blood pressure.
3. **Antidiuretic Hormone (ADH) Release**:
    a. **Mechanism**: Angiotensin II stimulates the release of ADH (vasopressin) from the posterior pituitary gland.
    b. **Effect**: ADH promotes water reabsorption in the kidneys, contributing to increased blood volume and pressure.
4. **Renal Effects**:
    a. **Mechanism**: Angiotensin II constricts the efferent arterioles of the kidneys, increasing glomerular filtration pressure and maintaining glomerular filtration rate.
    b. **Effect**: This helps in preserving kidney function and ensuring adequate filtration.
5. **Sympathetic Nervous System Stimulation**:

a. **Mechanism**: Angiotensin II can stimulate the sympathetic nervous system, enhancing vasoconstriction and increasing blood pressure.

Clinical Relevance and Drugs

1. **Angiotensin-Converting Enzyme (ACE) Inhibitors**:
   a. **Examples**: Enalapril, Lisinopril, Ramipril, Captopril.
   b. **Uses**: These drugs inhibit the enzyme ACE, preventing the conversion of angiotensin I to angiotensin II. They are used to treat hypertension, heart failure, and chronic kidney disease.
   c. **Mechanism**: Reduce levels of angiotensin II, leading to vasodilation, decreased aldosterone secretion, and reduced blood pressure.
2. **Angiotensin II Receptor Blockers (ARBs)**:
   a. **Examples**: Losartan, Valsartan, Irbesartan, Candesartan.
   b. **Uses**: These drugs block the action of angiotensin II at the AT1 receptors, preventing its effects on blood vessels and aldosterone secretion. They are used to manage hypertension, heart failure, and diabetic nephropathy.
   c. **Mechanism**: Block angiotensin II from binding to AT1 receptors, leading to vasodilation and decreased blood pressure.
3. **Direct Renin Inhibitors**:
   a. **Examples**: Aliskiren.
   b. **Uses**: These drugs directly inhibit renin, the enzyme responsible for converting angiotensinogen to angiotensin I. They are used for the treatment of hypertension.
   c. **Mechanism**: Reduce the formation of angiotensin I, leading to lower levels of angiotensin II and reduced blood pressure.
4. **Aldosterone Antagonists**:
   a. **Examples**: Spironolactone, Eplerenone.

b. **Uses**: These drugs block the action of aldosterone at its receptors in the kidneys, reducing sodium and water reabsorption and lowering blood pressure. They are used in heart failure, hypertension, and conditions like primary hyperaldosteronism.

c. **Mechanism**: Antagonize the effects of aldosterone, leading to increased sodium and water excretion and decreased blood pressure.

Mechanism of Action

1. **Angiotensin II**: Acts primarily through AT1 receptors, which are G-protein-coupled receptors. Binding of angiotensin II to these receptors triggers a cascade of intracellular events leading to vasoconstriction, aldosterone release, ADH release, and sympathetic activation.

Pathophysiology and Implications

1. **Hypertension**: Overactivity of the RAAS can lead to chronic hypertension, which is a risk factor for cardiovascular disease.
2. **Heart Failure**: In heart failure, increased levels of angiotensin II contribute to fluid retention, increased blood pressure, and worsening of heart failure symptoms.
3. **Chronic Kidney Disease**: Angiotensin II plays a role in kidney damage and progression of chronic kidney disease through its effects on renal hemodynamics and inflammation.

BRADYKININ

Bradykinin is a peptide that functions as an important autocoid in the body, primarily involved in the regulation of blood pressure and inflammatory responses. It is a member of the kallikrein-kinin system.

Synthesis and Release

1. **Synthesis**: Bradykinin is generated from kininogen, a plasma protein, through the action of the enzyme kallikrein. The conversion involves the following steps: Kininogen→KallikreinBradykinin\text{Kininogen}

\xrightarrow{\text{Kallikrein}} \text{Bradykinin}KininogenKallikrein Bradykinin

2. **Release**: Bradykinin is released locally from tissues and has autocrine and paracrine effects.

Actions of Bradykinin

1. **Vasodilation**:
   a. **Mechanism**: Bradykinin acts on B2 receptors on vascular smooth muscle cells, leading to increased production of nitric oxide (NO) and prostacyclin (PGI2), which cause vasodilation and reduce blood pressure.
2. **Increased Vascular Permeability**:
   a. **Mechanism**: Bradykinin increases the permeability of blood vessels, contributing to edema and the extravasation of fluids and proteins into the tissues.
3. **Pain Sensation**:
   a. **Mechanism**: Bradykinin sensitizes nociceptors (pain receptors) and can cause pain and discomfort. It is involved in inflammatory pain.
4. **Bronchoconstriction**:
   a. **Mechanism**: Bradykinin can induce bronchoconstriction, contributing to respiratory symptoms in conditions like asthma.

Clinical Relevance and Drugs

1. **ACE Inhibitors**:
   a. **Examples**: Enalapril, Lisinopril.
   b. **Uses**: ACE inhibitors increase bradykinin levels by blocking its degradation. This contributes to their antihypertensive effect and has implications for cough and angioedema as side effects.
2. **Bradykinin Receptor Antagonists**:
   a. **Examples**: Icatibant.

b. **Uses**: These drugs are used to treat angioedema, especially in hereditary angioedema, by blocking the effects of bradykinin.

Mechanism of Action

1. **Bradykinin**: Binds to B2 receptors, activating pathways that lead to vasodilation, increased vascular permeability, and pain. It also stimulates the release of NO and prostacyclin, which enhance its effects.

SUBSTANCE P

Substance P is a neuropeptide that functions as an autocoid involved in a range of physiological processes, including pain perception, inflammation, and stress responses. It is part of the tachykinin family of peptides.

Synthesis and Release

1. **Synthesis**: Substance P is synthesized from its precursor, preprotachykinin, in neurons and neuroendocrine cells. It is then processed to its active form, substance P.

$$\text{Kininogen} \xrightarrow{\text{Kallikrein}} \text{Bradykinin}$$

2. **Release**: Substance P is released from sensory neurons and other cells in response to various stimuli. It acts locally at the site of release and can also affect distant tissues.

Actions of Substance P

1. **Pain Perception**:
   a. **Mechanism**: Substance P is involved in the transmission of pain signals from peripheral nerves to the central nervous system. It is released from primary afferent neurons and acts on neurokinin-1 (NK1) receptors in the spinal cord and brain.
   b. **Effect**: Enhances pain perception and contributes to inflammatory pain.
2. **Inflammation**:

a. **Mechanism**: Substance P increases vascular permeability, leading to edema and inflammation. It also stimulates the release of other pro-inflammatory mediators from immune cells.
b. **Effect**: Contributes to the inflammatory response and exacerbates conditions such as arthritis and asthma.

3. **Stress and Anxiety**:
   a. **Mechanism**: Substance P is involved in the regulation of stress and anxiety by acting on neurokinin receptors in the brain.
   b. **Effect**: Modulates emotional responses and stress-related behaviors.
4. **Gastrointestinal Function**:
   a. **Mechanism**: Substance P affects gastrointestinal motility and secretion. It can influence peristalsis and gastric acid secretion.
   b. **Effect**: Plays a role in gastrointestinal disorders such as irritable bowel syndrome (IBS).

Clinical Relevance and Drugs

1. **Neurokinin-1 (NK1) Receptor Antagonists**:
   a. **Examples**: Aprepitant, Fosaprepitant.
   b. **Uses**: These drugs block the action of substance P at NK1 receptors and are used primarily to prevent nausea and vomiting associated with chemotherapy.
   c. **Mechanism**: By inhibiting NK1 receptors, these antagonists reduce the emetic (vomiting) response and improve patient comfort during cancer treatment.
2. **Substance P and Pain Management**:
   a. **Research**: Investigational drugs targeting substance P and its receptors are being studied for their potential to manage chronic pain and inflammatory conditions.

b. **Mechanism**: Potential drugs aim to reduce the impact of substance P on pain pathways and inflammatory responses.

Mechanism of Action

1. **Substance P**: Acts primarily through neurokinin-1 (NK1) receptors, which are G-protein-coupled receptors. Binding of substance P to these receptors activates intracellular signaling pathways that lead to:
   a. **Enhanced Pain Transmission**: Increases the release of neurotransmitters and sensitizes neurons involved in pain perception.
   b. **Inflammatory Response**: Promotes vasodilation and increases vascular permeability, leading to edema and inflammation.

Pathophysiology and Implications

1. **Chronic Pain**: Elevated levels of substance P are associated with various chronic pain conditions, including neuropathic pain and fibromyalgia.
2. **Inflammatory Diseases**: Substance P plays a role in the pathogenesis of inflammatory diseases such as rheumatoid arthritis and asthma.
3. **Gastrointestinal Disorders**: Substance P's influence on gastrointestinal motility and secretion is relevant in conditions like IBS and peptic ulcers.

Multiple Choice Questions (MCQs)

1. Which enzyme is responsible for converting histidine into histamine?
   a) Cyclooxygenase
   b) Histidine decarboxylase
   c) Lipoxygenase
   d) Aromatic L-amino acid decarboxylase
2. What type of receptor is involved in allergic reactions mediated by histamine?
   a) H1 receptor
   b) H2 receptor

c) H3 receptor
d) H4 receptor

3. Which prostaglandin is primarily involved in regulating blood flow and inhibiting platelet aggregation?
   a) PGE2
   b) PGI2 (Prostacyclin)
   c) PGF2α
   d) PGD2
4. What is the primary action of leukotrienes in asthma?
   a) Bronchodilation
   b) Bronchoconstriction
   c) Vasodilation
   d) Inhibition of mucus production
5. Which enzyme is involved in the synthesis of bradykinin from kininogen?
   a) Kallikrein
   b) Renin
   c) Lipoxygenase
   d) Cyclooxygenase
6. What is the clinical use of leukotriene receptor antagonists like montelukast?
   a) Treating hypertension
   b) Managing asthma and allergic rhinitis
   c) Reducing gastric acid secretion
   d) Preventing nausea and vomiting
7. Which autocoid is a potent vasodilator and modulates neurotransmission and immune responses?
   a) Histamine
   b) Serotonin
   c) Nitric oxide
   d) Bradykinin

8. What is the mechanism of action of ACE inhibitors in relation to bradykinin?
    a) Increase bradykinin degradation
    b) Decrease bradykinin levels
    c) Prevent bradykinin breakdown
    d) Block bradykinin receptors
9. Which drug is a serotonin reuptake inhibitor (SSRI) used to treat depression?
    a) Ondansetron
    b) Clozapine
    c) Buspirone
    d) Fluoxetine
10. What is the primary action of thromboxane A2 (TXA2)?
    a) Inhibiting platelet aggregation
    b) Promoting platelet aggregation and vasoconstriction
    c) Causing vasodilation
    d) Reducing vascular permeability
11. Which prostaglandin analog is used to induce labor?
    a) Iloprost
    b) Misoprostol
    c) Dinoprostone
    d) Latanoprost
12. What effect does substance P have on pain perception?
    a) Inhibits pain signals
    b) Enhances pain perception
    c) Neutralizes pain receptors
    d) Decreases pain threshold
13. Which drug is a neurokinin-1 (NK1) receptor antagonist used to prevent chemotherapy-induced nausea?
    a) Aprepitant
    b) Montelukast

c) Zileuton

d) Icatibant

14. What is the role of nitric oxide in the cardiovascular system?

a) Promoting platelet aggregation

b) Causing vasodilation

c) Increasing vascular permeability

d) Inducing bronchoconstriction

15. Which receptor type does serotonin act on to regulate gastrointestinal motility?

a) H1 receptor

b) 5-HT3 receptor

c) NK1 receptor

d) CystLT receptor

16. Which drug is an H2 antagonist used to reduce gastric acid secretion?

a) Diphenhydramine

b) Loratadine

c) Ranitidine

d) Fexofenadine

17. What is the primary action of prostaglandin F2α (PGF2α)?

a) Vasodilation

b) Bronchodilation

c) Stimulating uterine contractions

d) Inhibiting platelet aggregation

18. Which autocoid is derived from arachidonic acid via the lipoxygenase pathway?

a) Histamine

b) Prostaglandin

c) Leukotriene

d) Nitric oxide

19. Which enzyme converts angiotensin I to angiotensin II?

a) Renin

b) ACE (Angiotensin-Converting Enzyme)

c) Kallikrein

d) Thromboxane synthase

20. What is the clinical application of thromboxane receptor antagonists?

a) Treating asthma

b) Managing thrombotic disorders

c) Reducing blood pressure

d) Preventing nausea and vomiting

Short Answer Type Questions (Subjective)

1. Explain the synthesis and release of histamine in the body.
2. Describe the clinical uses of H1 and H2 antihistamines.
3. What are the physiological roles of prostaglandin E2 (PGE2)?
4. How do leukotriene receptor antagonists work in the management of asthma?
5. Describe the actions of bradykinin in the body.
6. What is the role of nitric oxide in regulating blood pressure?
7. Explain the synthesis and release of serotonin in the body.
8. Describe the clinical uses of serotonin reuptake inhibitors (SSRIs).
9. What are the primary actions of thromboxane A2 (TXA2)?
10. How do ACE inhibitors affect the levels of bradykinin?
11. Describe the mechanism of action of neurokinin-1 (NK1) receptor antagonists.
12. What are the therapeutic uses of prostaglandin analogs like misoprostol and dinoprostone?
13. Explain the mechanism of action of thromboxane receptor antagonists.
14. Describe the synthesis and release of substance P.

15. How does substance P contribute to pain perception?
16. Explain the physiological roles of leukotriene B4 (LTB4).
17. What are the effects of serotonin on gastrointestinal motility?
18. Describe the clinical relevance of angiotensin II in the regulation of blood pressure.
19. How do nonsteroidal anti-inflammatory drugs (NSAIDs) inhibit prostaglandin synthesis?
20. What is the role of aldosterone in fluid and electrolyte balance?

Long Answer Type Questions (Subjective)

1. Discuss the pharmacology of histamine, including its synthesis, release, receptors, and clinical applications of histamine antagonists.
2. Explain the synthesis, release, and actions of prostaglandins, and describe the clinical uses of prostaglandin analogs.
3. Describe the synthesis, release, and actions of leukotrienes, and explain the clinical applications of leukotriene receptor antagonists.
4. Discuss the synthesis, release, and actions of bradykinin, and describe the clinical relevance of drugs affecting bradykinin levels.
5. Explain the synthesis, release, and actions of serotonin, and discuss the clinical applications of serotonin modulators.
6. Describe the synthesis, release, and actions of nitric oxide, and explain the clinical uses of nitric oxide donors and inhibitors.
7. Discuss the synthesis, release, and actions of thromboxanes, and explain the clinical relevance of thromboxane inhibitors.
8. Explain the synthesis, release, and actions of substance P, and describe the clinical applications of neurokinin-1 (NK1) receptor antagonists.
9. Describe the renin-angiotensin-aldosterone system (RAAS), and explain the clinical applications of ACE inhibitors, ARBs, and direct renin inhibitors.
10. Discuss the physiological roles and clinical relevance of autocoids in the regulation of inflammation, blood pressure, and pain perception.

Answer Key for MCQs

1. b) Histidine decarboxylase
2. a) H1 receptor
3. b) PGI2 (Prostacyclin)
4. b) Bronchoconstriction
5. a) Kallikrein
6. b) Managing asthma and allergic rhinitis
7. c) Nitric oxide
8. c) Prevent bradykinin breakdown
9. d) Fluoxetine
10. b) Promoting platelet aggregation and vasoconstriction
11. c) Dinoprostone
12. b) Enhances pain perception
13. a) Aprepitant
14. b) Causing vasodilation
15. b) 5-HT3 receptor
16. c) Ranitidine
17. c) Stimulating uterine contractions
18. c) Leukotriene
19. b) ACE (Angiotensin-Converting Enzyme)
20. b) Managing thrombotic disorders

CHAPTER – 13

NON-STEROIDAL ANTI – INFLAMMATORY AGENTS

Mr. Satyendra Garg

Assistant Professor, Rajiv Gandhi Institute of Pharmacy, Faculty of Pharmaceutical Science & Technology, AKS University Satna, (M.P.)

ABSTRACT:

Non-steroidal anti-inflammatory drugs (NSAIDs) are a class of medications widely used to reduce inflammation, alleviate pain, and decrease fever. They work by inhibiting the cyclooxygenase (COX) enzymes, COX-1 and COX-2, which play a crucial role in the synthesis of prostaglandins. Prostaglandins are lipid compounds that mediate inflammation, pain, and fever. By reducing prostaglandin production, NSAIDs effectively manage symptoms associated with conditions such as arthritis, menstrual cramps, muscle aches, and headaches. Common NSAIDs include ibuprofen, naproxen, and aspirin. These drugs are available over-the-counter and by prescription, making them accessible for both acute and chronic conditions. While NSAIDs are effective and widely used, they can have adverse effects, including gastrointestinal irritation, ulcers, and an increased risk of cardiovascular events, especially with long-term use. Additionally, they may cause renal impairment and exacerbate hypertension. Patients with a history of gastrointestinal issues, heart disease, or kidney problems should use NSAIDs cautiously and under medical supervision. Despite these potential side effects, NSAIDs remain a cornerstone in the management of pain and inflammation, providing significant relief for millions of people worldwide. Their benefits often outweigh the risks when used appropriately and for the correct indications.

NON-STEROIDAL ANTI-INFLAMMATORY AGENTS

Non-steroidal anti-inflammatory drugs (NSAIDs) are a diverse group of medications used to reduce inflammation, pain, and fever. They exert their effects primarily through the inhibition of cyclooxygenase (COX) enzymes, which are involved in the synthesis of prostaglandins. Prostaglandins are autocoids that mediate inflammation, pain, and fever, making NSAIDs effective in managing conditions related to these processes.

Mechanism of Action

NSAIDs exert their effects primarily through the inhibition of cyclooxygenase (COX) enzymes, which are crucial for the biosynthesis of prostaglandins from arachidonic acid. Prostaglandins are mediators of inflammation, pain, and fever. There are two main isoforms of the COX enzyme:

- **COX-1**: Constitutively expressed in most tissues, involved in maintaining normal physiological functions such as gastric mucosal protection, platelet aggregation, and renal blood flow.
- **COX-2**: Inducible and primarily involved in the inflammatory response, expressed in response to inflammatory stimuli.

By inhibiting these enzymes, NSAIDs reduce the production of prostaglandins, thereby decreasing inflammation, pain, and fever.

Therapeutic Uses

1. **Anti-inflammatory**: Used to reduce inflammation in conditions such as rheumatoid arthritis, osteoarthritis, and other inflammatory arthropathies.
2. **Analgesic**: Effective in relieving mild to moderate pain from conditions like musculoskeletal injuries, dental pain, and menstrual cramps.
3. **Antipyretic**: Used to reduce fever in conditions like infections or autoimmune diseases.
4. **Antiplatelet**: Low-dose aspirin is used for its antiplatelet effects to prevent cardiovascular events like myocardial infarction and stroke.

Adverse Effects

1. **Gastrointestinal**: Irritation, ulcers, bleeding, and perforation due to inhibition of COX-1, which reduces the protective prostaglandins in the stomach lining.
2. **Renal**: Impairment of renal function, fluid retention, and hypertension, particularly in patients with pre-existing kidney conditions.
3. **Cardiovascular**: Increased risk of myocardial infarction and stroke, especially with selective COX-2 inhibitors.
4. **Hematological**: Prolonged bleeding time due to inhibition of platelet aggregation (primarily with aspirin).

Contraindications

1. **Peptic Ulcer Disease**: Increased risk of gastrointestinal bleeding and ulceration.
2. **Renal Impairment**: Risk of worsening renal function.
3. **Cardiovascular Disease**: Particularly for COX-2 selective inhibitors, which may increase the risk of thrombotic events.
4. **Hypersensitivity**: History of allergic reactions to NSAIDs, including asthma, urticaria, or anaphylaxis.

Common NSAIDs

1. **Ibuprofen**: Commonly used for pain, inflammation, and fever. It is available over-the-counter and by prescription.
2. **Naproxen**: Similar uses to ibuprofen, often preferred for its longer duration of action.
3. **Aspirin**: Used for pain, inflammation, and its unique antiplatelet effect in low doses for cardiovascular protection.

4. **Celecoxib**: A selective COX-2 inhibitor with a lower risk of gastrointestinal side effects but a higher risk of cardiovascular events.
5. **Diclofenac**: Effective for pain and inflammation, available in oral and topical forms.

Classification of NSAIDs

NSAIDs can be classified into different categories based on their selectivity for COX-1 and COX-2, as well as their chemical structure:

1. Non-selective NSAIDs

These inhibit both COX-1 and COX-2, which can lead to both therapeutic effects and adverse effects (e.g., gastrointestinal irritation).

a. **Aspirin (Acetylsalicylic Acid)**
   i. **Uses**: Pain, inflammation, fever, cardiovascular protection (antiplatelet effect).
   ii. **Mechanism**: Irreversibly inhibits COX-1 and COX-2.
   iii. **Side Effects**: Gastrointestinal ulcers, bleeding, renal impairment, Reye's syndrome in children.

b. **Ibuprofen**
   i. **Uses**: Pain, inflammation, fever.
   ii. **Mechanism**: Reversibly inhibits COX-1 and COX-2.
   iii. **Side Effects**: Gastrointestinal disturbances, renal impairment, cardiovascular risks.

c. **Naproxen**
   i. **Uses**: Pain, inflammation, fever, and some chronic inflammatory conditions.
   ii. **Mechanism**: Reversibly inhibits COX-1 and COX-2.
   iii. **Side Effects**: Gastrointestinal issues, renal problems, cardiovascular risks.

d. **Indomethacin**
   i. **Uses**: Acute gout, osteoarthritis, rheumatoid arthritis.

ii. **Mechanism**: Non-selective COX inhibition.

iii. **Side Effects**: Gastrointestinal toxicity, headaches, dizziness.

2. Selective COX-2 Inhibitors (Coxibs)

These preferentially inhibit COX-2, reducing inflammation and pain with less impact on COX-1, which helps in minimizing gastrointestinal side effects.

a. **Celecoxib**

i. **Uses**: Osteoarthritis, rheumatoid arthritis, acute pain.

ii. **Mechanism**: Selectively inhibits COX-2.

iii. **Side Effects**: Cardiovascular risks, renal issues.

b. **Rofecoxib** (withdrawn due to cardiovascular concerns)

i. **Uses**: Pain, inflammation.

ii. **Mechanism**: Selectively inhibits COX-2.

iii. **Side Effects**: Increased risk of myocardial infarction and stroke.

3. Acetic Acid Derivatives

These have a similar mechanism to non-selective NSAIDs but differ in their chemical structure.

a. **Diclofenac**

i. **Uses**: Pain, inflammation, and some chronic conditions.

ii. **Mechanism**: Non-selective COX inhibition.

iii. **Side Effects**: Gastrointestinal, hepatic, and renal adverse effects.

b. **Ketorolac**

i. **Uses**: Short-term management of severe pain.

ii. **Mechanism**: Non-selective COX inhibition.

iii. **Side Effects**: Gastrointestinal bleeding, renal impairment.

4. Propionic Acid Derivatives

These are a common class of NSAIDs with moderate COX-1 and COX-2 inhibition.

a. **Oxaprozin**

i. **Uses**: Chronic arthritis.

ii. **Mechanism**: Non-selective COX inhibition.

iii. **Side Effects**: Similar to other NSAIDs, including gastrointestinal and renal issues.

b. **Naproxen**

i. **Uses**: As mentioned above.

ii. **Mechanism**: Non-selective COX inhibition.

iii. **Side Effects**: Similar to other NSAIDs.

Adverse Effects

NSAIDs can cause a range of adverse effects, including:

a. **Gastrointestinal Issues**: Ulcers, bleeding, and gastritis.

b. **Renal Impairment**: Reduced renal function and fluid retention.

c. **Cardiovascular Risks**: Increased risk of heart attack and stroke, particularly with COX-2 inhibitors.

d. **Allergic Reactions**: Rashes, anaphylaxis in rare cases.

Clinical Use

NSAIDs are used in a variety of clinical settings, including:

a. **Acute Pain**: Relief of mild to moderate pain.

b. **Chronic Inflammatory Conditions**: Such as arthritis and osteoarthritis.

c. **Fever**: Reduction of elevated body temperature.

d. **Cardiovascular Protection**: Aspirin for secondary prevention of cardiovascular events.

CHAPTER – 14

ANTI – GOUT DRUGS

Mrs. Neelam Singh

Assistant Professor, Rajiv Gandhi Institute of Pharmacy, Faculty of Pharmaceutical Science & Technology, AKS University Satna, (M.P.)

ABSTRACT:

Anti-gout drugs are medications designed to prevent and treat gout, a form of arthritis characterized by sudden, severe attacks of pain, redness, and swelling in joints due to the accumulation of uric acid crystals. These drugs can be categorized into those that manage acute attacks and those that prevent future episodes. For acute gout attacks, non-steroidal anti-inflammatory drugs (NSAIDs) like indomethacin and ibuprofen, corticosteroids like prednisone, and colchicine are commonly used. Colchicine helps reduce inflammation by inhibiting the migration of white blood cells to the affected area. To prevent recurrent gout, medications such as allopurinol, febuxostat, and probenecid are prescribed. Allopurinol and febuxostat inhibit xanthine oxidase, an enzyme involved in the production of uric acid, thereby reducing its levels in the blood. Probenecid increases the excretion of uric acid by the kidneys. While effective, these medications can have side effects, such as gastrointestinal disturbances with NSAIDs and colchicine, and hypersensitivity reactions with allopurinol. Regular monitoring and lifestyle modifications, including dietary changes, are also important in managing gout effectively, reducing the frequency of attacks, and preventing long-term joint damage.

ANTI-GOUT DRUGS

Anti-gout drugs are used to manage and treat gout, a type of inflammatory arthritis caused by the accumulation of uric acid crystals in the joints. The treatment of gout involves both acute management of symptoms and long-term control of uric acid levels. Here's a detailed overview of the main classes of anti-gout drugs:

Uric Acid Lowering Drugs:

Uric acid lowering drugs are critical in the management of gout, a condition characterized by high levels of uric acid in the blood leading to the formation of uric acid crystals and causing painful inflammatory attacks. These drugs help to reduce serum uric acid levels, prevent the formation of uric acid crystals, and manage chronic gout. They can be broadly classified into two main categories: xanthine oxidase inhibitors and uricosuric agents.

1. Xanthine Oxidase Inhibitors

These drugs work by inhibiting xanthine oxidase, an enzyme involved in the production of uric acid from purines. By reducing uric acid production, these drugs help to lower serum uric acid levels and prevent gout attacks.

a. Allopurinol

1. **Mechanism of Action**: Allopurinol inhibits xanthine oxidase, which is responsible for the conversion of hypoxanthine and xanthine to uric acid. This reduces the production of uric acid.
2. **Uses**:
    i. Chronic gout
    ii. Hyperuricemia associated with chemotherapy or malignancy
3. **Administration**: Oral.
4. **Dosage**: Typically started at 100 mg daily, adjusted based on uric acid levels and patient tolerance.
5. **Side Effects**:
    i. **Common**: Gastrointestinal symptoms (nausea, diarrhea).
    ii. **Serious**: Rash, including severe hypersensitivity reactions such as Stevens-Johnson syndrome, liver toxicity, renal impairment.
6. **Monitoring**: Regular monitoring of renal function and liver enzymes; caution in patients with renal impairment.

b. Febuxostat

1. **Mechanism of Action**: Febuxostat is a selective inhibitor of xanthine oxidase, providing a more targeted approach to reducing uric acid levels.
2. **Uses**:
    i. Chronic gout
    ii. Hyperuricemia
3. **Administration**: Oral.
4. **Dosage**: Typically 40 to 80 mg daily, adjusted based on uric acid levels.
5. **Side Effects**:
    i. **Common**: Liver enzyme abnormalities, gastrointestinal symptoms.
    ii. **Serious**: Cardiovascular events (e.g., myocardial infarction), severe hypersensitivity reactions.
6. **Monitoring**: Regular liver function tests; caution in patients with a history of cardiovascular disease.

2. Uricosuric Agents

Uricosuric agents enhance the excretion of uric acid by inhibiting its reabsorption in the kidneys. This helps to lower serum uric acid levels and prevent gout attacks.

a. Probenecid

1. **Mechanism of Action**: Probenecid inhibits the reabsorption of uric acid in the renal tubules, leading to increased uric acid excretion.
2. **Uses**:
    i. Chronic gout
    ii. Hyperuricemia
3. **Administration**: Oral.
4. **Dosage**: Typically started at 250 mg twice daily, increased gradually to 500-1000 mg daily in divided doses.
5. **Side Effects**:
    i. **Common**: Gastrointestinal upset, rash.

ii. **Serious**: Renal stones (nephrolithiasis), hypersensitivity reactions.

6. **Monitoring**: Regular assessment of uric acid levels and renal function; ensure adequate hydration to reduce the risk of renal stones.

b. Sulfinpyrazone

1. **Mechanism of Action**: Similar to probenecid, sulfinpyrazone inhibits uric acid reabsorption in the renal tubules, increasing uric acid excretion.
2. **Uses**:
   i. Chronic gout
3. **Administration**: Oral.
4. **Dosage**: Typically 100-200 mg twice daily, increased gradually as needed.
5. **Side Effects**:
   i. **Common**: Gastrointestinal symptoms, rash.
   ii. **Serious**: Hematologic effects (e.g., leukopenia), renal issues.
6. **Monitoring**: Regular blood counts and renal function tests.

3. Combination Therapies

In some cases, a combination of uric acid lowering drugs may be used to achieve better control of serum uric acid levels. For example, a patient might be prescribed a xanthine oxidase inhibitor (e.g., allopurinol) for long-term uric acid control and a uricosuric agent (e.g., probenecid) to enhance uric acid excretion.

4. Additional Considerations

a. **Initiation of Therapy**: Uric acid lowering therapy should be initiated during an intercritical period (not during an acute gout attack) to avoid exacerbating the attack.

b. **Titration and Monitoring**: Regular monitoring of serum uric acid levels is essential to ensure effectiveness and adjust dosages accordingly.

c. **Lifestyle Modifications**: Patients should be encouraged to make dietary changes, reduce alcohol intake, and stay hydrated to support the effectiveness of uric acid lowering therapy.

Anti-inflammatory Drugs for Acute Gout Attacks:

Anti-inflammatory drugs are essential in managing acute gout attacks, which are characterized by sudden and severe pain, redness, and swelling in the affected joint(s). These drugs aim to reduce inflammation and alleviate pain, providing relief during acute episodes. Here's a detailed overview of the main classes of anti-inflammatory drugs used for acute gout attacks:

1. Non-Steroidal Anti-Inflammatory Drugs (NSAIDs)

NSAIDs are commonly used to manage acute gout attacks by reducing inflammation and pain. They work by inhibiting cyclooxygenase (COX) enzymes, which decreases the production of prostaglandins that mediate inflammation.

a. Indomethacin

1. **Mechanism of Action**: Non-selective COX inhibitor, reducing the production of prostaglandins and alleviating inflammation and pain.
2. **Uses**: Acute gout attacks.
3. **Administration**: Oral or intravenous.
4. **Dosage**: Typically started at 50 mg three times daily, adjusted based on response and tolerance.
5. **Side Effects**:
    i. **Common**: Gastrointestinal symptoms (nausea, vomiting, dyspepsia), headache, dizziness.
    ii. **Serious**: Gastrointestinal bleeding or ulceration, renal impairment, cardiovascular effects.

b. Naproxen

1. **Mechanism of Action**: Non-selective COX inhibitor, reducing inflammation and pain through prostaglandin synthesis inhibition.
2. **Uses**: Acute gout attacks.
3. **Administration**: Oral.
4. **Dosage**: Typically 250-500 mg twice daily.

5. **Side Effects**:
    i. **Common**: Gastrointestinal upset, headache, dizziness.
    ii. **Serious**: Gastrointestinal bleeding, renal impairment, cardiovascular issues.

c. Ibuprofen

1. **Mechanism of Action**: Non-selective COX inhibitor, decreasing prostaglandin production and reducing inflammation and pain.
2. **Uses**: Acute gout attacks.
3. **Administration**: Oral.
4. **Dosage**: Typically 400-800 mg every 6-8 hours.
5. **Side Effects**:
    i. **Common**: Gastrointestinal discomfort, headache, dizziness.
    ii. **Serious**: Gastrointestinal bleeding, renal issues, cardiovascular risks.

2. Colchicine

Colchicine is a specific anti-inflammatory drug for gout that helps to alleviate acute gout attacks and prevent future flares.

a. **Mechanism of Action**: Inhibits microtubule formation, which disrupts leukocyte migration and reduces inflammation.
b. **Uses**: Acute gout attacks, prevention of recurrent attacks.
c. **Administration**: Oral.
d. **Dosage**:
    i. **Acute Attack**: Initial dose of 1.2 mg, followed by 0.6 mg after 1 hour; total dose should not exceed 1.8 mg in a 24-hour period.
    ii. **Prophylaxis**: 0.6 mg once or twice daily.
e. **Side Effects**:
    i. **Common**: Gastrointestinal symptoms (nausea, vomiting, diarrhea).
    ii. **Serious**: Muscle weakness, bone marrow suppression, peripheral neuropathy (in high doses).

3. Corticosteroids

Corticosteroids are used for their potent anti-inflammatory effects, especially when NSAIDs and colchicine are contraindicated or ineffective.

a. Prednisone

1. **Mechanism of Action**: Reduces inflammation by suppressing the immune response and decreasing the production of inflammatory cytokines.
2. **Uses**: Acute gout attacks, particularly in cases where NSAIDs or colchicine are contraindicated.
3. **Administration**: Oral.
4. **Dosage**: Typically 20-60 mg daily, tapered over a few days.
5. **Side Effects**:
   i. **Common**: Weight gain, mood changes, insomnia.
   ii. **Serious**: Hyperglycemia, hypertension, osteoporosis, increased risk of infections.

b. Methylprednisolone

1. **Mechanism of Action**: Similar to prednisone, it reduces inflammation through immune suppression and cytokine inhibition.
2. **Uses**: Acute gout attacks.
3. **Administration**: Oral or intra-articular injection.
4. **Dosage**: For oral use, typically 16-64 mg daily, tapered as needed. For intra-articular use, the dosage varies based on the joint involved.
5. **Side Effects**:
   i. **Common**: Gastrointestinal symptoms, mood changes, weight gain.
   ii. **Serious**: Similar to prednisone, including the risk of infections and metabolic effects.

4. Combination Therapy

In some cases, a combination of the above drugs may be used to achieve better control of acute gout attacks. For instance, a patient may be treated with NSAIDs or colchicine and may receive corticosteroids if their symptoms are not adequately controlled or if they have contraindications to NSAIDs or colchicine.

5. Additional Considerations

a. **Initiation of Therapy**: Anti-inflammatory therapy should be initiated as soon as possible after the onset of an acute gout attack for optimal relief.
b. **Monitoring**: Regular monitoring for side effects is important, especially with long-term use or high doses.
c. **Patient Education**: Patients should be advised on the potential side effects of these medications and the importance of adhering to the prescribed dosage.

Drugs for Specific Indications

In addition to the main categories of uric acid lowering and anti-inflammatory drugs, specific indications for gout management include medications that address particular challenges or severe forms of gout. These drugs are used in scenarios where conventional therapies may not be sufficient or where there are unique clinical situations. Here's a detailed look at some of these drugs:

1. Pegloticase

Mechanism of Action: Pegloticase is a recombinant uricase enzyme that converts uric acid into allantoin, a more soluble substance that can be excreted in the urine. This significantly lowers serum uric acid levels.

a. **Uses**:
   i. Severe, refractory gout
   ii. Chronic gout where traditional uric acid-lowering treatments are ineffective
b. **Administration**: Intravenous infusion every 2 weeks.

c. **Dosage**: Typically 8 mg every 2 weeks.

d. **Side Effects**:

    i. **Common**: Infusion reactions (e.g., fever, chills, rash).

    ii. **Serious**: Gout flares during initiation, allergic reactions, potential for development of anti-pegloticase antibodies which may reduce effectiveness.

e. **Monitoring**: Regular monitoring of uric acid levels, as well as observation during infusions for any immediate reactions.

2. Rasburicase

Mechanism of Action: Similar to pegloticase, rasburicase is a recombinant uricase enzyme that converts uric acid to allantoin.

a. **Uses**:

    i. Hyperuricemia associated with tumor lysis syndrome (TLS) in cancer patients undergoing chemotherapy.

b. **Administration**: Intravenous infusion.

c. **Dosage**: Typically 0.2 mg/kg once daily for 1-2 days.

d. **Side Effects**:

    i. **Common**: Allergic reactions, infusion reactions.

    ii. **Serious**: Hemolysis in patients with glucose-6-phosphate dehydrogenase (G6PD) deficiency, severe allergic reactions.

e. **Monitoring**: Regular monitoring of uric acid levels, renal function, and for signs of hemolysis.

3. Lesinurad

Mechanism of Action: Lesinurad inhibits the renal uric acid transporters (URAT1 and OAT4), which increases uric acid excretion.

a. **Uses**:

    i. Chronic gout in combination with a xanthine oxidase inhibitor (e.g., allopurinol) when uric acid levels are not adequately controlled.

b. **Administration**: Oral.

c. **Dosage**: Typically 200 mg once daily.

d. **Side Effects**:

   i. **Common**: Headache, gastroesophageal reflux disease (GERD), and elevated creatinine levels.

   ii. **Serious**: Renal impairment, increased risk of kidney stones.

e. **Monitoring**: Regular monitoring of renal function and uric acid levels.

4. Pegloticase (Revisited)

Given its role in severe and refractory cases, it's worth reiterating that pegloticase is used specifically when other uric acid-lowering therapies fail. Its unique mechanism provides an option for patients with advanced disease who do not respond to conventional treatments.

5. Uric Acid-Lowering Combination Therapy

Sometimes, a combination of medications is necessary to manage severe or refractory gout effectively. For example:

a. **Allopurinol + Probenecid**: Used in cases where uric acid levels are inadequately controlled by a single agent.

b. **Febuxostat + Probenecid**: Combines a xanthine oxidase inhibitor with a uricosuric agent to enhance uric acid lowering.

Additional Considerations

a. **Patient Selection**: Drugs like pegloticase and rasburicase are reserved for severe cases or specific indications such as TLS, and are typically used under specialist supervision.

b. **Patient Education**: Patients should be informed about the potential side effects, signs of allergic reactions, and the need for regular monitoring.

c. **Lifestyle Modifications**: As with other gout treatments, patients should be advised on lifestyle changes to support the effectiveness of medications, such as dietary modifications and hydration.

CHAPTER – 15

ANTIRHEUMATIC DRUGS

Mr. Abu Tahir

Assistant Professor, Rajiv Gandhi Institute of Pharmacy, Faculty of Pharmaceutical Science & Technology, AKS University Satna, (M.P.)

ABSTRACT:

Antirheumatic drugs are a diverse group of medications used to treat rheumatoid arthritis (RA) and other autoimmune and inflammatory conditions affecting the joints. These drugs aim to reduce inflammation, alleviate pain, and slow the progression of joint damage. The main categories of antirheumatic drugs include non-steroidal anti-inflammatory drugs (NSAIDs), corticosteroids, disease-modifying antirheumatic drugs (DMARDs), and biologic agents. NSAIDs, like ibuprofen and naproxen, provide symptomatic relief by reducing inflammation and pain but do not alter disease progression. Corticosteroids, such as prednisone, offer powerful anti-inflammatory effects and can rapidly control acute flare-ups but are not suitable for long-term use due to significant side effects. DMARDs, such as methotrexate, hydroxychloroquine, and sulfasalazine, target the underlying immune processes driving the disease, helping to prevent joint damage and preserve function. Biologic agents, including TNF inhibitors like etanercept and adalimumab, and interleukin inhibitors like tocilizumab, offer targeted therapy by interfering with specific immune system pathways. While highly effective, these medications require careful monitoring for potential side effects, including liver toxicity, infections, and gastrointestinal issues. Combining pharmacologic treatment with lifestyle modifications, physical therapy, and regular monitoring can significantly improve outcomes for patients with rheumatoid arthritis, enhancing their quality of life and reducing disease progression.

Introduction:

Antirheumatic drugs are used to treat rheumatic diseases, such as rheumatoid arthritis (RA), systemic lupus erythematosus (SLE), and other autoimmune or inflammatory disorders. These drugs aim to reduce inflammation, relieve symptoms, and slow disease progression. They can be broadly categorized into several classes:

Non-Steroidal Anti-Inflammatory Drugs (NSAIDs):

Non-Steroidal Anti-Inflammatory Drugs (NSAIDs) play a significant role in the management of various rheumatic conditions by alleviating pain, reducing inflammation, and improving joint function. They are commonly used in the treatment of conditions such as rheumatoid arthritis (RA), osteoarthritis (OA), and other inflammatory joint diseases. Here's a detailed overview of NSAIDs used in rheumatology:

1. Mechanism of Action

NSAIDs exert their therapeutic effects primarily through the inhibition of cyclooxygenase (COX) enzymes. These enzymes are involved in the conversion of arachidonic acid to prostaglandins, which are key mediators of inflammation, pain, and fever.

a. **COX-1**: Enzyme involved in the production of prostaglandins that protect the gastrointestinal lining and support platelet function.

b. **COX-2**: Enzyme induced during inflammation, responsible for the production of prostaglandins that mediate pain and inflammation.

By inhibiting these enzymes, NSAIDs reduce the production of inflammatory prostaglandins, thereby alleviating symptoms.

2. Categories of NSAIDs

a. Non-Selective COX Inhibitors

These NSAIDs inhibit both COX-1 and COX-2 enzymes. While effective in reducing inflammation and pain, they can also lead to gastrointestinal and renal side effects due to COX-1 inhibition.

1. **Aspirin**

i. **Mechanism of Action**: Irreversibly inhibits COX-1 and COX-2, reducing prostaglandin production.
ii. **Uses**: RA, OA, acute gout, cardiovascular protection.
iii. **Administration**: Oral.
iv. **Dosage**: Typically 300-600 mg every 4-6 hours for acute symptoms.
v. **Side Effects**: Gastrointestinal irritation, bleeding, renal impairment, tinnitus.

2. **Indomethacin**
   i. **Mechanism of Action**: Non-selective COX inhibitor.
   ii. **Uses**: RA, OA, acute gout.
   iii. **Administration**: Oral or intravenous.
   iv. **Dosage**: Typically 50 mg three times daily.
   v. **Side Effects**: Gastrointestinal distress, headache, dizziness, renal impairment.
3. **Naproxen**
   i. **Mechanism of Action**: Non-selective COX inhibitor.
   ii. **Uses**: RA, OA, acute gout.
   iii. **Administration**: Oral.
   iv. **Dosage**: Typically 250-500 mg twice daily.
   v. **Side Effects**: Gastrointestinal upset, headache, dizziness.
4. **Ibuprofen**
   i. **Mechanism of Action**: Non-selective COX inhibitor.
   ii. **Uses**: RA, OA, acute gout.
   iii. **Administration**: Oral.
   iv. **Dosage**: Typically 400-800 mg every 6-8 hours.
   v. **Side Effects**: Gastrointestinal discomfort, headache, dizziness.

b. Selective COX-2 Inhibitors

These NSAIDs specifically inhibit COX-2, which is primarily involved in inflammation. They are designed to reduce the risk of gastrointestinal side effects associated with non-selective NSAIDs.

1. **Celecoxib**
   i. **Mechanism of Action**: Selective COX-2 inhibitor.
   ii. **Uses**: RA, OA, acute pain.
   iii. **Administration**: Oral.
   iv. **Dosage**: Typically 100-200 mg once or twice daily.
   v. **Side Effects**: Gastrointestinal issues (less than non-selective NSAIDs), cardiovascular risks, renal impairment.

c. Other NSAIDs

1. **Diclofenac**
   i. **Mechanism of Action**: Non-selective COX inhibitor.
   ii. **Uses**: RA, OA, acute pain.
   iii. **Administration**: Oral, topical, or intramuscular.
   iv. **Dosage**: Typically 50 mg two to three times daily.
   v. **Side Effects**: Gastrointestinal upset, headache, dizziness.
2. **Ketorolac**
   i. **Mechanism of Action**: Non-selective COX inhibitor.
   ii. **Uses**: Short-term management of moderate to severe pain.
   iii. **Administration**: Oral or intramuscular.
   iv. **Dosage**: Typically 10 mg every 4-6 hours as needed.
   v. **Side Effects**: Gastrointestinal irritation, renal impairment, bleeding.

3. Considerations and Monitoring

a. **Gastrointestinal Effects**: NSAIDs can cause gastrointestinal irritation, ulcers, and bleeding. To mitigate these risks, use the lowest effective dose for the shortest duration necessary. Consider prescribing proton pump inhibitors (PPIs) for patients at high risk of gastrointestinal complications.

b. **Renal Effects**: NSAIDs can impair renal function, particularly in patients with pre-existing renal conditions or those taking other nephrotoxic drugs. Monitor renal function periodically in long-term NSAID users.
c. **Cardiovascular Risks**: Some NSAIDs, especially COX-2 inhibitors, may increase the risk of cardiovascular events. Assess cardiovascular risk factors before initiating therapy and monitor accordingly.
d. **Drug Interactions**: NSAIDs can interact with various medications, including anticoagulants, other anti-inflammatory drugs, and antihypertensives. Review the patient's medication list and adjust dosages as necessary.
e. **Patient Education**: Inform patients about the potential side effects, signs of gastrointestinal bleeding (e.g., black stools, abdominal pain), and the importance of adherence to prescribed dosages.

Disease-Modifying Anti-Rheumatic Drugs (DMARDs):

Disease-Modifying Anti-Rheumatic Drugs (DMARDs) are a class of medications used to slow the progression of rheumatic diseases, particularly rheumatoid arthritis (RA) and other autoimmune conditions. Unlike Non-Steroidal Anti-Inflammatory Drugs (NSAIDs) and corticosteroids, which primarily alleviate symptoms, DMARDs aim to modify the underlying disease process, reduce joint damage, and improve long-term outcomes.

Here's a detailed overview of DMARDs, including their mechanisms of action, uses, administration, and potential side effects:

1. Conventional DMARDs

a. Methotrexate

1. **Mechanism of Action**: Methotrexate is a folate antagonist that inhibits dihydrofolate reductase, leading to a decrease in nucleotide synthesis.

This results in reduced proliferation of immune cells and decreased production of inflammatory mediators.

2. **Uses**:
    i. RA
    ii. Psoriasis
    iii. Some forms of cancer
3. **Administration**: Oral or subcutaneous injection.
4. **Dosage**: Typically 7.5-25 mg once weekly.
5. **Side Effects**:
    i. **Common**: Gastrointestinal symptoms (nausea, vomiting), mucosal ulcers, liver enzyme abnormalities.
    ii. **Serious**: Hepatotoxicity, bone marrow suppression, pneumonitis, renal impairment.
6. **Monitoring**: Regular monitoring of liver function, renal function, and complete blood counts.

b. Sulfasalazine

1. **Mechanism of Action**: Sulfasalazine is broken down into sulfapyridine and 5-aminosalicylic acid (5-ASA). The exact mechanism is not fully understood, but it is believed to have anti-inflammatory and immunomodulatory effects.
2. **Uses**:
    i. RA
    ii. Inflammatory bowel disease (IBD)
3. **Administration**: Oral.
4. **Dosage**: Typically 500 mg to 2 g daily, in divided doses.
5. **Side Effects**:
    i. **Common**: Gastrointestinal symptoms, rash, headache.
    ii. **Serious**: Hematologic effects (e.g., agranulocytosis), liver toxicity, hypersensitivity reactions.

6. **Monitoring**: Regular monitoring of blood counts and liver function.

c. Hydroxychloroquine

1. **Mechanism of Action**: Hydroxychloroquine is an antimalarial drug with immunomodulatory effects. It inhibits the activation of toll-like receptors (TLRs) and decreases the production of pro-inflammatory cytokines.
2. **Uses**:
    i. RA
    ii. Systemic lupus erythematosus (SLE)
3. **Administration**: Oral.
4. **Dosage**: Typically 200-400 mg daily.
5. **Side Effects**:
    i. **Common**: Gastrointestinal symptoms, skin rash.
    ii. **Serious**: Retinal toxicity (maculopathy), muscle weakness.
6. **Monitoring**: Regular eye examinations and monitoring of liver function.

d. Leflunomide

1. **Mechanism of Action**: Leflunomide inhibits dihydroorotate dehydrogenase, leading to a reduction in pyrimidine synthesis, which impairs lymphocyte proliferation and activity.
2. **Uses**:
    i. RA
    ii. Psoriatic arthritis
3. **Administration**: Oral.
4. **Dosage**: Typically 20 mg daily.
5. **Side Effects**:
    i. **Common**: Gastrointestinal symptoms, rash, hair loss.
    ii. **Serious**: Hepatotoxicity, bone marrow suppression, teratogenic effects.
6. **Monitoring**: Regular monitoring of liver function, blood counts, and screening for pregnancy.

2. Biological DMARDs

Biological DMARDs are targeted therapies that act on specific components of the immune system involved in inflammation. They are often used when conventional DMARDs are insufficient or contraindicated.

a. Tumor Necrosis Factor (TNF) Inhibitors

1. **Examples**:
    i. **Infliximab**: Monoclonal antibody that binds to TNF-alpha, preventing its interaction with TNF receptors.
    ii. **Etanercept**: A fusion protein that binds to TNF-alpha and TNF-beta, inhibiting their activity.
    iii. **Adalimumab**: Monoclonal antibody that binds to TNF-alpha, blocking its interaction with its receptor.
2. **Uses**:
    i. RA
    ii. Psoriasis
    iii. Ankylosing spondylitis
    iv. Crohn's disease
3. **Administration**:
    i. **Infliximab**: Intravenous infusion.
    ii. **Etanercept**: Subcutaneous injection.
    iii. **Adalimumab**: Subcutaneous injection.
4. **Dosage**: Varies by drug and condition.
5. **Side Effects**:
    i. **Common**: Injection site reactions, upper respiratory infections.
    ii. **Serious**: Increased risk of infections, including tuberculosis, and potential for malignancies.
6. **Monitoring**: Regular screening for infections, monitoring for signs of malignancy, and routine lab tests.

b. Interleukin-6 (IL-6) Inhibitors

1. **Examples**:
    i. **Tocilizumab**: Monoclonal antibody that inhibits the IL-6 receptor.
2. **Uses**:
    i. RA
    ii. Systemic juvenile idiopathic arthritis
3. **Administration**: Intravenous or subcutaneous injection.
4. **Dosage**: Typically 4-8 mg/kg every 4 weeks (IV) or 162 mg every other week (SC).
5. **Side Effects**:
    i. **Common**: Upper respiratory infections, headache.
    ii. **Serious**: Increased risk of infections, liver enzyme abnormalities, lipid abnormalities.
6. **Monitoring**: Regular monitoring of liver function, lipid levels, and for signs of infections.

c. Janus Kinase (JAK) Inhibitors

1. **Examples**:
    i. **Tofacitinib**: Oral JAK inhibitor that blocks intracellular signaling pathways involved in inflammation.
    ii. **Baricitinib**: Similar mechanism to tofacitinib.
2. **Uses**:
    i. RA
    ii. Some other autoimmune conditions
3. **Administration**: Oral.
4. **Dosage**: Typically 5-10 mg twice daily.
5. **Side Effects**:
    i. **Common**: Gastrointestinal symptoms, headache.
    ii. **Serious**: Increased risk of infections, blood clots, liver enzyme abnormalities.

6. **Monitoring**: Regular blood counts, liver function tests, and monitoring for infections.

3. Targeted Synthetic DMARDs

These are newer agents designed to target specific pathways involved in inflammation, with a more targeted mechanism than conventional DMARDs.

a. **Examples**:
    i. **Apremilast**: Inhibits phosphodiesterase 4 (PDE4), reducing the production of pro-inflammatory cytokines.
b. **Uses**:
    i. Psoriatic arthritis
    ii. Behçet's disease
c. **Administration**: Oral.
d. **Dosage**: Typically 30 mg twice daily.
e. **Side Effects**:
    i. **Common**: Gastrointestinal symptoms, headache.
    ii. **Serious**: Weight loss, depression.

4. Considerations and Monitoring

a. **Efficacy and Safety**: The choice of DMARD depends on the specific condition, disease severity, patient comorbidities, and response to previous treatments.
b. **Monitoring**: Regular monitoring is crucial for all DMARDs to check for adverse effects and ensure efficacy. This includes blood tests, liver function tests, and monitoring for infections.
c. **Patient Education**: Patients should be educated about potential side effects, the importance of adherence to treatment, and the need for regular monitoring.

Corticosteroids:

Corticosteroids are a class of drugs used in the management of various rheumatic and inflammatory diseases. They are potent anti-inflammatory agents and are used to control symptoms and disease activity in conditions like rheumatoid arthritis (RA), lupus, and other autoimmune and inflammatory disorders. Here's a detailed overview of corticosteroids in the context of antirheumatic drugs:

1. Mechanism of Action

Corticosteroids exert their effects through several mechanisms:

a. **Anti-Inflammatory Effects**: They inhibit the release of inflammatory mediators such as prostaglandins and leukotrienes by blocking phospholipase A2. This reduces inflammation and edema.

b. **Immunosuppressive Effects**: Corticosteroids suppress the function of immune cells, including lymphocytes and macrophages, which reduces the immune response and subsequent inflammation.

c. **Metabolic Effects**: They influence glucose metabolism, protein synthesis, and fat distribution.

2. Types of Corticosteroids

a. Glucocorticoids

Glucocorticoids are the most commonly used corticosteroids in rheumatic diseases. They primarily affect glucose metabolism and have potent anti-inflammatory and immunosuppressive properties.

1. **Prednisone**
    a. **Mechanism of Action**: Prednisone is a prodrug that is converted to prednisolone in the liver. It acts by binding to glucocorticoid receptors, affecting gene expression and reducing inflammation.
    b. **Uses**:
        i. RA
        ii. Systemic lupus erythematosus (SLE)
        iii. Psoriasis
        iv. Inflammatory bowel disease (IBD)
    c. **Administration**: Oral.

d. **Dosage**: Typically 5-60 mg daily, depending on the condition and severity.
e. **Side Effects**:
    i. **Common**: Weight gain, fluid retention, increased appetite, mood changes.
    ii. **Serious**: Osteoporosis, hypertension, diabetes mellitus, increased risk of infections.
f. **Monitoring**: Regular monitoring for side effects such as blood glucose levels, bone density, and blood pressure.

2. **Prednisolone**
    a. **Mechanism of Action**: Active form of prednisone with similar actions.
    b. **Uses**: Similar to prednisone.
    c. **Administration**: Oral.
    d. **Dosage**: Typically 5-60 mg daily.
    e. **Side Effects**: Similar to prednisone.
    f. **Monitoring**: Similar to prednisone.
3. **Dexamethasone**
    a. **Mechanism of Action**: Highly potent glucocorticoid with strong anti-inflammatory effects.
    b. **Uses**:
        i. RA
        ii. SLE
        iii. Severe allergic reactions
    c. **Administration**: Oral, intravenous, or intramuscular.
    d. **Dosage**: Typically 0.75-10 mg daily, depending on the condition.
    e. **Side Effects**: Similar to other glucocorticoids but may be more pronounced due to its potency.
    f. **Monitoring**: Regular monitoring similar to other corticosteroids.

4. **Hydrocortisone**
    a. **Mechanism of Action**: Similar to prednisone, but less potent.
    b. **Uses**:
        i. RA
        ii. Acute adrenal insufficiency
    c. **Administration**: Oral, intravenous, or topical.
    d. **Dosage**: Typically 20-240 mg daily.
    e. **Side Effects**: Similar to other glucocorticoids.
    f. **Monitoring**: Similar to other glucocorticoids.

b. Mineralocorticoids

Mineralocorticoids primarily affect electrolyte and fluid balance rather than inflammation. The most commonly used mineralocorticoid is:

1. **Fludrocortisone**
    a. **Mechanism of Action**: It acts on mineralocorticoid receptors to increase sodium reabsorption and potassium excretion.
    b. **Uses**:
        i. Addison's disease
        ii. Orthostatic hypotension
    c. **Administration**: Oral.
    d. **Dosage**: Typically 0.1-0.2 mg daily.
    e. **Side Effects**:
        i. **Common**: Edema, hypertension, hypokalemia.
        ii. **Serious**: Heart failure, metabolic alkalosis.
    f. **Monitoring**: Regular monitoring of electrolytes and blood pressure.

3. Administration Routes and Regimens

a. **Oral**: Most commonly used for chronic conditions. Dosages are adjusted based on disease activity and response.

b. **Intravenous**: Used for acute flare-ups or severe conditions. Provides rapid relief of symptoms.
c. **Intramuscular**: Can be used for localized treatment, such as in injections for joint inflammation.
d. **Topical**: Used for localized conditions like psoriasis or eczema.

4. Long-Term Considerations and Side Effects

a. **Osteoporosis**: Corticosteroids can lead to bone loss. Patients may require calcium and vitamin D supplementation, and bisphosphonates may be prescribed.
b. **Diabetes Mellitus**: Steroids can induce hyperglycemia. Blood glucose levels should be monitored, and diabetic management may need adjustment.
c. **Hypertension**: Monitoring and management of blood pressure are important.
d. **Gastrointestinal Issues**: Risk of peptic ulcers. Patients should be monitored for gastrointestinal symptoms and may need prophylactic treatment with proton pump inhibitors.
e. **Infections**: Increased risk due to immunosuppressive effects. Patients should be monitored for signs of infections and vaccinated as appropriate.

5. Tapering and Withdrawal

a. **Tapering**: Long-term use of corticosteroids should be tapered gradually rather than abruptly discontinued to avoid adrenal insufficiency. The rate of tapering depends on the dose and duration of therapy.
b. **Withdrawal Symptoms**: Patients may experience withdrawal symptoms, including fatigue, joint pain, and fever when discontinuing corticosteroids.

Janus inase (JAK) Inhibitors:

Janus Kinase (JAK) inhibitors are a newer class of oral medications used in the management of various rheumatic diseases. They target specific intracellular signaling pathways involved in the inflammatory process. By inhibiting these pathways, JAK inhibitors help to control disease activity and improve symptoms in conditions such as rheumatoid arthritis (RA), psoriatic arthritis, and other autoimmune disorders. Here's a detailed overview of JAK inhibitors used in rheumatology:

1. Mechanism of Action

JAK inhibitors work by blocking the activity of Janus kinases, which are crucial enzymes in the JAK-STAT signaling pathway. This pathway is involved in the regulation of various cytokines and growth factors that contribute to inflammation and immune responses.

a. **JAK Family**: The JAK family includes four isoforms: JAK1, JAK2, JAK3, and Tyk2. These kinases mediate the signaling of various cytokine receptors, influencing the activation and proliferation of immune cells.

b. **Inhibition**: JAK inhibitors selectively inhibit one or more of these kinases, thereby reducing the signaling of inflammatory cytokines such as interleukins (e.g., IL-6, IL-17) and tumor necrosis factor-alpha (TNF-alpha).

2. Types of JAK Inhibitors

a. Tofacitinib

1. **Mechanism of Action**: Tofacitinib inhibits JAK1 and JAK3, leading to reduced signaling of cytokine receptors involved in inflammation.
2. **Uses**:
    i. RA
    ii. Psoriatic arthritis
    iii. Ulcerative colitis
3. **Administration**: Oral.
4. **Dosage**: Typically 5 mg twice daily or 11 mg once daily for RA; dosage may vary for other conditions.
5. **Side Effects**:

i. **Common**: Headache, diarrhea, nasopharyngitis.

ii. **Serious**: Risk of infections (e.g., tuberculosis), increased risk of blood clots, liver enzyme abnormalities, elevated cholesterol levels.

6. **Monitoring**: Regular monitoring of blood counts, liver function, lipid levels, and screening for infections.

b. Baricitinib

1. **Mechanism of Action**: Baricitinib inhibits JAK1 and JAK2, affecting cytokine signaling pathways that contribute to inflammation.
2. **Uses**:
   i. RA
   ii. Atopic dermatitis (FDA approval pending)
3. **Administration**: Oral.
4. **Dosage**: Typically 2 mg or 4 mg once daily.
5. **Side Effects**:
   i. **Common**: Upper respiratory tract infections, headache, nausea.
   ii. **Serious**: Risk of infections, thrombosis, elevated liver enzymes, lipid abnormalities.
6. **Monitoring**: Similar to tofacitinib, with regular monitoring of blood counts, liver function, and infection screening.

c. Upadacitinib

1. **Mechanism of Action**: Upadacitinib selectively inhibits JAK1, with a focus on reducing inflammation by blocking specific cytokine signaling.
2. **Uses**:
   i. RA
   ii. Psoriatic arthritis
   iii. Atopic dermatitis
3. **Administration**: Oral.
4. **Dosage**: Typically 15 mg once daily.

5. **Side Effects**:
    i. **Common**: Upper respiratory infections, nausea, headache.
    ii. **Serious**: Risk of infections, thromboembolic events, liver enzyme elevations, increased cholesterol levels.
6. **Monitoring**: Regular monitoring for infections, blood counts, liver function, and lipid levels.

d. Filgotinib

1. **Mechanism of Action**: Filgotinib inhibits JAK1, impacting the signaling pathways of inflammatory cytokines.
2. **Uses**:
    i. RA
    ii. Ulcerative colitis
3. **Administration**: Oral.
4. **Dosage**: Typically 200 mg once daily.
5. **Side Effects**:
    i. **Common**: Nausea, headache, upper respiratory infections.
    ii. **Serious**: Risk of infections, liver enzyme abnormalities, lipid abnormalities.
6. **Monitoring**: Similar to other JAK inhibitors, with regular monitoring for infections, liver function, and blood counts.

3. Considerations and Monitoring

a. **Infection Risk**: JAK inhibitors increase the risk of infections due to their immunosuppressive effects. Patients should be screened for latent tuberculosis and other infections before starting therapy and monitored regularly during treatment.

b. **Cardiovascular Risk**: There is a potential increased risk of cardiovascular events, such as thrombosis. Patients should be monitored for signs of cardiovascular issues and have their lipid levels checked periodically.

c. **Liver Function**: Liver enzyme abnormalities can occur with JAK inhibitors. Regular monitoring of liver function tests is necessary.
d. **Blood Counts**: JAK inhibitors can affect blood cell counts, leading to conditions such as anemia or leukopenia. Regular complete blood counts are recommended.
e. **Pregnancy and Lactation**: The safety of JAK inhibitors during pregnancy and lactation is not well established. They should be used with caution, and alternative therapies may be considered.

4. Patient Education

a. **Adherence**: Patients should be advised to take their medication as prescribed and report any side effects or symptoms of infections immediately.
b. **Infection Prevention**: Educate patients on the importance of infection prevention measures, such as avoiding exposure to sick individuals and practicing good hygiene.
c. **Monitoring**: Inform patients about the need for regular follow-up appointments and laboratory tests to monitor for potential side effects and ensure effective management of their condition.

Other Medications:

a. **Azathioprine**
    i. **Mechanism of Action**: Inhibits purine synthesis, affecting lymphocyte proliferation.
    ii. **Uses**: RA, SLE, other autoimmune diseases.
    iii. **Side Effects**: Bone marrow suppression, liver toxicity.
b. **Cyclophosphamide**
    i. **Mechanism of Action**: Alkylates DNA, affecting rapidly dividing cells.
    ii. **Uses**: Severe autoimmune diseases like SLE.

iii. **Side Effects**: Bone marrow suppression, hemorrhagic cystitis, infertility.

Multiple Choice Questions (MCQs)

1. What is the primary function of histamine H2 receptors?
   a) Mediate allergic responses
   b) Regulate gastric acid secretion
   c) Involved in neurotransmission
   d) Play a role in immune cell chemotaxis
2. Which drug is an example of a selective COX-2 inhibitor?
   a) Aspirin
   b) Ibuprofen
   c) Celecoxib
   d) Naproxen
3. What is the mechanism of action of Montelukast?
   a) COX-2 inhibition
   b) Leukotriene receptor antagonism
   c) Serotonin reuptake inhibition
   d) ACE inhibition
4. Which drug is a serotonin receptor agonist used in migraine treatment?
   a) Fluoxetine
   b) Sertraline
   c) Sumatriptan
   d) Loratadine
5. What is the primary action of bradykinin?
   a) Vasoconstriction
   b) Vasodilation
   c) Inhibition of pain
   d) Increase in gastric acid secretion

6. Which enzyme do NSAIDs primarily inhibit?
   a) Lipoxygenase
   b) Cyclooxygenase (COX)
   c) Histidine decarboxylase
   d) Aromatic L-amino acid decarboxylase
7. What is a common side effect of non-selective NSAIDs?
   a) Bronchoconstriction
   b) Hypotension
   c) Gastrointestinal irritation
   d) Hyperglycemia
8. Which of the following is a xanthine oxidase inhibitor used to treat chronic gout?
   a) Colchicine
   b) Allopurinol
   c) Probenecid
   d) Pegloticase
9. What is the primary use of corticosteroids in rheumatic diseases?
   a) Increase uric acid excretion
   b) Provide cardiovascular protection
   c) Reduce inflammation and immune response
   d) Enhance prostaglandin synthesis
10. Which drug is a Janus Kinase (JAK) inhibitor used in the management of rheumatoid arthritis?
   a) Tofacitinib
   b) Sulfasalazine
   c) Leflunomide
   d) Hydroxychloroquine
11. What is the mechanism of action of disease-modifying antirheumatic drugs (DMARDs)?

a) Provide symptomatic relief
b) Modify the underlying disease process
c) Increase gastrointestinal motility
d) Enhance neurotransmitter release

12. Which prostaglandin analog is used to treat glaucoma?

a) Dinoprostone
b) Misoprostol
c) Latanoprost
d) Iloprost

13. What is the primary clinical use of leukotriene synthesis inhibitors like Zileuton?

a) Hypertension
b) Asthma management
c) Gastric ulcer treatment
d) Depression treatment

14. Which drug class does ibuprofen belong to?

a) Xanthine oxidase inhibitors
b) Selective COX-2 inhibitors
c) Non-selective NSAIDs
d) Leukotriene receptor antagonists

15. What is the main adverse effect associated with colchicine use in gout treatment?

a) Hyperglycemia
b) Muscle weakness
c) Hypotension
d) Hepatotoxicity

16. Which antirheumatic drug is an antimalarial with immunomodulatory effects?

a) Methotrexate

b) Sulfasalazine
c) Hydroxychloroquine
d) Leflunomide

17. Which enzyme converts arachidonic acid to leukotrienes?
a) Cyclooxygenase
b) Lipoxygenase
c) Xanthine oxidase
d) Phospholipase A2

18. Which corticosteroid is often used for its potent anti-inflammatory effects in severe rheumatic conditions?
a) Prednisone
b) Methotrexate
c) Sulfasalazine
d) Hydroxychloroquine

19. What is the primary function of prostaglandins in inflammation?
a) Decrease vascular permeability
b) Promote platelet aggregation
c) Mediate pain, fever, and inflammation
d) Enhance neurotransmission

20. Which drug is a mineralocorticoid used in the treatment of Addison's disease?
a) Prednisone
b) Fludrocortisone
c) Dexamethasone
d) Hydrocortisone

Short Answer Type Questions (Subjective)

1. Explain the mechanism of action of NSAIDs.
2. What are the clinical uses of selective serotonin reuptake inhibitors (SSRIs)?

3. Describe the primary actions of bradykinin in the body.
4. How do leukotriene receptor antagonists help in asthma management?
5. What are the potential side effects of long-term corticosteroid use?
6. Explain the role of prostaglandins in inflammation and pain.
7. What are the primary clinical applications of disease-modifying antirheumatic drugs (DMARDs)?
8. Describe the mechanism of action of xanthine oxidase inhibitors in gout treatment.
9. How does colchicine help in managing acute gout attacks?
10. What is the significance of monitoring liver function in patients taking methotrexate?
11. Explain the therapeutic uses of prostaglandin analogs.
12. Describe the side effects associated with non-selective NSAIDs.
13. How do ACE inhibitors affect bradykinin levels?
14. What are the primary actions of thromboxane A2?
15. Describe the mechanism of action of JAK inhibitors in rheumatic diseases.
16. What is the role of hydroxychloroquine in treating systemic lupus erythematosus (SLE)?
17. How do uricosuric agents help in the management of chronic gout?
18. Explain the potential cardiovascular risks associated with COX-2 inhibitors.
19. What is the role of phospholipase A2 in the synthesis of autocoids?
20. Describe the mechanism of action of anti-gout drugs like pegloticase.

Long Answer Type Questions (Subjective)

1. Discuss the pharmacology of histamine, including its synthesis, release, receptors, and clinical applications of histamine antagonists.
2. Explain the synthesis, release, and actions of prostaglandins, and describe the clinical uses of prostaglandin analogs.

3. Describe the synthesis, release, and actions of leukotrienes, and explain the clinical applications of leukotriene receptor antagonists.
4. Discuss the synthesis, release, and actions of bradykinin, and describe the clinical relevance of drugs affecting bradykinin levels.
5. Explain the synthesis, release, and actions of serotonin, and discuss the clinical applications of serotonin modulators.
6. Describe the synthesis, release, and actions of nitric oxide, and explain the clinical uses of nitric oxide donors and inhibitors.
7. Discuss the synthesis, release, and actions of thromboxanes, and explain the clinical relevance of thromboxane inhibitors.
8. Explain the synthesis, release, and actions of substance P, and describe the clinical applications of neurokinin-1 (NK1) receptor antagonists.
9. Describe the pharmacology of non-steroidal anti-inflammatory drugs (NSAIDs), including their mechanisms, classifications, and clinical uses.
10. Discuss the pharmacology of disease-modifying antirheumatic drugs (DMARDs), including conventional and biological DMARDs, their mechanisms, uses, and monitoring requirements.

Answer Key for MCQs

1. b) Regulate gastric acid secretion
2. c) Celecoxib
3. b) Leukotriene receptor antagonism
4. c) Sumatriptan
5. b) Vasodilation
6. b) Cyclooxygenase (COX)
7. c) Gastrointestinal irritation
8. b) Allopurinol
9. c) Reduce inflammation and immune response
10. a) Tofacitinib

11.b) Modify the underlying disease process

12.c) Latanoprost

13.b) Asthma management

14.c) Non-selective NSAIDs

15.b) Muscle weakness

16.c) Hydroxychloroquine

17.b) Lipoxygenase

18.a) Prednisone

19.c) Mediate pain, fever, and inflammation

20.b) Fludrocortisone

CHAPTER – 16

PHARMACOLOGY OF DRUGS ACTING ON ENDOCRINE SYSTEM –I

Mr. Ashutosh Jain

Assistant Professor, Rajiv Gandhi Institute of Pharmacy, Faculty of Pharmaceutical Science & Technology, AKS University Satna, (M.P.)

ABSTRACT:

Endocrine pharmacology involves the study of drugs that influence the function of endocrine glands, which secrete hormones regulating various bodily functions. These drugs can either mimic natural hormones (analogues) or inhibit hormone production and action. Understanding hormone receptors, signal transduction pathways, and feedback mechanisms is crucial for effectively using these drugs in treating hormonal imbalances and endocrine disorders. Endocrine pharmacology is vital in managing diseases such as diabetes, thyroid disorders, and growth hormone deficiencies, providing therapeutic options that restore normal hormonal balance and function. The anterior pituitary gland secretes several critical hormones, including growth hormone (GH), adrenocorticotropic hormone (ACTH), and gonadotropins (LH and FSH). Analogues of these hormones, such as somatropin for GH deficiency and cosyntropin for ACTH testing, are used to treat deficiencies and stimulate hormone production. Inhibitors, such as octreotide, a somatostatin analogue, are used to treat conditions like acromegaly by inhibiting excessive GH release. Additionally, drugs like cabergoline inhibit prolactin secretion, addressing disorders like prolactinomas. These therapies help manage various endocrine disorders by modulating hormone levels effectively. Thyroid hormones, primarily thyroxine (T4) and triiodothyronine (T3), regulate metabolism, growth, and development. Levothyroxine, a synthetic T4, is the standard treatment for hypothyroidism, restoring normal metabolic function. For hyperthyroidism, inhibitors like methimazole and propylthiouracil (PTU) reduce thyroid hormone production by inhibiting the enzyme thyroid peroxidase, which is essential for hormone synthesis. Radioactive iodine therapy is another approach to destroy overactive thyroid tissue. These drugs are crucial in managing thyroid disorders, ensuring appropriate hormone levels to maintain metabolic balance and overall health.

INTRODUCTION:

The endocrine system is a complex network of glands and organs that produce and release hormones to regulate various physiological processes in the body. The pharmacology of drugs acting on the endocrine system involves the study of how these drugs interact with hormone-producing glands and their receptors to modify hormonal activity and treat endocrine disorders. Here's a detailed overview of this field:

1. Endocrine Glands and Hormones

a. **Hypothalamus and Pituitary Gland:** These are the master glands that control other endocrine glands. The hypothalamus releases hormones that regulate the pituitary gland, which in turn releases hormones affecting various organs.

b. **Thyroid Gland:** Produces thyroid hormones (T3 and T4) that regulate metabolism, growth, and development.

c. **Parathyroid Glands:** Regulate calcium and phosphate balance through the secretion of parathyroid hormone (PTH).

d. **Adrenal Glands:** Produce corticosteroids (e.g., cortisol), mineralocorticoids (e.g., aldosterone), and catecholamines (e.g., adrenaline).

e. **Pancreas:** Secretes insulin and glucagon to regulate blood glucose levels.

f. **Gonads:** The ovaries and testes produce sex hormones (estrogens, progesterone, and testosterone) that influence reproductive and sexual functions.

2. Drug Categories Acting on the Endocrine System

a. **Thyroid Hormones and Antithyroid Agents:**

   i. **Thyroid Hormones:** Levothyroxine (T4) and Liothyronine (T3) are used to treat hypothyroidism.

   ii. **Antithyroid Agents:** Methimazole and Propylthiouracil (PTU) are used to manage hyperthyroidism by inhibiting thyroid hormone synthesis.

b. **Corticosteroids:**

   i. **Glucocorticoids:** Hydrocortisone, Prednisone, and Dexamethasone are used to treat inflammatory and autoimmune conditions.

   ii. **Mineralocorticoids:** Fludrocortisone is used to manage conditions involving aldosterone deficiency or excess.

c. **Sex Hormones and Hormone Antagonists:**

   i. **Estrogens and Progestins:** Used in contraceptives and hormone replacement therapy (e.g., Ethinyl estradiol, Norgestrel).

   ii. **Androgens:** Testosterone and its derivatives are used in hormone replacement therapy and for certain cancers.

   iii. **Antagonists:** Drugs like Tamoxifen and Anastrozole are used in the treatment of hormone-sensitive cancers.

d. **Insulin and Antidiabetic Agents:**

   i. **Insulin:** Various forms of insulin (e.g., Regular, NPH, Lantus) are used to manage diabetes mellitus.

   ii. **Oral Hypoglycemics:** Metformin, Sulfonylureas, and DPP-4 inhibitors help manage blood glucose levels in type 2 diabetes.

e. **Parathyroid Hormone Analogues:**

   i. **Teriparatide:** Used for osteoporosis by stimulating bone formation.

f. **Other Endocrine Drugs:**
    i. **Growth Hormone:** Recombinant human growth hormone (e.g., Somatropin) is used to treat growth disorders.
    ii. **Oxytocin:** Used to induce labor and manage postpartum bleeding.

3. Mechanism of Action

Drugs acting on the endocrine system can have various mechanisms of action depending on their targets:

a. **Receptor Agonists/Antagonists:** Drugs may mimic or block the action of endogenous hormones by binding to their specific receptors.
b. **Enzyme Inhibitors:** Some drugs inhibit enzymes involved in hormone synthesis or metabolism (e.g., aromatase inhibitors in breast cancer).
c. **Hormone Replacement:** Administering exogenous hormones to replace deficient levels (e.g., thyroid hormones in hypothyroidism).

4. Therapeutic Uses

a. **Thyroid Disorders:** Management of hypothyroidism and hyperthyroidism.
b. **Adrenal Disorders:** Treatment of Addison's disease, Cushing's syndrome, and other adrenal dysfunctions.
c. **Diabetes Management:** Regulation of blood glucose levels and treatment of complications.
d. **Reproductive Health:** Management of hormonal imbalances, contraception, and hormone replacement therapy.
e. **Bone Health:** Treatment of osteoporosis and related conditions.

5. Adverse Effects and Drug Interactions

Drugs affecting the endocrine system can have significant side effects, including:

a. **Thyroid Drugs:** Risk of hyperthyroidism or hypothyroidism if not properly dosed.

b. **Corticosteroids:** Potential for weight gain, osteoporosis, and increased infection risk.
c. **Insulin:** Risk of hypoglycemia and weight gain.
d. **Sex Hormones:** Risk of thromboembolic events, mood changes, and cancer.

BASIC CONCEPTS IN ENDOCRINE PHARMACOLOGY

Endocrine pharmacology focuses on how drugs influence the function of the endocrine system, which consists of glands that release hormones into the bloodstream to regulate various bodily functions. Here's a detailed breakdown of the fundamental concepts in this field:

1. Hormone Function and Regulation

a. **Hormone Production and Release:**
   i. Hormones are produced by endocrine glands and secreted directly into the bloodstream. They travel to target tissues or organs where they exert their effects.

b. **Feedback Mechanisms:**
   i. **Negative Feedback:** Most endocrine systems operate on a negative feedback mechanism, where an increase in hormone levels inhibits further hormone release. For example, high levels of thyroid hormones inhibit the release of Thyroid-Stimulating Hormone (TSH) from the pituitary gland.
   ii. **Positive Feedback:** Less common, positive feedback mechanisms enhance the release of hormones. An example is the release of oxytocin during childbirth, which stimulates uterine contractions.

2. Receptor Binding and Signal Transduction

a. **Hormone-Receptor Interaction:**
   i. Hormones exert their effects by binding to specific receptors on or within target cells. The nature of the receptor determines the subsequent cellular response.

b. **Types of Hormone Receptors:**

   i. **Cell Surface Receptors:** These include G-protein coupled receptors (GPCRs) and enzyme-linked receptors (e.g., receptor tyrosine kinases). Hormones that cannot cross the cell membrane (e.g., insulin) bind to these receptors.

   ii. **Intracellular Receptors:** These receptors are located inside the cell, usually in the cytoplasm or nucleus. Hormones that can cross the cell membrane (e.g., thyroid hormones, steroid hormones) bind to these receptors, affecting gene expression.

c. **Signal Transduction Pathways:**

   i. Upon hormone binding, various intracellular signaling pathways are activated, such as second messengers (e.g., cAMP, IP3) or direct modulation of gene expression.

3. Drug Action on Hormone Systems

a. **Agonists and Antagonists:**

   i. **Agonists:** Drugs that mimic the action of endogenous hormones by activating their receptors (e.g., synthetic thyroid hormones like levothyroxine).

   ii. **Antagonists:** Drugs that block the action of endogenous hormones by inhibiting their receptors (e.g., Tamoxifen as an estrogen receptor antagonist).

b. **Hormone Replacement Therapy (HRT):**

   i. Administering synthetic or natural hormones to replace deficient levels in conditions such as hypothyroidism, adrenal insufficiency, and menopausal symptoms.

c. **Enzyme Inhibitors:**

   i. Drugs that inhibit enzymes involved in hormone synthesis or metabolism (e.g., aromatase inhibitors in breast cancer).

4. Pharmacokinetics and Pharmacodynamics

a. **Pharmacokinetics:**

   i. **Absorption:** Hormonal drugs may be administered orally, transdermally, or via injection. Their absorption can be influenced by factors like food and other medications.

   ii. **Distribution:** Hormones and their analogs are distributed throughout the body, and their effects depend on their ability to reach target tissues.

   iii. **Metabolism:** Hormones are metabolized in the liver and other tissues, affecting their duration of action.

   iv. **Excretion:** Hormonal drugs and their metabolites are excreted primarily through the kidneys or bile.

b. **Pharmacodynamics:**

   i. The study of how drugs affect the endocrine system, including their potency, efficacy, and the relationship between dose and response.

5. Therapeutic Uses and Clinical Applications

a. **Thyroid Disorders:** Management of hypothyroidism and hyperthyroidism with thyroid hormones or antithyroid drugs.

b. **Adrenal Disorders:** Treatment of conditions like Addison's disease and Cushing's syndrome with corticosteroids or adrenal enzyme inhibitors.

c. **Diabetes Management:** Use of insulin and oral hypoglycemics to regulate blood glucose levels.

d. **Reproductive Health:** Hormonal therapies for contraception, hormone replacement, and reproductive disorders.

6. Adverse Effects and Drug Interactions

a. **Adverse Effects:**

   i. **Endocrine Drugs:** Potential side effects include weight gain, mood changes, cardiovascular effects, and risk of infections, depending on the drug and its action.

b. **Drug Interactions:**

i. Endocrine drugs may interact with other medications, altering their effects or increasing the risk of side effects. For instance, corticosteroids can affect the metabolism of other drugs, and certain antidiabetic drugs may interact with other medications affecting glucose levels.

7. Diagnostic and Monitoring Considerations

a. **Hormone Levels:** Monitoring hormone levels is essential for adjusting drug dosages and ensuring therapeutic efficacy.

b. **Clinical Symptoms:** Regular assessment of clinical symptoms helps in evaluating the effectiveness of treatment and managing any adverse effects.

ANTERIOR PITUITARY HORMONES- ANALOGUES AND THEIR INHIBITORS

The anterior pituitary gland produces several key hormones that regulate various physiological processes by acting on other endocrine glands. These hormones include:

1. Adrenocorticotropic Hormone (ACTH)
2. Thyroid-Stimulating Hormone (TSH)
3. Luteinizing Hormone (LH)
4. Follicle-Stimulating Hormone (FSH)
5. Growth Hormone (GH)
6. Prolactin (PRL)

1. Adrenocorticotropic Hormone (ACTH):

Function:

a. Stimulates the adrenal cortex to release cortisol and other corticosteroids.

Analogues:

a. **Cosyntropin (Synthetic ACTH):** Used in diagnostic tests to evaluate adrenal function. It stimulates the adrenal glands to produce cortisol, helping to assess the integrity of the hypothalamic-pituitary-adrenal (HPA) axis.

Inhibitors:

a. **Metyrapone:** Inhibits cortisol synthesis, used in diagnostic tests to assess ACTH production and adrenal function.
b. **Ketoconazole:** An antifungal drug that inhibits several steroidogenic enzymes, leading to reduced cortisol production and is used off-label for Cushing's syndrome.

2. Thyroid-Stimulating Hormone (TSH):

Function:

a. Stimulates the thyroid gland to produce thyroid hormones (T3 and T4).

Analogues:

a. **Thyrotropin alfa:** A recombinant form of TSH used in diagnostic imaging to enhance the visualization of thyroid cancer cells.

Inhibitors:

a. **Anti-TSH Antibodies:** These can be present in some autoimmune thyroid diseases, such as Hashimoto's thyroiditis, and can interfere with TSH function.

3. Luteinizing Hormone (LH):

Function:

a. In females, LH triggers ovulation and stimulates the production of estrogen and progesterone.
b. In males, LH stimulates testosterone production.

Analogues:

a. **Leuprolide:** A GnRH analog that initially stimulates LH and FSH release but ultimately suppresses their secretion when used continuously (used in treating hormone-sensitive cancers and precocious puberty).

Inhibitors:

a. **Goserelin:** Another GnRH analog that suppresses LH and FSH release and is used in hormone-sensitive cancers and endometriosis.
b. **Cetrorelix and Ganirelix:** GnRH antagonists used in controlled ovarian stimulation protocols to prevent premature ovulation.

4. Follicle-Stimulating Hormone (FSH):

Function:

a. In females, FSH stimulates follicle development and estrogen production.
b. In males, FSH supports sperm production.

Analogues:

a. **Follitropin alfa (rFSH):** Recombinant FSH used in fertility treatments to stimulate follicular development in women and sperm production in men.
b. **Urofollitropin:** Purified FSH obtained from the urine of postmenopausal women, used for similar purposes as recombinant FSH.

Inhibitors:

a. **Inhibin:** A naturally occurring hormone that inhibits FSH release; no specific pharmacological inhibitors for FSH are used clinically.

5. Growth Hormone (GH):

Function:

a. Stimulates growth, cell repair, and metabolism.

Analogues:

a. **Somatropin:** Recombinant human growth hormone used to treat growth hormone deficiency in children and adults.
b. **Somatrem:** Another form of recombinant GH with similar uses.

Inhibitors:

a. **Octreotide:** A somatostatin analogue that inhibits GH release, used in acromegaly (excess GH) and certain neuroendocrine tumors.
b. **Lanreotide:** Another somatostatin analogue used to manage acromegaly and some types of tumors.

6. Prolactin (PRL):

Function:

a. Stimulates milk production in lactating women and affects reproductive functions.

Analogues:

a. No direct analogues are used clinically; however, medications that modulate prolactin levels can be utilized.

Inhibitors:

a. **Dopamine Agonists:** Used to treat hyperprolactinemia (high prolactin levels) by stimulating dopamine receptors that inhibit prolactin release. Examples include:
   i. **Cabergoline:** A potent dopamine agonist used to treat prolactin-secreting tumors (prolactinomas) and other causes of hyperprolactinemia.
   ii. **Bromocriptine:** An older dopamine agonist with similar uses.

THYROID HORMONES- ANALOGUES AND THEIR INHIBITORS

Thyroid hormones are crucial for regulating metabolism, growth, and development. They are produced by the thyroid gland and consist primarily of:

1. Thyroxine (T4)
2. Triiodothyronine (T3)

1. Thyroid Hormones

Thyroxine (T4) and Triiodothyronine (T3)

Function:

a. **T4 (Thyroxine):** The primary thyroid hormone produced by the thyroid gland. It is converted into T3 in peripheral tissues.
b. **T3 (Triiodothyronine):** The more active form of thyroid hormone, responsible for stimulating metabolism, growth, and development.

Analogues of Thyroid Hormones:

1. Levothyroxine (Synthetic T4)

a. **Use:** The most commonly prescribed thyroid hormone replacement therapy for hypothyroidism. It is a synthetic form of T4 that is converted to T3 in the body.

b. **Brand Names:** Synthroid, Eltroxin, Levoxyl.

2. Liothyronine (Synthetic T3)

a. **Use:** Used in cases where a more rapid onset of action is needed or when T4 conversion is impaired. It can be used alone or in combination with levothyroxine.

b. **Brand Names:** Cytomel, Triostat.

3. Liotrix (Combination of T3 and T4)

a. **Use:** A fixed combination of T3 and T4. It is less commonly used than levothyroxine alone but may be prescribed in certain situations.

b. **Brand Name:** Thyrolar.

4. Natural Thyroid Extracts

a. **Use:** Derived from animal thyroid glands, containing both T4 and T3. These are less commonly used due to variability in potency.

b. **Brand Name:** Armour Thyroid, Nature-Throid.

Inhibitors of Thyroid Hormones:

1. Antithyroid Agents

a. Methimazole

a. **Use:** The first-line treatment for hyperthyroidism (overactive thyroid). It inhibits thyroid peroxidase, which is essential for the synthesis of thyroid hormones.

b. **Brand Names:** Tapazole.

b. Propylthiouracil (PTU)

a. **Use:** Used to treat hyperthyroidism. It inhibits thyroid peroxidase and also inhibits the peripheral conversion of T4 to T3.

b. **Brand Names:** PTU (generic).

2. Iodine Compounds

a. Radioactive Iodine (I-131)

a. **Use:** A form of radioactive iodine used to destroy overactive thyroid tissue in hyperthyroidism and thyroid cancer. It works by concentrating in the thyroid gland and emitting radiation that destroys thyroid cells.
b. **Brand Name:** Not applicable (used as a specific therapeutic procedure rather than a branded medication).

b. Non-Radioactive Iodine Solutions (e.g., Lugol's Solution)

a. **Use:** Used in certain conditions to decrease thyroid hormone release. Lugol's solution can be used to prepare patients for thyroid surgery or manage thyroid storm.
b. **Brand Names:** Lugol's Solution, potassium iodide.

3. Other Agents

a. Potassium Iodide

a. **Use:** In high doses, it can reduce the release of thyroid hormones, often used in acute situations like thyroid storm or before thyroid surgery.
b. **Brand Names:** SSKI (Saturated Solution of Potassium Iodide), ThyroSafe.

b. Beta-Blockers (e.g., Propranolol)

a. **Use:** Not direct inhibitors of thyroid hormone synthesis, but they can help manage symptoms of hyperthyroidism by blocking the effects of thyroid hormones on the heart and other tissues.
b. **Brand Names:** Inderal.

Mechanism of Action

a. **Thyroid Hormone Analogues:** These drugs work by substituting the natural thyroid hormones that are deficient or absent, helping to normalize metabolic functions.
b. **Antithyroid Agents:** Inhibit the synthesis of thyroid hormones by blocking the enzymes needed for thyroid hormone production or reducing the conversion of T4 to T3.

c. **Iodine Compounds:** Radioactive iodine destroys thyroid tissue, while non-radioactive iodine can reduce hormone release temporarily.
d. **Beta-Blockers:** Manage symptoms associated with excess thyroid hormone, such as tachycardia and anxiety.

Clinical Applications

a. **Hypothyroidism:** Treated with synthetic thyroid hormones (levothyroxine, liothyronine).
b. **Hyperthyroidism:** Managed with antithyroid drugs (methimazole, propylthiouracil), radioactive iodine, and iodine solutions.
c. **Thyroid Cancer:** Treated with radioactive iodine and thyroid hormone therapy to suppress TSH and prevent cancer recurrence.

Adverse Effects and Considerations

a. **Thyroid Hormone Analogues:** Potential side effects include weight loss, palpitations, heat intolerance, and bone loss if overdosed.
b. **Antithyroid Agents:** Can cause rash, agranulocytosis, and liver dysfunction.
c. **Iodine Compounds:** Risk of allergic reactions, iodism, and potential thyroid dysfunction.
d. **Beta-Blockers:** May cause fatigue, bradycardia, and exacerbation of respiratory conditions.

CHAPTER – 17

PHARMACOLOGY OF DRUGS ACTING ON ENDOCRINE SYSTEM –I

Ms. Shikha Singh

Assistant Professor, Rajiv Gandhi Institute of Pharmacy, Faculty of Pharmaceutical Science & Technology, AKS University Satna, (M.P.)

ABSTRACT:

The regulation of plasma calcium levels is critical for various physiological processes, including bone health, muscle contraction, and nerve function. Parathyroid hormone (PTH) increases blood calcium levels by stimulating bone resorption, enhancing renal reabsorption of calcium, and activating vitamin D synthesis. Calcitonin, secreted by the thyroid gland, lowers blood calcium levels by inhibiting bone resorption and increasing renal calcium excretion. Vitamin D, obtained from diet or synthesized in the skin, enhances calcium absorption in the intestines. Insulin, while primarily involved in glucose metabolism, also influences calcium homeostasis by modulating bone formation and resorption. These hormones work in concert to maintain calcium balance and overall metabolic health. Oral hypoglycemic agents are used to manage type 2 diabetes by lowering blood glucose levels. Classes include sulfonylureas (e.g., glipizide), which stimulate insulin secretion; biguanides (e.g., metformin), which reduce hepatic glucose production; and SGLT2 inhibitors (e.g., empagliflozin), which increase renal glucose excretion. Glucagon, a hormone produced by the pancreas, raises blood glucose levels by promoting glycogenolysis and gluconeogenesis in the liver. It is used in emergency situations to treat severe hypoglycemia in diabetic patients. Together, these agents help maintain glucose homeostasis and prevent complications associated with diabetes. Adrenocorticotropic hormone (ACTH) stimulates the adrenal cortex to produce corticosteroids, including glucocorticoids (e.g., cortisol) and mineralocorticoids (e.g., aldosterone). Glucocorticoids regulate metabolism, immune response, and stress, while mineralocorticoids control electrolyte and water balance. Synthetic corticosteroids, such as prednisone and dexamethasone, are used to treat a wide range of conditions, including inflammatory diseases, autoimmune disorders, and adrenal insufficiency. While effective, these drugs can cause side effects like immunosuppression, osteoporosis, and metabolic disturbances, requiring careful monitoring and management to minimize risks and ensure therapeutic efficacy.

HORMONES REGULATING PLASMA CALCIUM LEVEL- PARATHORMONE, CALCITONIN AND VITAMIN- D, INSULIN

Maintaining plasma calcium levels is essential for various physiological functions, including bone health, muscle function, and nerve transmission. The primary hormones involved in regulating plasma calcium levels are:

1. Parathyroid Hormone (PTH)
2. Calcitonin
3. Vitamin D
4. Insulin (though not a primary regulator, it influences calcium metabolism indirectly)

1. Parathyroid Hormone (PTH)

Function:

a. Produced by the parathyroid glands.
b. **Increases Plasma Calcium Levels** by:
    i. Stimulating osteoclast activity in bones, leading to bone resorption and release of calcium into the bloodstream.
    ii. Enhancing renal reabsorption of calcium and reducing renal phosphate reabsorption.
    iii. Stimulating the conversion of vitamin D to its active form, which increases intestinal calcium absorption.

Therapeutic Uses:

a. **Synthetic PTH (Teriparatide):** Used in the treatment of osteoporosis to stimulate bone formation and improve bone density.

   i. **Brand Name:** Forteo

Adverse Effects:

a. Possible side effects include dizziness, headache, nausea, and increased risk of osteosarcoma with long-term use.

2. Calcitonin

Function:

a. Produced by the C cells of the thyroid gland.

b. **Decreases Plasma Calcium Levels** by:

   i. Inhibiting osteoclast activity, leading to reduced bone resorption and decreased calcium release from bones.

   ii. Increasing renal excretion of calcium by promoting its excretion in the urine.

Therapeutic Uses:

a. **Synthetic Calcitonin:** Used in conditions like osteoporosis and Paget's disease of bone to reduce bone resorption and pain.

   i. **Brand Names:** Miacalcin (intranasal), Calcimar (injectable)

Adverse Effects:

a. Common side effects include nasal irritation (for intranasal forms), flushing, and nausea. Rarely, allergic reactions may occur.

3. Vitamin D

Function:

a. Essential for the absorption of calcium from the intestine.

b. **Active Form (Calcitriol, 1,25-dihydroxyvitamin D3):** Increases intestinal calcium absorption, enhances bone mineralization, and works synergistically with PTH to regulate calcium levels.

Therapeutic Uses:

a. **Vitamin D Supplements:** Used to prevent and treat vitamin D deficiency, rickets, and osteomalacia. Commonly used forms include:

   i. **Cholecalciferol (Vitamin D3):** Preferred for its efficacy and long-term benefits.

   ii. **Ergocalciferol (Vitamin D2):** Another form of vitamin D used in supplementation.

   iii. **Calcitriol (Active Form):** Used in conditions like chronic kidney disease to manage calcium and phosphate balance.

Adverse Effects:

a. Excessive vitamin D can cause hypercalcemia, leading to symptoms like nausea, vomiting, and kidney stones. Long-term overuse can also affect kidney function.

4. Insulin

Function:

a. Primarily regulates glucose metabolism but also influences calcium metabolism indirectly.

b. **Effects on Calcium:**

   i. **Calcium Absorption:** Insulin can affect bone mineralization and calcium deposition in bones.

   ii. **Bone Health:** Adequate insulin levels are necessary for bone health, and insulin resistance or deficiency may negatively impact bone density and calcium balance.

Therapeutic Uses:

a. **Insulin Therapy:** Used in the management of diabetes mellitus. Proper management of diabetes can indirectly support bone health and calcium metabolism by preventing hyperglycemia and related complications.

Adverse Effects:

a. Potential side effects of insulin include hypoglycemia, weight gain, and, with chronic uncontrolled diabetes, potential negative impacts on bone health.

ORAL HYPOGLYCEMIC AGENTS AND GLUCAGON

Managing blood glucose levels is crucial in the treatment of diabetes mellitus. Oral hypoglycemic agents are primarily used in type 2 diabetes to lower blood glucose levels, while glucagon is used in emergency situations to raise blood glucose levels when hypoglycemia occurs.

1. Oral Hypoglycemic Agents

Oral hypoglycemic agents are a diverse group of medications that work through different mechanisms to control blood glucose levels in individuals with type 2 diabetes. They include:

a. Sulfonylureas

1. **Mechanism of Action:** Stimulate the pancreas to release more insulin by closing ATP-sensitive potassium channels on beta cells.
2. **Examples:**
    i. **Glyburide:** Effective in lowering blood glucose levels and has a long history of use.
    ii. **Glipizide:** Used for its shorter duration of action compared to other sulfonylureas.
    iii. **Glimepiride:** A newer sulfonylurea with fewer side effects and a lower risk of hypoglycemia.
3. **Adverse Effects:** Hypoglycemia, weight gain, and possible allergic reactions.

b. Biguanides

1. **Mechanism of Action:** Decrease glucose production by the liver and improve insulin sensitivity in peripheral tissues.
2. **Example:**

i. **Metformin:** The first-line treatment for type 2 diabetes. It is also used for its cardiovascular benefits and low risk of hypoglycemia.

3. **Adverse Effects:** Gastrointestinal issues (e.g., diarrhea, nausea) and a rare risk of lactic acidosis.

c. Thiazolidinediones (TZDs)

1. **Mechanism of Action:** Improve insulin sensitivity by activating peroxisome proliferator-activated receptor-gamma (PPAR-γ).
2. **Examples:**
   i. **Pioglitazone:** Helps lower blood glucose levels and may have additional cardiovascular benefits.
   ii. **Rosiglitazone:** Associated with cardiovascular risks but effective in glycemic control.
3. **Adverse Effects:** Weight gain, fluid retention, and potential risk of heart failure.

d. Dipeptidyl Peptidase-4 (DPP-4) Inhibitors

1. **Mechanism of Action:** Prevent the breakdown of incretin hormones, which enhance insulin secretion and inhibit glucagon release.
2. **Examples:**
   i. **Sitagliptin:** Used for its efficacy in controlling blood glucose levels with a low risk of hypoglycemia.
   ii. **Saxagliptin:** Similar to sitagliptin, with a slightly different side effect profile.
3. **Adverse Effects:** Upper respiratory tract infections, headache, and gastrointestinal issues.

e. Sodium-Glucose Cotransporter-2 (SGLT2) Inhibitors

1. **Mechanism of Action:** Block the reabsorption of glucose in the kidneys, leading to increased glucose excretion in urine.
2. **Examples:**

i. **Empagliflozin:** Reduces blood glucose levels and has benefits for cardiovascular health.

ii. **Canagliflozin:** Also associated with cardiovascular benefits and weight loss.

3. **Adverse Effects:** Genital infections, urinary tract infections, and dehydration.

f. Alpha-Glucosidase Inhibitors

1. **Mechanism of Action:** Delay the digestion and absorption of carbohydrates in the intestine, leading to a slower rise in blood glucose levels.
2. **Examples:**
   i. **Acarbose:** Used to manage postprandial blood glucose levels.
   ii. **Miglitol:** Similar to acarbose with slightly different gastrointestinal side effects.
3. **Adverse Effects:** Gastrointestinal discomfort, flatulence, and diarrhea.

g. Meglitinides

1. **Mechanism of Action:** Stimulate insulin release from the pancreas in a glucose-dependent manner.
2. **Examples:**
   i. **Repaglinide:** Effective in lowering postprandial blood glucose levels.
   ii. **Nateglinide:** Similar to repaglinide with a shorter duration of action.
3. **Adverse Effects:** Hypoglycemia and weight gain.

2. Glucagon

Function:

a. **Mechanism of Action:** Increases blood glucose levels by stimulating glycogenolysis (breakdown of glycogen) in the liver and promoting gluconeogenesis (production of glucose from non-carbohydrate sources).

b. **Indications:** Used in emergency situations to treat severe hypoglycemia, especially when a patient is unconscious or unable to consume glucose orally.

Administration:

a. **Forms:** Available as an injectable solution or prefilled auto-injectors.

b. **Usage:** Administered subcutaneously or intramuscularly in cases of severe hypoglycemia.

Adverse Effects:

a. **Nausea and Vomiting:** Common side effects after administration.

b. **Allergic Reactions:** Rare but possible.

Precautions:

a. **Blood Glucose Monitoring:** After glucagon administration, blood glucose levels should be monitored, and follow-up treatment with oral glucose or carbohydrates is often needed.

Summary

a. **Oral Hypoglycemic Agents:** A wide array of medications used to manage type 2 diabetes through various mechanisms, including increasing insulin secretion, improving insulin sensitivity, and enhancing glucose excretion. Common classes include sulfonylureas, biguanides, TZDs, DPP-4 inhibitors, SGLT2 inhibitors, alpha-glucosidase inhibitors, and meglitinides.

b. **Glucagon:** Used for rapid management of severe hypoglycemia, increasing blood glucose levels through glycogenolysis and gluconeogenesis.

ACTH AND CORTICOSTEROIDS

Adrenocorticotropic Hormone (ACTH) and **corticosteroids** are crucial in the regulation of stress responses, metabolism, and immune function. Here's a detailed overview of each:

1. Adrenocorticotropic Hormone (ACTH)

Function:

a. ACTH is produced by the anterior pituitary gland.

b. It stimulates the adrenal cortex to produce and release corticosteroids, primarily cortisol.

Mechanism of Action:

a. ACTH binds to melanocortin 2 receptors (MC2R) on adrenal cortical cells.

b. This binding activates adenylate cyclase, increasing cyclic AMP (cAMP) levels, which in turn stimulates the synthesis and release of corticosteroids.

Therapeutic Uses:

a. **Diagnostic Testing:** Synthetic ACTH (Cosyntropin) is used to assess adrenal gland function by stimulating cortisol production. This test helps diagnose conditions like Addison's disease and primary adrenal insufficiency.

Adverse Effects:

a. **Synthetic ACTH (Cosyntropin):** Generally well-tolerated but can cause effects like nausea, headache, and hypertension. Rarely, prolonged use can lead to adrenal suppression.

2. Corticosteroids

Corticosteroids are classified into two main types based on their functions:

a. Glucocorticoids

Function:

a. Regulate metabolism, immune response, and stress adaptation.

b. Major glucocorticoid: **Cortisol**

Mechanism of Action:

a. **Receptor Binding:** Cortisol binds to glucocorticoid receptors in target cells, influencing gene expression.

b. **Effects:** Increases gluconeogenesis, decreases glucose uptake in peripheral tissues, suppresses inflammation, and modulates immune response.

Therapeutic Uses:

a. **Replacement Therapy:** In conditions like Addison's disease, where endogenous cortisol production is insufficient.

b. **Anti-inflammatory and Immunosuppressive Therapy:** Used in conditions like asthma, rheumatoid arthritis, and lupus.

c. **Allergic Reactions and Autoimmune Disorders:** Effective in controlling severe allergic reactions and autoimmune diseases.

Examples:

a. **Hydrocortisone:** Used for replacement therapy and anti-inflammatory purposes.

    i. **Brand Names:** Cortef, Solu-Cortef.

b. **Prednisolone:** A potent anti-inflammatory and immunosuppressive agent.

    i. **Brand Names:** Prelone, Orapred.

c. **Dexamethasone:** A highly potent glucocorticoid with a long duration of action.

    i. **Brand Names:** Decadron, DexPak.

d. **Betamethasone:** Used in dermatologic and inflammatory conditions.

    i. **Brand Names:** Celestone, Diprolene.

Adverse Effects:

a. **Short-Term Use:** Insomnia, mood changes, increased appetite, and gastrointestinal upset.

b. **Long-Term Use:** Osteoporosis, hypertension, diabetes, Cushing's syndrome, and increased susceptibility to infections.

b. Mineralocorticoids

Function:

a. Regulate electrolyte and fluid balance, primarily through sodium and potassium retention.
b. Major mineralocorticoid: **Aldosterone**

Mechanism of Action:

a. **Receptor Binding:** Aldosterone binds to mineralocorticoid receptors in the kidneys, promoting sodium reabsorption and potassium excretion.
b. **Effects:** Increases blood volume and blood pressure.

Therapeutic Uses:

a. **Replacement Therapy:** Used in conditions like Addison's disease where mineralocorticoid production is deficient.
b. **Treatment of Primary Aldosteronism:** Spironolactone, a mineralocorticoid antagonist, is used to treat conditions of excessive aldosterone production.

Examples:

a. **Fludrocortisone:** A synthetic mineralocorticoid used in replacement therapy.
    i. **Brand Names:** Florinef.

Adverse Effects:

a. **Fludrocortisone:** Can cause hypertension, hypokalemia, and fluid retention.

Summary

a. **ACTH:** Stimulates the adrenal cortex to produce corticosteroids. Used primarily in diagnostic testing and as a therapeutic agent in certain conditions.
b. **Corticosteroids:** Include glucocorticoids (e.g., cortisol, hydrocortisone, prednisolone, dexamethasone) and mineralocorticoids (e.g., aldosterone, fludrocortisone). They play critical roles in managing inflammation, immune response, and electrolyte balance but can have significant side effects, especially with long-term use.

Multiple Choice Questions (MCQs)

1. What hormone stimulates the adrenal cortex to release cortisol?
    a) Thyroid-Stimulating Hormone (TSH)
    b) Adrenocorticotropic Hormone (ACTH)
    c) Luteinizing Hormone (LH)
    d) Follicle-Stimulating Hormone (FSH)
2. Which of the following is a synthetic form of T4 used to treat hypothyroidism?
    a) Liothyronine
    b) Levothyroxine
    c) Liotrix
    d) Methimazole
3. What is the primary action of calcitonin?
    a) Increase plasma calcium levels
    b) Decrease plasma calcium levels
    c) Stimulate insulin release
    d) Inhibit glucagon release
4. Which oral hypoglycemic agent is known for its cardiovascular benefits and low risk of hypoglycemia?
    a) Glyburide
    b) Metformin
    c) Pioglitazone
    d) Sitagliptin
5. What is the mechanism of action of glucagon?
    a) Stimulates glycogenolysis and gluconeogenesis
    b) Inhibits insulin release
    c) Promotes glucose uptake in cells
    d) Reduces renal glucose reabsorption

6. Which drug is a recombinant form of TSH used in diagnostic imaging?
    a) Cosyntropin
    b) Thyrotropin alfa
    c) Leuprolide
    d) Follitropin alfa
7. What is the primary function of parathyroid hormone (PTH)?
    a) Decrease plasma calcium levels
    b) Increase plasma calcium levels
    c) Stimulate insulin secretion
    d) Inhibit cortisol release
8. Which of the following is a synthetic ACTH used to assess adrenal function?
    a) Cosyntropin
    b) Prednisolone
    c) Dexamethasone
    d) Fludrocortisone
9. What is the mechanism of action of methimazole?
    a) Stimulates thyroid hormone synthesis
    b) Inhibits thyroid peroxidase
    c) Blocks TSH receptors
    d) Enhances T4 to T3 conversion
10. Which drug is a somatostatin analogue used to treat acromegaly?
    a) Somatropin
    b) Lanreotide
    c) Bromocriptine
    d) Levothyroxine
11. What is the primary clinical use of fludrocortisone?
    a) Treat hypothyroidism
    b) Manage Addison's disease
    c) Treat hyperthyroidism

d) Manage acromegaly

12. Which of the following is an example of a thiazolidinedione?

a) Sitagliptin

b) Glipizide

c) Pioglitazone

d) Metformin

13. What is the primary adverse effect of sulfonylureas?

a) Hypoglycemia

b) Hypercalcemia

c) Hyperglycemia

d) Hypocalcemia

14. Which drug is used to treat hyperprolactinemia by stimulating dopamine receptors?

a) Bromocriptine

b) Cabergoline

c) Leuprolide

d) Follitropin alfa

15. What is the primary therapeutic use of teriparatide?

a) Treat hyperthyroidism

b) Stimulate bone formation in osteoporosis

c) Reduce blood glucose levels

d) Inhibit cortisol synthesis

16. Which hormone is responsible for increasing intestinal calcium absorption?

a) Calcitonin

b) Insulin

c) Vitamin D

d) Glucagon

17. What is the mechanism of action of DPP-4 inhibitors?

a) Inhibit glucose reabsorption in the kidneys

b) Enhance insulin secretion and inhibit glucagon release

c) Stimulate insulin release from the pancreas

d) Delay carbohydrate absorption in the intestine

18. Which drug is a synthetic form of T3 used in hypothyroidism?

a) Levothyroxine

b) Liothyronine

c) Liotrix

d) Methimazole

19. What is the primary function of mineralocorticoids?

a) Regulate glucose metabolism

b) Regulate electrolyte and fluid balance

c) Stimulate immune response

d) Inhibit inflammatory processes

20. Which hormone is primarily involved in regulating plasma glucose levels?

a) Parathyroid Hormone (PTH)

b) Calcitonin

c) Insulin

d) Thyroid-Stimulating Hormone (TSH)

Short Answer Type Questions (Subjective)

1. Describe the mechanism of action of glucocorticoids.
2. What are the clinical uses of levothyroxine?
3. Explain the function of parathyroid hormone (PTH) in calcium regulation.
4. How do sulfonylureas help in managing type 2 diabetes?
5. What are the adverse effects of long-term corticosteroid use?
6. Describe the therapeutic uses of methimazole.
7. How does glucagon function in the body?
8. What is the role of calcitonin in calcium homeostasis?
9. Explain the mechanism of action of insulin in glucose metabolism.

10. What are the uses of recombinant human growth hormone (somatropin)?
11. Describe the mechanism of action of DPP-4 inhibitors.
12. What is the clinical significance of using radioactive iodine in thyroid disorders?
13. How does metformin help in managing type 2 diabetes?
14. What are the primary adverse effects of thiazolidinediones?
15. Describe the function of ACTH in the endocrine system.
16. What are the therapeutic applications of teriparatide?
17. Explain the mechanism of action of beta-blockers in managing hyperthyroidism symptoms.
18. How do alpha-glucosidase inhibitors work in diabetes management?
19. Describe the role of vitamin D in calcium metabolism.
20. What are the clinical uses of antithyroid agents like propylthiouracil?

Long Answer Type Questions (Subjective)

1. Discuss the pharmacology of thyroid hormones, including their synthesis, release, analogues, and inhibitors.
2. Explain the role of ACTH and corticosteroids in the endocrine system, including their mechanisms, therapeutic uses, and adverse effects.
3. Describe the different classes of oral hypoglycemic agents, their mechanisms of action, therapeutic uses, and side effects.
4. Discuss the hormones involved in regulating plasma calcium levels, including parathyroid hormone, calcitonin, and vitamin D, and their clinical applications.
5. Explain the pharmacology of insulin and glucagon, including their mechanisms, therapeutic uses, and management of diabetes.
6. Describe the therapeutic applications of anterior pituitary hormone analogues and their inhibitors.

7. Discuss the role of DPP-4 inhibitors and SGLT2 inhibitors in managing type 2 diabetes, including their mechanisms and clinical benefits.
8. Explain the clinical significance and therapeutic uses of recombinant human growth hormone (somatropin).
9. Discuss the mechanisms, uses, and adverse effects of glucocorticoids in treating inflammatory and autoimmune conditions.
10. Describe the various drugs used in the treatment of hyperthyroidism, including their mechanisms, uses, and potential side effects.

Answer Key for MCQs

1. b) Adrenocorticotropic Hormone (ACTH)
2. b) Levothyroxine
3. b) Decrease plasma calcium levels
4. b) Metformin
5. a) Stimulates glycogenolysis and gluconeogenesis
6. b) Thyrotropin alfa
7. b) Increase plasma calcium levels
8. a) Cosyntropin
9. b) Inhibits thyroid peroxidase
10. b) Lanreotide
11. b) Manage Addison's disease
12. c) Pioglitazone
13. a) Hypoglycemia
14. b) Cabergoline
15. b) Stimulate bone formation in osteoporosis
16. c) Vitamin D
17. b) Enhance insulin secretion and inhibit glucagon release
18. b) Liothyronine
19. b) Regulate electrolyte and fluid balance
20. c) Insulin

CHAPTER – 18

PHARMACOLOGY OF DRUGS ACTING ON ENDOCRINE SYSTEM – III

Mrs. Saba Ruksaar

Assistant Professor, Rajiv Gandhi Institute of Pharmacy, Faculty of Pharmaceutical Science & Technology, AKS University Satna, (M.P.)

ABSTRACT:

Androgens, such as testosterone, are male sex hormones responsible for the development and maintenance of male characteristics. They promote protein synthesis and muscle growth, which is why synthetic derivatives, known as anabolic steroids, are often abused for performance enhancement. Medically, androgens are used to treat conditions like hypogonadism, delayed puberty, and muscle wasting diseases. However, their misuse can lead to adverse effects such as liver damage, cardiovascular issues, and hormonal imbalances. Estrogens are primary female sex hormones involved in the regulation of the menstrual cycle, reproductive system, and secondary sexual characteristics. They are used therapeutically in hormone replacement therapy (HRT) for menopausal symptoms, osteoporosis prevention, and certain types of breast cancer. Common synthetic estrogens include ethinylestradiol and conjugated estrogens. Potential side effects include an increased risk of thromboembolic events, breast cancer, and endometrial hyperplasia, necessitating careful patient monitoring. Progesterone is a hormone crucial for regulating the menstrual cycle and maintaining pregnancy. It is used in hormone replacement therapy, to treat menstrual disorders, and to support early pregnancy in cases of recurrent miscarriage or assisted reproductive technologies. Synthetic forms, known as progestins, are also used in combination with estrogens in contraceptives. Side effects can include mood changes, weight gain, and increased risk of cardiovascular events. Oral contraceptives are medications taken to prevent pregnancy. They typically contain synthetic forms of estrogen and progesterone (progestins). These hormones work by inhibiting ovulation, thickening cervical mucus to prevent sperm penetration, and altering the uterine lining to prevent implantation. Combined oral contraceptives (COCs) and progestin-only pills (POPs) are common types. Benefits include regulation of menstrual cycles and reduced risk of ovarian and endometrial cancers. Risks include thromboembolic events, hypertension, and potential interactions with other medications. Drugs acting on the uterus include uterotonics and tocolytics. Uterotonics, like oxytocin and misoprostol, stimulate uterine contractions and are used to induce labor, control postpartum hemorrhage, and manage incomplete abortion. Tocolytics, such as nifedipine and magnesium sulfate, inhibit uterine contractions and are used to delay preterm labor, allowing for fetal maturation and transfer to a specialized facility. While effective, these drugs must be carefully managed due to potential side effects such as hypertension, arrhythmias, and uterine hyperstimulation.

INTRODUCTION:

Pharmacology of drugs acting on the endocrine system focuses on how medications interact with hormonal pathways to influence various physiological functions. Here's an overview of the key classes of drugs acting on the endocrine system:

1. Hormone Replacement Therapy (HRT)

a. Thyroid Hormones:

i. **L-Thyroxine (T4)** and **L-Triiodothyronine (T3)**: These are synthetic forms of thyroid hormones used to treat hypothyroidism. They help normalize metabolic processes.

   1. **Mechanism of Action:** They bind to thyroid hormone receptors in cells, affecting transcription and regulating gene expression involved in metabolism.
   2. **Uses:** Hypothyroidism, goiter, and certain types of thyroid cancer.

3. **Side Effects:** Overdosage can lead to symptoms of hyperthyroidism, such as tachycardia, weight loss, and insomnia.

b. Antithyroid Agents:

i. **Propylthiouracil (PTU)** and **Methimazole**: These drugs inhibit thyroid hormone synthesis, used to manage hyperthyroidism.

1. **Mechanism of Action:** They block the enzyme thyroid peroxidase, reducing the synthesis of T3 and T4.
2. **Uses:** Graves' disease, hyperthyroidism.
3. **Side Effects:** Rash, agranulocytosis, liver toxicity.

2. Adrenal Hormones and Antagonists

a. Corticosteroids:

i. **Cortisone, Hydrocortisone, Prednisolone, and Betamethasone**: These are synthetic corticosteroids used to treat inflammatory and autoimmune conditions.

1. **Mechanism of Action:** They bind to glucocorticoid receptors, influencing gene expression to reduce inflammation and immune responses.
2. **Uses:** Allergic reactions, autoimmune diseases, and chronic inflammatory conditions.
3. **Side Effects:** Weight gain, osteoporosis, hypertension, and increased susceptibility to infections.

b. Mineralocorticoids:

i. **Fludrocortisone**: A synthetic mineralocorticoid used to treat conditions like Addison's disease.

1. **Mechanism of Action:** It acts on the kidneys to promote sodium and water retention, increasing blood volume and blood pressure.
2. **Uses:** Addison's disease, orthostatic hypotension.
3. **Side Effects:** Edema, hypertension, hypokalemia.

c. Adrenal Androgen Inhibitors:

i. **Ketoconazole**: An antifungal agent with adrenal enzyme-inhibiting properties, used off-label to reduce adrenal androgen production.

1. **Mechanism of Action:** Inhibits adrenal steroidogenesis, reducing androgen levels.
2. **Uses:** Cushing's syndrome, prostate cancer.
3. **Side Effects:** Hepatotoxicity, gastrointestinal issues.

3. Sex Hormones and Modulators

a. Estrogens:

i. **Estradiol, Estrone**: Natural estrogens used in HRT for menopausal symptoms and osteoporosis prevention.

1. **Mechanism of Action:** They bind to estrogen receptors, influencing gene expression related to reproductive tissues and bone health.
2. **Uses:** Menopausal symptoms, osteoporosis prevention.
3. **Side Effects:** Risk of thromboembolism, breast cancer.

b. Progestins:

i. **Medroxyprogesterone acetate, Norgestrel, Levonorgestrel**: Synthetic progestins used in contraceptives and HRT.

1. **Mechanism of Action:** They bind to progesterone receptors, affecting the uterine lining and ovulation.
2. **Uses:** Contraception, endometriosis, HRT.
3. **Side Effects:** Weight gain, mood changes, nausea.

c. Androgens:

i. **Testosterone, Dihydrotestosterone**: Natural androgens used in hormone replacement therapy and to treat hypogonadism.

1. **Mechanism of Action:** They bind to androgen receptors, influencing muscle mass, libido, and secondary sexual characteristics.

2. **Uses:** Hypogonadism, muscle wasting.
3. **Side Effects:** Acne, aggression, liver toxicity.

d. Anti-Estrogens and Anti-Androgens:

i. **Tamoxifen, Letrozole**: Used in hormone-sensitive cancers like breast cancer.
   1. **Mechanism of Action:** Tamoxifen acts as an estrogen receptor antagonist, while letrozole inhibits estrogen synthesis.
   2. **Uses:** Estrogen receptor-positive breast cancer.
   3. **Side Effects:** Hot flashes, bone loss, risk of blood clots.

4. Hypothalamic and Pituitary Hormones

a. Growth Hormone (GH) Analogues:

i. **Somatropin**: Recombinant growth hormone used to treat growth disorders.
   1. **Mechanism of Action:** Mimics natural GH, promoting growth and metabolism.
   2. **Uses:** Growth hormone deficiency, Turner syndrome.
   3. **Side Effects:** Joint pain, edema, insulin resistance.

b. Antidiuretic Hormone (ADH) Analogues:

i. **Desmopressin**: Used in the treatment of diabetes insipidus and bedwetting.
   1. **Mechanism of Action:** Acts on V2 receptors in the kidney to increase water reabsorption.
   2. **Uses:** Diabetes insipidus, nocturnal enuresis.
   3. **Side Effects:** Hyponatremia, headache.

c. Gonadotropins:

i. **Follicle-stimulating hormone (FSH) and Luteinizing hormone (LH)**: Used in fertility treatments.
   1. **Mechanism of Action:** Stimulate ovarian follicle development and testosterone production.

2. **Uses:** Infertility treatment.
3. **Side Effects:** Ovarian hyperstimulation syndrome, multiple pregnancies.

ANDROGENS AND ANABOLIC STEROIDS

Androgens and anabolic steroids are crucial in pharmacology for their roles in managing hormonal imbalances, enhancing muscle growth, and treating certain medical conditions. Here's a detailed look at both categories:

1. Androgens

Androgens are a class of hormones that play a role in male characteristics and reproductive activity. The most well-known androgen is **testosterone**, but other androgens also play significant roles.

a. Testosterone

i. **Mechanism of Action:**

1. Testosterone binds to androgen receptors in various tissues, including muscle, bone, and the prostate. This binding influences gene expression, leading to anabolic effects (muscle growth) and development of male secondary sexual characteristics (e.g., facial hair, deeper voice).

ii. **Uses:**

1. **Hypogonadism:** Treatment for men with low testosterone levels.
2. **Delayed Puberty:** Helps induce puberty in adolescents with delayed development.
3. **Muscle Wasting Conditions:** Used in conditions like HIV/AIDS to counteract muscle loss.
4. **Certain Types of Breast Cancer:** As part of hormone therapy in some cases.

iii. **Administration:**

1. Available in various forms, including intramuscular injections, transdermal patches, gels, and oral tablets.

iv. **Side Effects:**

1. Acne, oily skin, increased libido, mood swings, aggression, and potentially liver damage. Long-term use can lead to cardiovascular issues, liver problems, and endocrine disturbances.
2. In women, excessive testosterone can cause virilization (e.g., deepening of the voice, excessive hair growth).

b. Dihydrotestosterone (DHT)

i. **Mechanism of Action:**

1. DHT is a potent androgen converted from testosterone by the enzyme 5-alpha reductase. It binds to androgen receptors with higher affinity than testosterone, influencing hair growth and prostate development.

ii. **Uses:**

1. **Benign Prostatic Hyperplasia (BPH):** Medications like finasteride, which inhibit 5-alpha reductase, can reduce DHT levels and alleviate symptoms of BPH.
2. **Androgenic Alopecia:** Drugs like finasteride are used to treat male pattern baldness by reducing DHT levels.

iii. **Side Effects:**

1. Sexual dysfunction, including decreased libido and erectile dysfunction. Reduced DHT levels can also impact hair growth patterns and prostate health.

2. Anabolic Steroids

Anabolic steroids are synthetic derivatives of testosterone designed to maximize anabolic effects (muscle-building) while minimizing androgenic effects (development of male characteristics).

a. Common Anabolic Steroids

i. **Testosterone Derivatives:**

1. **Methandrostenolone (Dianabol):** Known for its powerful anabolic effects, leading to significant muscle growth.
2. **Nandrolone (Deca-Durabolin):** Used for its anabolic properties with fewer androgenic side effects compared to testosterone.
3. **Oxandrolone (Anavar):** Known for its mild androgenic effects, often used for muscle wasting diseases.

ii. **Mechanism of Action:**

1. Anabolic steroids bind to androgen receptors in muscle cells, enhancing protein synthesis, increasing muscle mass, and promoting recovery. They also influence the metabolism of fats and proteins.

iii. **Uses:**

1. **Medical Uses:** Treating conditions like anemia, muscle wasting, and osteoporosis. Sometimes used in hormone replacement therapy for men with low testosterone.
2. **Performance Enhancement:** Although banned in most sports, anabolic steroids are used illicitly to enhance athletic performance and muscle growth.

iv. **Administration:**

1. Can be administered orally or via intramuscular injections. Some are also available in topical forms.

v. **Side Effects:**

1. **Androgenic Effects:** Acne, hair loss, and voice changes. In women, it can lead to male-pattern baldness, hirsutism, and menstrual irregularities.
2. **Cardiovascular Issues:** Increased risk of heart disease, hypertension, and altered cholesterol levels.
3. **Liver Damage:** Oral anabolic steroids can be hepatotoxic.

4. **Psychiatric Effects:** Mood swings, aggression, and even psychiatric disorders like mania or depression.
5. **Hormonal Imbalances:** Long-term use can lead to suppression of natural testosterone production, testicular atrophy, and infertility in men.

ESTROGENS

Estrogens are a group of hormones essential for the development and regulation of the female reproductive system and secondary sexual characteristics. They also have significant roles in other tissues, such as bone and cardiovascular systems. Here's a detailed look at estrogens in pharmacology:

1. Types of Estrogens

a. Natural Estrogens:

i. **Estradiol (E2):** The most potent and prevalent form of estrogen in premenopausal women.

ii. **Estrone (E1):** The primary estrogen in postmenopausal women.

iii. **Estriol (E3):** Predominantly found during pregnancy, produced by the placenta.

b. Synthetic Estrogens:

i. **Ethinyl Estradiol:** A common synthetic estrogen used in oral contraceptives and hormone replacement therapy.

ii. **Conjugated Estrogens:** A mixture of estrogen compounds derived from pregnant mare urine, used in various HRT formulations.

2. Mechanism of Action

i. **Estrogen Receptors:** Estrogens exert their effects by binding to estrogen receptors (ERα and ERβ) in target tissues. This binding leads to the activation or repression of gene transcription, influencing cell function and growth.

ii. **Genomic Effects:** Estrogen receptor activation affects the transcription of genes involved in reproductive tissue development, bone density maintenance, and lipid metabolism.

iii. **Non-Genomic Effects:** Estrogens can also activate signaling pathways independent of direct gene transcription, influencing cell signaling and function.

3. Uses of Estrogens

a. **Hormone Replacement Therapy (HRT):**

i. **Postmenopausal Symptoms:** Estrogens are used to alleviate symptoms of menopause, such as hot flashes, vaginal dryness, and mood swings.

ii. **Osteoporosis Prevention:** HRT can help maintain bone density and reduce the risk of fractures in postmenopausal women.

iii. **Premature Ovarian Insufficiency:** Used in younger women with early menopause to mimic natural hormonal levels.

b. **Contraception:**

i. **Oral Contraceptives:** Combination pills containing ethinyl estradiol and a progestin prevent ovulation and regulate menstrual cycles.

ii. **Transdermal Patches and Vaginal Rings:** Deliver estrogens in combination with progestins for effective contraception.

c. **Menstrual Disorders:**

i. **Amenorrhea and Dysmenorrhea:** Estrogens are used to regulate menstrual cycles and manage conditions like amenorrhea (absence of menstruation) and dysmenorrhea (painful menstruation).

d. **Cancer Treatment:**

i. **Estrogen-Receptor Positive Breast Cancer:** Estrogens or anti-estrogens are used in hormone-sensitive cancers to modulate disease progression.

4. Side Effects of Estrogen Therapy

i. **Cardiovascular Risks:**

1. **Thromboembolism:** Increased risk of blood clots, stroke, and heart attack.
2. **Hypertension:** Possible elevation of blood pressure with long-term use.

ii. **Cancer Risks:**

1. **Breast Cancer:** Prolonged use of estrogen-only HRT can increase the risk of breast cancer.
2. **Endometrial Cancer:** Estrogen can stimulate the growth of the endometrial lining, increasing the risk of endometrial cancer if not balanced with progestins.

iii. **Other Effects:**

1. **Weight Gain:** Fluid retention and changes in fat distribution.
2. **Mood Changes:** Emotional lability and depression.
3. **Nausea and Vomiting:** Common initial side effects of oral estrogens.

5. Administration Routes

i. **Oral:** Tablets or capsules, commonly used for HRT and contraception.

ii. **Transdermal:** Patches or gels that provide a steady release of estrogen.

iii. **Intravaginal:** Rings or creams for localized effects in the vaginal area.

iv. **Injectable:** Less common but used for certain therapeutic purposes.

6. Monitoring and Management

i. **Regular Check-ups:** Women on long-term estrogen therapy should undergo regular monitoring for side effects and risks, such as cardiovascular health and cancer screening.

ii. **Personalization of Therapy:** Estrogen therapy should be individualized based on the patient's health profile, risk factors, and therapeutic goals.

PROGESTERONE

Progesterone is a key hormone in the endocrine system, primarily involved in the regulation of the menstrual cycle, pregnancy, and various other physiological processes. Here's a detailed overview of progesterone in pharmacology:

1. Overview of Progesterone

Progesterone is a steroid hormone produced mainly by the corpus luteum in the ovaries during the luteal phase of the menstrual cycle and by the placenta during pregnancy. It plays a crucial role in preparing the endometrium for implantation and maintaining pregnancy.

2. Mechanism of Action

i. **Progesterone Receptors:** Progesterone acts by binding to progesterone receptors (PR) in target tissues. These receptors are nuclear receptors that, when activated, modulate gene expression related to reproductive functions.

ii. **Genomic Effects:** Progesterone receptor activation leads to changes in gene transcription that prepare the endometrium for implantation, suppress uterine contractions, and maintain pregnancy.

iii. **Non-Genomic Effects:** Progesterone may also have rapid effects on cell signaling pathways, influencing various physiological processes.

3. Uses of Progesterone

a. **Hormone Replacement Therapy (HRT):**

i. **Menopausal Symptoms:** Progesterone is used in combination with estrogens in HRT to manage symptoms of menopause, such as hot flashes and vaginal dryness, and to prevent endometrial hyperplasia.

ii. **Postmenopausal Bone Health:** Helps maintain bone density when used in conjunction with estrogen in postmenopausal women.

b. **Contraception:**

i. **Progestin-Only Pills:** These contain synthetic forms of progesterone (progestins) and prevent ovulation, thicken cervical mucus, and alter the endometrial lining to prevent pregnancy.

ii. **Long-Acting Reversible Contraceptives:** Methods like the progestin-only implant and hormonal intrauterine devices (IUDs) provide effective contraception by releasing progesterone over time.

c. **Menstrual Disorders:**

i. **Amenorrhea and Dysmenorrhea:** Progesterone can regulate menstrual cycles, manage abnormal bleeding, and treat conditions like amenorrhea (absence of menstruation) and dysmenorrhea (painful menstruation).

ii. **Endometrial Hyperplasia:** Progesterone therapy helps in managing abnormal thickening of the endometrial lining, often caused by excessive estrogen.

d. **Pregnancy Support:**

i. **Luteal Phase Support:** In assisted reproductive technologies (ART), progesterone is used to support the luteal phase and enhance the chances of implantation and pregnancy.

ii. **Preterm Birth Prevention:** Progesterone is administered to pregnant women at risk of preterm birth to reduce the risk of premature labor.

4. Forms of Progesterone Administration

i. **Oral:** Tablets or capsules are commonly used for hormonal therapy and menstrual regulation.

ii. **Transdermal:** Creams or gels that provide a steady release of progesterone through the skin.

iii. **Intravaginal:** Suppositories or gels used for localized effects, often for fertility treatments or hormone support during pregnancy.

iv. **Injectable:** Used for specific therapeutic purposes, such as in ART or for endometrial conditions.

v. **Intrauterine Device (IUD):** A hormonal IUD releases progestin locally within the uterus for long-term contraception.

5. Side Effects of Progesterone Therapy

i. **Common Side Effects:**

1. **Mood Changes:** Depression, irritability, and mood swings.
2. **Weight Gain:** Fluid retention and changes in fat distribution.
3. **Breast Tenderness:** Common in hormonal therapies.
4. **Nausea and Vomiting:** Especially with high doses or oral forms.

ii. **Serious Side Effects:**

1. **Venous Thromboembolism:** Increased risk of blood clots, especially with combined hormonal therapies.
2. **Cardiovascular Risks:** Potential for increased blood pressure and other cardiovascular issues.
3. **Endometrial Changes:** Prolonged use of unopposed progesterone can affect the endometrial lining and lead to abnormal bleeding.

6. Monitoring and Management

i. **Regular Check-ups:** Women on long-term progesterone therapy should be monitored for side effects and cardiovascular risks.

ii. **Individualized Therapy:** Progesterone therapy should be tailored based on the patient's specific needs, health profile, and therapeutic goals.

ORAL CONTRACEPTIVES

Oral contraceptives, also known as birth control pills, are a primary method of hormonal contraception used to prevent pregnancy. They are designed to regulate the hormonal balance in the body, primarily through the use of synthetic hormones. Here's a detailed overview of oral contraceptives in pharmacology:

1. Types of Oral Contraceptives

a. Combination Oral Contraceptives (COCs):

i. **Components:** Contain both an estrogen and a progestin (synthetic progesterone).

ii. **Common Formulations:**

1. **Estrogen:** Typically ethinyl estradiol or mestranol.

2. **Progestin:** Various forms including levonorgestrel, norethindrone, desogestrel, and drospirenone.

iii. **Mechanism of Action:**

1. **Suppression of Ovulation:** Estrogens and progestins work together to inhibit the release of luteinizing hormone (LH) and follicle-stimulating hormone (FSH), preventing ovulation.
2. **Thickening of Cervical Mucus:** Progestins thicken the cervical mucus, making it more difficult for sperm to enter the uterus.
3. **Endometrial Alteration:** Changes the endometrial lining, making it less suitable for implantation.

b. Progestin-Only Pills (POPs):

i. **Components:** Contain only a progestin without estrogen.

ii. **Common Formulations:**

1. **Progestins:** Norethindrone, desogestrel, or other forms.

iii. **Mechanism of Action:**

1. **Cervical Mucus Thickening:** Primarily acts by thickening cervical mucus to prevent sperm penetration.
2. **Endometrial Effects:** Alters the endometrial lining, but may not consistently suppress ovulation in all users.

c. Extended-Cycle Pills:

i. **Components:** Similar to combination oral contraceptives but designed to extend the menstrual cycle, typically providing menstruation only once every 3 months or fewer.

ii. **Mechanism of Action:** Functions similarly to COCs but reduces the frequency of menstrual periods.

2. Administration and Dosage

i. **Daily Administration:** Most oral contraceptives are taken once daily. Combination pills are usually taken for 21 days followed by a 7-day break or placebo period, while progestin-only pills are taken continuously without a break.

ii. **Start Timing:** Pills can be started at any time during the menstrual cycle, though it may take a few days for the contraceptive effect to become effective if started outside of the menstrual period.

3. Effectiveness

i. **Typical Use:** About 91% effective, with typical use including occasional missed doses.

ii. **Perfect Use:** Up to 99% effective when taken exactly as prescribed without missing any doses.

4. Side Effects

a. Common Side Effects:

i. **Nausea and Vomiting:** Often occurs initially and may resolve with continued use.

ii. **Headaches:** Hormonal changes can lead to headaches or migraines.

iii. **Breast Tenderness:** Common due to hormonal fluctuations.

iv. **Weight Gain:** Some users may experience weight gain due to fluid retention or changes in appetite.

b. Serious Side Effects:

i. **Thromboembolism:** Increased risk of blood clots, stroke, and deep vein thrombosis, particularly with formulations containing higher doses of estrogen.

ii. **Hypertension:** Possible elevation in blood pressure.

iii. **Mood Changes:** Some users may experience mood swings or depressive symptoms.

iv. **Increased Risk of Certain Cancers:** Slight increase in the risk of breast and cervical cancers, though it may also reduce the risk of ovarian and endometrial cancers.

5. Contraindications

i. **Smoking:** Especially in women over 35 years old who smoke, due to increased risk of cardiovascular events.
ii. **History of Blood Clots:** Individuals with a history of deep vein thrombosis, pulmonary embolism, or other clotting disorders should generally avoid COCs.
iii. **Certain Medical Conditions:** Conditions such as liver disease, certain types of cancers, and uncontrolled hypertension may be contraindications.

6. Interactions

i. **Drug Interactions:**
   1. **Antibiotics:** Some antibiotics may reduce the effectiveness of oral contraceptives, though this is less common with newer antibiotics.
   2. **Antiepileptics:** Certain antiepileptic drugs can decrease the efficacy of oral contraceptives.
   3. **St. John's Wort:** May reduce the effectiveness of hormonal contraceptives.

7. Monitoring and Management

i. **Regular Check-ups:** Routine medical check-ups are recommended to monitor for side effects, assess blood pressure, and ensure continued suitability.
ii. **Alternative Methods:** If side effects are problematic or contraindications arise, alternative forms of contraception should be considered.

DRUGS ACTING ON THE UTERUS

Drugs acting on the uterus play crucial roles in managing various uterine conditions, controlling labor, and addressing reproductive health issues. Here's a detailed overview of these drugs in pharmacology:

1. Uterotonics

Uterotonics are drugs that stimulate uterine contractions. They are often used to induce labor or manage postpartum hemorrhage.

a. Oxytocin

i. **Mechanism of Action:**
    1. Oxytocin binds to specific receptors in the uterus, leading to increased intracellular calcium levels and enhanced uterine muscle contractions.

ii. **Uses:**
    1. **Labor Induction:** To stimulate contractions during labor and facilitate childbirth.
    2. **Postpartum Hemorrhage:** To control bleeding by promoting uterine contraction and reducing the risk of hemorrhage.

iii. **Administration:**
    1. Typically administered intravenously (IV) in a hospital setting, especially during labor.

iv. **Side Effects:**
    1. **Uterine Hyperstimulation:** Excessive contractions can lead to fetal distress or uterine rupture.
    2. **Water Intoxication:** High doses may cause fluid retention and electrolyte imbalances.

b. Methylergometrine (Methergine)

i. **Mechanism of Action:**
    1. A derivative of ergometrine, it stimulates smooth muscle contractions by acting on serotonin and adrenergic receptors.

ii. **Uses:**
    1. **Postpartum Hemorrhage:** Used to control bleeding after childbirth by enhancing uterine contractions.

iii. **Administration:**
    1. Typically administered intramuscularly (IM) or orally.

iv. **Side Effects:**
    1. **Hypertension:** Can cause significant increases in blood pressure.
    2. **Nausea and Vomiting:** Common gastrointestinal side effects.

c. Carbetocin

i. **Mechanism of Action:**

   1. A synthetic analog of oxytocin with a longer duration of action.

ii. **Uses:**

   1. **Postpartum Hemorrhage:** Used to prevent excessive bleeding after delivery.

iii. **Administration:**

   1. Typically administered intravenously (IV) or intramuscularly (IM).

iv. **Side Effects:**

   1. Similar to oxytocin, including uterine hyperstimulation and water intoxication.

2. Tocolytics

Tocolytics are drugs used to suppress premature labor by inhibiting uterine contractions.

a. Beta-Adrenergic Agonists (e.g., Terbutaline)

i. **Mechanism of Action:**

   1. Beta-adrenergic agonists relax the uterine smooth muscle by stimulating beta-2 adrenergic receptors.

ii. **Uses:**

   1. **Preterm Labor:** To delay preterm labor and allow time for corticosteroid therapy to mature the fetus's lungs.

iii. **Administration:**

   1. Typically administered subcutaneously (SC) or intravenously (IV).

iv. **Side Effects:**

   1. **Tachycardia:** Increased heart rate.
   2. **Tremors:** Common with beta-adrenergic stimulation.
   3. **Hyperglycemia:** Elevated blood glucose levels.

b. Calcium Channel Blockers (e.g., Nifedipine)

i. **Mechanism of Action:**

1. Calcium channel blockers inhibit calcium entry into uterine smooth muscle cells, reducing contraction frequency and intensity.

ii. **Uses:**

1. **Preterm Labor:** To manage and delay premature labor.

iii. **Administration:**

1. Typically administered orally.

iv. **Side Effects:**

1. **Hypotension:** Reduced blood pressure.
2. **Headache:** Common side effect due to vasodilation.
3. **Flushing:** Warmth and redness in the skin.

c. Magnesium Sulfate

i. **Mechanism of Action:**

1. Magnesium sulfate acts as a smooth muscle relaxant by competing with calcium for binding sites.

ii. **Uses:**

1. **Preterm Labor:** Used to delay delivery and manage preterm labor.
2. **Neuroprotection:** Administered to reduce the risk of cerebral palsy in preterm infants.

iii. **Administration:**

1. Typically administered intravenously (IV).

iv. **Side Effects:**

1. **Neurotoxicity:** High levels can lead to respiratory depression and decreased reflexes.
2. **Flushing and Sweating:** Common side effects.

3. Abortifacients

Abortifacients are drugs used to terminate pregnancy. They can be used in medical abortions or to manage miscarriage.

a. Mifepristone (RU-486)

i. **Mechanism of Action:**

1. Mifepristone is a progesterone receptor antagonist that blocks the effects of progesterone, leading to the detachment of the embryo from the uterine lining.

ii. **Uses:**

1. **Medical Abortion:** Used in combination with misoprostol to terminate early pregnancies.

iii. **Administration:**

1. Taken orally.

iv. **Side Effects:**

1. **Bleeding:** Heavy bleeding and cramping.
2. **Nausea and Vomiting:** Common gastrointestinal side effects.

b. Misoprostol

i. **Mechanism of Action:**

1. Misoprostol is a prostaglandin analog that induces uterine contractions and cervical ripening.

ii. **Uses:**

1. **Medical Abortion:** Used in combination with mifepristone or alone for medical abortion.
2. **Miscarriage Management:** Used to expel retained products of conception.

iii. **Administration:**

1. Taken orally, buccally, or vaginally.

iv. **Side Effects:**

1. **Abdominal Pain and Cramping:** Common due to uterine contractions.
2. **Diarrhea:** Frequent gastrointestinal side effect.

4. Hormonal Agents for Uterine Disorders

Hormonal agents can be used to treat various uterine disorders such as endometriosis and uterine fibroids.

a. Levonorgestrel-Releasing Intrauterine Device (IUD)

i. **Mechanism of Action:**

1. Releases a progestin that thins the endometrial lining and thickens cervical mucus.

ii. **Uses:**

1. **Contraception:** Long-term reversible contraception.
2. **Menstrual Regulation:** Reduces menstrual bleeding and can help manage uterine fibroids and endometriosis.

iii. **Administration:**

1. Inserted into the uterus by a healthcare provider.

iv. **Side Effects:**

1. **Irregular Bleeding:** Common initially, may improve over time.
2. **Cramping:** May occur during or after insertion.

Multiple Choice Questions (MCQs)

1. Which synthetic thyroid hormones are used to treat hypothyroidism?
   a) Methimazole and PTU
   b) L-Thyroxine (T4) and L-Triiodothyronine (T3)
   c) Hydrocortisone and Prednisolone
   d) Fludrocortisone and Ketoconazole
2. What is the mechanism of action for antithyroid agents like propylthiouracil (PTU) and methimazole?
   a) Stimulating thyroid hormone synthesis
   b) Blocking the enzyme thyroid peroxidase
   c) Increasing thyroid hormone receptor sensitivity
   d) Reducing thyroid gland size
3. Which condition is treated with synthetic mineralocorticoid Fludrocortisone?
   a) Hyperthyroidism

b) Addison’s disease
c) Graves' disease
d) Hypogonadism

4. What is a common side effect of corticosteroid therapy?
a) Hypoglycemia
b) Osteoporosis
c) Hypotension
d) Hyperkalemia

5. Which drug is an adrenal androgen inhibitor used off-label for reducing adrenal androgen production?
a) Hydrocortisone
b) Betamethasone
c) Ketoconazole
d) Fludrocortisone

6. What is the mechanism of action for estrogens like estradiol and estrone?
a) Binding to androgen receptors
b) Inhibiting estrogen synthesis
c) Binding to estrogen receptors
d) Blocking estrogen receptors

7. Which synthetic progestin is commonly used in contraceptives?
a) Levonorgestrel
b) Estradiol
c) Testosterone
d) Oxytocin

8. What are the uses of anti-estrogens like tamoxifen and letrozole?
a) Contraception
b) Treating hormone-sensitive cancers
c) Managing Addison's disease
d) Inducing labor

9. Which growth hormone analogue is used to treat growth disorders?
    a) Desmopressin
    b) Somatropin
    c) FSH
    d) LH
10. What is the primary use of desmopressin?
    a) Treating growth hormone deficiency
    b) Managing diabetes insipidus
    c) Inducing labor
    d) Treating hypogonadism
11. What is a common side effect of testosterone therapy?
    a) Hypoglycemia
    b) Liver toxicity
    c) Hypotension
    d) Weight loss
12. Which androgen is known for its potent effect on hair growth and prostate development?
    a) Estradiol
    b) Dihydrotestosterone (DHT)
    c) Levonorgestrel
    d) Desmopressin
13. What is the mechanism of action for anabolic steroids?
    a) Blocking androgen receptors
    b) Binding to estrogen receptors
    c) Enhancing protein synthesis and muscle mass
    d) Inhibiting testosterone production
14. What is a serious side effect of oral contraceptives?
    a) Hypoglycemia
    b) Thromboembolism

c) Weight loss
d) Hair loss

15. Which drug is used to control postpartum hemorrhage by enhancing uterine contractions?
a) Methylergometrine
b) Terbutaline
c) Nifedipine
d) Mifepristone

16. What is the primary mechanism of action for tocolytics like nifedipine?
a) Stimulating uterine contractions
b) Inhibiting calcium entry into uterine smooth muscle cells
c) Enhancing uterine muscle contractility
d) Blocking oxytocin receptors

17. Which drug is a progesterone receptor antagonist used in medical abortion?
a) Methylergometrine
b) Misoprostol
c) Mifepristone
d) Terbutaline

18. What is a common administration route for long-acting reversible contraceptives like the hormonal IUD?
a) Oral
b) Transdermal
c) Intramuscular
d) Intrauterine

19. What is a serious side effect of progesterone therapy?
a) Hypoglycemia
b) Venous thromboembolism
c) Hair loss
d) Weight loss

20. Which drug is used to suppress premature labor by inhibiting uterine contractions?
    a) Oxytocin
    b) Methylergometrine
    c) Terbutaline
    d) Misoprostol

Short Answer Type Questions (Subjective)

1. Define hormone replacement therapy (HRT) and its primary uses.
2. Explain the mechanism of action of thyroid hormones L-Thyroxine (T4) and L-Triiodothyronine (T3).
3. What are the common side effects of corticosteroid therapy?
4. Describe the therapeutic uses of anti-estrogens like tamoxifen.
5. Explain the mechanism of action of androgens like testosterone.
6. What are the uses and side effects of the synthetic progestin levonorgestrel?
7. Discuss the primary uses of growth hormone analogue somatropin.
8. What are the common side effects of oral contraceptives?
9. Explain the mechanism of action of tocolytics like nifedipine.
10. Describe the uses and side effects of desmopressin.
11. What is the role of estrogens in hormone replacement therapy?
12. Explain the mechanism of action of progesterone in menstrual regulation.
13. What are the uses of androgen inhibitors like ketoconazole?
14. Describe the therapeutic uses of oxytocin in obstetrics.
15. Explain the side effects and risks associated with anabolic steroid use.
16. What is the significance of anti-androgens in treating prostate cancer?
17. Discuss the mechanism of action of abortifacients like mifepristone.
18. Explain the role of levonorgestrel-releasing intrauterine devices (IUDs) in contraception.
19. What are the potential cardiovascular risks associated with estrogen therapy?

20. Describe the therapeutic applications of hypothalamic and pituitary hormones in fertility treatments.

Long Answer Type Questions (Subjective)

1. Discuss the pharmacology of drugs acting on the thyroid gland, including hormone replacements and antithyroid agents.
2. Explain the mechanisms, therapeutic uses, and side effects of corticosteroids and mineralocorticoids.
3. Describe the role of sex hormones and their modulators in treating hormonal imbalances and cancers.
4. Discuss the use of growth hormone and antidiuretic hormone analogues in clinical therapy.
5. Explain the pharmacology, uses, and side effects of androgens and anabolic steroids.
6. Describe the therapeutic applications and risks of oral contraceptives.
7. Discuss the pharmacological management of uterine conditions using uterotonics and tocolytics.
8. Explain the mechanism of action, uses, and side effects of progesterone in various therapeutic contexts.
9. Describe the pharmacology and clinical applications of estrogen therapy.
10. Discuss the role of hypothalamic and pituitary hormones in fertility treatments and their mechanisms of action.

Answer Key for MCQs

1. b) L-Thyroxine (T4) and L-Triiodothyronine (T3)
2. b) Blocking the enzyme thyroid peroxidase
3. b) Addison's disease
4. b) Osteoporosis
5. c) Ketoconazole

6. c) Binding to estrogen receptors
7. a) Levonorgestrel
8. b) Treating hormone-sensitive cancers
9. b) Somatropin
10. b) Managing diabetes insipidus
11. b) Liver toxicity
12. b) Dihydrotestosterone (DHT)
13. c) Enhancing protein synthesis and muscle mass
14. b) Thromboembolism
15. a) Methylergometrine
16. b) Inhibiting calcium entry into uterine smooth muscle cells
17. c) Mifepristone
18. d) Intrauterine
19. b) Venous thromboembolism
20. c) Terbutaline

CHAPTER – 19

BIOASSAY – I

Ms. Neha Goel

Associate Professor, Rajiv Gandhi Institute of Pharmacy, Faculty of Pharmaceutical Science & Technology, AKS University Satna, (M.P.)

ABSTRACT:

Bioassay is a scientific method used to measure the concentration or potency of a substance by its effect on living cells or tissues. This method is essential in pharmacology for determining the biological activity of drugs, hormones, and other bioactive compounds. Bioassays rely on the principles of dose-response relationships, where the biological response is proportional to the concentration of the substance. Applications include drug development, quality control, and therapeutic monitoring, ensuring that pharmaceuticals meet efficacy and safety standards. Bioassays can be classified into two main types: qualitative and quantitative. Qualitative bioassays determine the presence or absence of a substance by observing its biological effect. Quantitative bioassays measure the exact amount of a substance by comparing its effect to a standard. Examples include endpoint assays, where a specific effect is measured at a single time point, and kinetic assays, where the rate of response is measured over time. Both types are crucial for different stages of drug development and testing.The bioassay of insulin typically involves its effect on blood glucose levels in animals or isolated tissue preparations. One common method is the rabbit blood sugar assay, where insulin's hypoglycemic effect is measured by monitoring blood glucose levels after administration. This assay ensures the potency and efficacy of insulin preparations used in diabetes treatment. Another method involves the use of adipocytes or hepatocytes to measure insulin's effect on glucose uptake or glycogen synthesis. The bioassay of oxytocin is often performed using isolated uterine muscle preparations from animals like rats or guinea pigs. Oxytocin induces uterine contractions, and the strength and frequency of these contractions are measured to determine the hormone's potency. This assay is crucial for ensuring the effectiveness of oxytocin used in labor induction and management of postpartum hemorrhage. The sensitivity of the uterine response to oxytocin makes this a reliable method for its bioassay. The bioassay of vasopressin involves measuring its antidiuretic effect on renal function. One method is the rat antidiuretic assay, where the reduction in urine output after vasopressin administration is quantified. Another approach is using isolated kidney tubules to measure vasopressin's effect on water reabsorption. These assays are vital for determining the potency of vasopressin preparations used in treating conditions like diabetes insipidus and vasodilatory shock, ensuring they meet therapeutic standards.

INTRODUCTION:

Bioassay is a method used to evaluate the biological activity of a substance by measuring its effect on living organisms or biological systems. It's commonly used in pharmacology, toxicology, and various fields of biomedical research to assess the potency, efficacy, and safety of drugs, hormones, and other chemical agents.

Introduction to Bioassay

1. Definition and Purpose

Bioassay involves the measurement of the biological response produced by a test substance compared to a standard or control. The primary purposes include:

a. **Determining Potency**: Assessing how much of a substance is required to produce a specific effect.
b. **Evaluating Efficacy**: Measuring how effective a substance is at achieving a desired biological response.
c. **Assessing Safety**: Identifying potential toxic effects or adverse reactions.

2. Types of Bioassays

a. **In Vivo Bioassay**: Performed on living organisms (e.g., animals or humans). Examples include testing the effect of a drug on blood pressure in rats or evaluating the therapeutic effects of a new medication in clinical trials.
b. **In Vitro Bioassay**: Conducted in a controlled environment outside a living organism, such as in cell cultures or tissue samples. Examples include assessing enzyme activity in a cell line or measuring the binding affinity of a drug to its receptor in isolated tissues.
c. **In Silico Bioassay**: Utilizes computational models to predict biological activity based on data from known interactions. This approach is used in drug discovery to identify potential candidates for further testing.

3. Methods of Bioassay

a. **Direct Method**: Measures the biological effect of a substance directly, such as the inhibition of enzyme activity or changes in cell growth.
b. **Indirect Method**: Uses secondary measures to assess biological activity, such as observing changes in physiological parameters or biochemical markers.

4. Design of a Bioassay

a. **Selection of Biological System**: Choosing an appropriate model (e.g., cell line, tissue, animal) based on the research question and substance being tested.
b. **Standardization**: Ensuring consistency in experimental conditions, such as temperature, pH, and nutrient availability, to obtain reliable results.
c. **Control Groups**: Including positive and negative controls to validate the assay and ensure that observed effects are due to the test substance.
d. **Dose-Response Relationship**: Evaluating how different concentrations of the test substance affect the biological system to determine its potency and efficacy.

5. Applications

a. **Drug Development**: Screening for new drugs, determining dosage, and assessing safety.
b. **Environmental Monitoring**: Evaluating the impact of pollutants and toxins on living organisms.
c. **Clinical Research**: Testing the effectiveness of new treatments and therapies in clinical trials.

6. Advantages and Limitations

a. **Advantages**:
   i. Provides direct measurement of biological effects.
   ii. Can be tailored to specific substances and biological systems.
b. **Limitations**:
   i. May not fully replicate complex interactions in a living organism.
   ii. Results can vary depending on the biological system used.

PRINCIPLES AND APPLICATIONS OF BIOASSAY

Principles of Bioassay:

The principles of bioassay are fundamental to understanding how biological activity is measured and interpreted. These principles ensure that bioassays are reliable, reproducible, and relevant to the biological question being studied.

a. Biological Response Measurement

i. **Quantitative Response**: Bioassays often measure a specific biological response, such as enzyme activity, cell proliferation, or changes in physiological parameters. This response is quantified to determine the potency or efficacy of the test substance.
ii. **Qualitative Response**: Sometimes, bioassays are used to observe qualitative effects, such as changes in behavior or appearance, which can provide insights into the biological impact of a substance.

b. Dose-Response Relationship

i. **Dose-Response Curve**: A key aspect of bioassays is establishing a dose-response curve, which plots the biological response against the concentration of the test substance. This curve helps determine the potency, efficacy, and possible side effects of the substance.

ii. **Threshold and Maximum Response**: Identifying the threshold dose (the lowest concentration at which a response is observed) and the maximum response (the highest effect achievable) is crucial for understanding the substance's biological activity.

c. Standardization

i. **Experimental Conditions**: Maintaining consistent experimental conditions (e.g., temperature, pH, and medium) ensures that the bioassay results are reliable and reproducible.

ii. **Controls**: Using positive controls (known substances that produce a specific response) and negative controls (substances with no expected effect) helps validate the bioassay and interpret results accurately.

d. Specificity and Sensitivity

i. **Specificity**: A bioassay should be specific to the test substance, meaning it should measure the response related to the substance's action and not other unrelated effects.

ii. **Sensitivity**: The assay should be sensitive enough to detect meaningful differences in biological response at various concentrations of the test substance.

e. Accuracy and Precision

i. **Accuracy**: The bioassay should provide results that are close to the true value or the known effect of the test substance.

ii. **Precision**: Repeated measurements should yield consistent results, indicating that the bioassay is reliable.

2. Applications of Bioassay

Bioassays have a wide range of applications in various fields, including pharmacology, toxicology, environmental science, and clinical research. Here are some key applications:

a. Drug Development and Testing

i. **Screening for New Drugs**: Bioassays are used to identify potential drug candidates by evaluating their effects on biological systems.

ii. **Determining Potency and Efficacy**: Measuring the biological response to different concentrations of a drug helps determine its potency and efficacy.

iii. **Safety Evaluation**: Bioassays help assess the safety of new drugs by identifying potential toxic effects and adverse reactions.

b. Clinical Research

i. **Assessing Therapeutic Effects**: In clinical trials, bioassays are used to evaluate the effectiveness of new treatments and therapies in patients.

ii. **Monitoring Disease Progression**: Bioassays can be used to measure biomarkers related to disease progression and treatment response.

c. Environmental Monitoring

i. **Evaluating Pollutants**: Bioassays are used to assess the impact of environmental pollutants and toxins on living organisms.

ii. **Ecotoxicology**: Studying the effects of chemicals on ecosystems and wildlife to ensure environmental safety.

d. Quality Control

i. **Pharmaceutical Industry**: Bioassays are employed to ensure the quality and consistency of pharmaceutical products by verifying their biological activity.

ii. **Food and Beverage Industry**: Ensuring that products meet safety standards and contain the desired active ingredients.

e. Basic Research

i. **Understanding Biological Mechanisms**: Bioassays are used to study the mechanisms of action of biological agents and drugs, providing insights into cellular and molecular processes.

ii. **Exploring Disease Pathogenesis**: Investigating how diseases affect biological systems and how they can be treated or managed.

TYPES OF BIOASSAY

Bioassays are classified into various types based on the biological systems used, the nature of the test substance, and the methods employed. Each type has specific applications and advantages, depending on the research or testing requirements.

Types of Bioassay

1. In Vivo Bioassay

Description: In vivo bioassays are conducted on whole living organisms, such as animals or humans, to measure the biological effect of a substance.

Characteristics:

a. **Complex Interactions**: Reflects the complex interactions within a living organism, including metabolism, absorption, distribution, and excretion of the test substance.

b. **Ethical Considerations**: Requires ethical considerations and approval, especially when using animals or human subjects.

c. **Applications**: Commonly used in drug development, toxicology, and clinical trials.

Examples:

a. **Animal Models**: Testing the efficacy of a new drug on rats or mice to observe its therapeutic effects or potential side effects.

b. **Clinical Trials**: Evaluating the effectiveness and safety of a new drug or therapy in human volunteers or patients.

Advantages:

a. Provides comprehensive data on the overall effect of a substance.

b. Allows for the study of systemic effects and interactions.

Limitations:

a. Ethical and logistical challenges in using animals or humans.

b. Variability in responses due to biological differences between individuals.

2. In Vitro Bioassay

Description: In vitro bioassays are performed outside of a living organism, typically using isolated cells, tissues, or organs in a controlled laboratory environment.

Characteristics:

a. **Controlled Conditions**: Offers controlled experimental conditions, allowing for precise measurement of biological responses.
b. **Reduced Complexity**: Focuses on specific cellular or molecular interactions, simplifying the system compared to whole organisms.
c. **Applications**: Widely used in pharmacology, toxicology, and biomedical research.

Examples:

a. **Cell Culture Assays**: Testing the effect of a drug on cancer cell lines to assess its cytotoxicity or therapeutic potential.
b. **Enzyme Activity Assays**: Measuring the inhibition or activation of specific enzymes in isolated enzyme preparations.

Advantages:

a. Greater control over experimental variables.
b. Faster and less expensive compared to in vivo studies.

Limitations:

a. May not fully replicate the complexity of a whole organism.
b. Limited ability to assess systemic effects or interactions.

3. In Silico Bioassay

Description: In silico bioassays use computational models and simulations to predict the biological activity of substances based on data from known interactions and molecular properties.

Characteristics:

a. **Model-Based**: Relies on mathematical models and algorithms to simulate biological processes.
b. **Data-Driven**: Uses existing data, such as molecular structures and interaction data, to make predictions.
c. **Applications**: Useful in early-stage drug discovery, toxicology, and pharmacogenomics.

Examples:

a. **Molecular Docking**: Predicting how a drug will bind to a target protein based on its molecular structure.
b. **Quantitative Structure-Activity Relationship (QSAR)**: Modeling the relationship between the chemical structure of a compound and its biological activity.

Advantages:

a. Can predict biological activity before experimental testing.
b. Reduces the need for extensive laboratory experiments.

Limitations:

a. Predictions are based on existing data and models, which may have limitations.
b. Requires accurate and comprehensive data to be effective.

4. Comparative Bioassay

Description: Comparative bioassays involve comparing the biological activity of different substances or formulations using the same biological system.

Characteristics:

a. **Relative Measurement**: Measures and compares the effects of different substances relative to each other or to a standard.
b. **Benchmarking**: Useful for determining which substance is more effective or potent.
c. **Applications**: Common in drug development and quality control.

Examples:

a. **Potency Testing**: Comparing the efficacy of different formulations of a drug or different drugs for the same condition.
b. **Standardization**: Ensuring that different batches of a drug or vaccine meet the same standards of efficacy and safety.

Advantages:

a. Provides relative comparisons between substances.
b. Helps in standardizing products and ensuring consistency.

Limitations:

a. Requires a reliable and consistent biological system for accurate comparisons.
b. May not provide absolute measures of biological activity.

5. Prophylactic and Therapeutic Bioassay

Description: Prophylactic bioassays evaluate the effectiveness of a substance in preventing a disease or condition, while therapeutic bioassays assess its ability to treat or manage an existing condition.

Characteristics:

a. **Prophylactic**: Focuses on prevention, such as testing vaccines or preventive medications.
b. **Therapeutic**: Focuses on treatment, such as evaluating the efficacy of drugs or therapies for active diseases.
c. **Applications**: Relevant in vaccine development, preventive medicine, and treatment protocols.

Examples:

a. **Vaccine Trials**: Assessing the ability of a vaccine to prevent infection or disease in animal models or clinical trials.
b. **Treatment Studies**: Evaluating the effectiveness of a new drug in managing symptoms or curing a disease.

Advantages:

a. Addresses different aspects of disease management (prevention vs. treatment).
b. Provides valuable data for developing comprehensive health strategies.

Limitations:

a. Requires appropriate models and conditions for testing preventive and therapeutic effects.
b. May involve complex and lengthy study designs.

BIOASSAY OF INSULIN

The bioassay of insulin is a method used to measure the biological activity of insulin, a crucial hormone involved in glucose metabolism. The primary aim is to assess the potency and efficacy of insulin preparations, which is essential for ensuring consistency and effectiveness in therapeutic use.

Bioassay of Insulin

1. Importance and Objectives

The bioassay of insulin is vital for:

a. **Quantifying Insulin Activity**: Determining the biological potency of insulin preparations.
b. **Quality Control**: Ensuring that insulin products meet required standards for clinical use.
c. **Comparing Different Insulin Formulations**: Evaluating various insulin formulations or brands to ensure they have equivalent therapeutic effects.

2. Types of Insulin Bioassays

a. In Vivo Bioassays

Description: In vivo bioassays involve testing insulin on living organisms, such as laboratory animals. These assays measure the physiological effects of insulin in a whole organism.

Methodology:

i. **Animal Models**: Commonly used animals include rats or rabbits. Animals are induced to have a diabetic-like state (e.g., through pancreatic damage or administration of diabetogenic agents).

ii. **Procedure**: Administer insulin to the animal and measure its effects on blood glucose levels. This is usually done by injecting a known quantity of insulin and monitoring the reduction in blood glucose.

iii. **Endpoints**: Primary endpoints include the decrease in blood glucose levels and the insulin dose required to achieve a specific reduction in glucose.

Advantages:

i. Reflects the overall physiological effect of insulin, including its pharmacokinetics and pharmacodynamics.

ii. Provides a direct measure of insulin potency in a living system.

Limitations:

i. Ethical considerations and the need for animal welfare approvals.

ii. Variability in animal responses and the complexity of the biological system.

b. In Vitro Bioassays

Description: In vitro bioassays are conducted using isolated cells or tissues to measure insulin activity.

Methodology:

i. **Cell Culture Assays**: Use of cultured cells, such as muscle or adipose cells, which are known to respond to insulin. Cells are exposed to insulin, and glucose uptake or metabolism is measured.

ii. **Insulin Receptor Binding Assay**: Measures how well insulin binds to its receptor on cell membranes. The binding affinity and capacity can be assessed using labeled insulin and receptor-expressing cells.

Advantages:

i. Provides controlled conditions and focuses on specific cellular or molecular interactions.
ii. Can be more reproducible and less variable than in vivo assays.

Limitations:

i. May not fully replicate the complex physiological effects of insulin.
ii. Limited ability to assess systemic effects and interactions.

c. Comparative Bioassays

Description: Comparative bioassays are used to compare the activity of different insulin preparations or formulations.

Methodology:

i. **Standardized Insulin**: Use a reference standard of insulin to compare the biological activity of different insulin samples.
ii. **Experimental Design**: Administer the test insulin and reference insulin under identical conditions and compare their effects on blood glucose levels or other relevant endpoints.

Advantages:

i. Useful for ensuring consistency and equivalence between different insulin products.
ii. Helps in standardizing insulin preparations across manufacturers.

Limitations:

i. Requires accurate and consistent reference standards.
ii. May not account for all differences in formulation or delivery methods.

3. Key Considerations in Insulin Bioassay

a. Calibration and Standardization

i. **Reference Standards**: Accurate and standardized reference preparations are crucial for comparing insulin activity. The World Health Organization (WHO) and other regulatory bodies provide standard insulin preparations for this purpose.

ii. **Calibration**: Bioassays must be calibrated using known standards to ensure accurate and reliable results.

b. Method Validation

i. **Precision and Accuracy**: Ensure that the bioassay method is precise and accurate by conducting validation studies.

ii. **Reproducibility**: The assay should produce consistent results across different laboratories and conditions.

c. Ethical and Regulatory Considerations

i. **Ethical Approval**: In vivo assays require ethical approval and adherence to animal welfare regulations.

ii. **Regulatory Guidelines**: Follow regulatory guidelines and standards for insulin bioassays to ensure compliance and validity of results.

4. Applications

a. Pharmaceutical Industry

i. **Quality Control**: Ensuring that insulin products meet required potency and quality standards.

ii. **New Formulation Development**: Comparing new insulin formulations with established products.

b. Clinical Research

i. **Drug Development**: Assessing the efficacy of new insulin analogs or delivery systems.

ii. **Safety Studies**: Evaluating potential differences in safety and efficacy between insulin products.

BIOASSAY OF OXYTOCIN

The bioassay of oxytocin is designed to measure the biological activity of oxytocin, a hormone crucial for various physiological functions such as uterine contractions during labor and milk ejection during lactation. Accurate bioassays of oxytocin are essential for evaluating the potency and efficacy of oxytocin preparations used in medical treatments and research.

Bioassay of Oxytocin

1. Importance and Objectives

The primary objectives of bioassaying oxytocin are:

a. **Quantifying Oxytocin Activity**: Determining the potency of oxytocin preparations.

b. **Quality Control**: Ensuring that oxytocin products meet required standards for clinical use.

c. **Comparing Formulations**: Evaluating different oxytocin formulations or brands to ensure consistent therapeutic effects.

2. Types of Oxytocin Bioassays

a. In Vivo Bioassays

Description: In vivo bioassays involve testing oxytocin on living animals to measure its physiological effects.

Methodology:

i. **Animal Models**: Common models include pregnant rats or mice, where oxytocin's effects on uterine contractions can be observed.

ii. **Procedure**: Administer oxytocin to the animal and measure its effects on uterine contractions or other physiological responses. This often involves monitoring uterine activity using techniques such as electromyography or direct observation.

iii. **Endpoints**: Primary endpoints include the frequency, amplitude, and duration of uterine contractions, as well as the overall responsiveness to oxytocin.

Advantages:

i. Provides comprehensive data on the physiological effects of oxytocin, including systemic interactions.

ii. Reflects the overall impact of oxytocin in a living system.

Limitations:

i. Ethical considerations and the need for animal welfare approvals.

ii. Variability in animal responses and complexity of the biological system.

b. In Vitro Bioassays

Description: In vitro bioassays are conducted using isolated tissues or cell cultures to measure oxytocin activity.

Methodology:

i. **Uterine Tissue Assays**: Use isolated uterine tissue or muscle strips from animals to study oxytocin's effect on contraction. The tissue is placed in a controlled environment, and oxytocin is applied to observe its effect on muscle contraction.

ii. **Cell Culture Assays**: Cultured cells expressing oxytocin receptors can be used to measure receptor binding or activation in response to oxytocin.

iii. **Procedures**: Assessments might involve measuring changes in tissue contractility or receptor activity using techniques such as contractile force measurements or receptor-binding assays.

Advantages:

i. Provides controlled conditions and focuses on specific cellular or tissue responses.

ii. Reduces variability and allows for more precise measurements.

Limitations:

i. May not fully replicate the complex physiological effects of oxytocin.

ii. Limited ability to assess systemic interactions and long-term effects.

c. Comparative Bioassays

Description: Comparative bioassays involve comparing the activity of different oxytocin preparations or formulations using standardized methods.

Methodology:

i. **Standardized Oxytocin**: Utilize reference oxytocin preparations to compare the biological activity of different samples.

ii. **Experimental Design**: Administer test oxytocin and reference oxytocin under identical conditions and compare their effects on uterine contractions or other relevant endpoints.

Advantages:

i. Ensures consistency and equivalence between different oxytocin products.

ii. Helps in standardizing oxytocin preparations across manufacturers.

Limitations:

i. Requires accurate and consistent reference standards.

ii. May not account for all differences in formulation or delivery methods.

3. Key Considerations in Oxytocin Bioassay

a. Calibration and Standardization

i. **Reference Standards**: Accurate and standardized reference oxytocin preparations are essential for comparing biological activity. Regulatory bodies provide standard oxytocin preparations for this purpose.

ii. **Calibration**: Bioassays must be calibrated using known standards to ensure accurate results.

b. Method Validation

i. **Precision and Accuracy**: Ensure that the bioassay method is precise and accurate by conducting validation studies.

ii. **Reproducibility**: The assay should yield consistent results across different laboratories and conditions.

c. Ethical and Regulatory Considerations

i. **Ethical Approval**: In vivo assays require ethical approval and adherence to animal welfare regulations.

ii. **Regulatory Guidelines**: Follow regulatory guidelines and standards for oxytocin bioassays to ensure compliance and validity of results.

4. Applications

a. Pharmaceutical Industry

i. **Quality Control**: Ensuring that oxytocin products meet required potency and quality standards.

ii. **Formulation Development**: Comparing new oxytocin formulations or delivery systems with established products.

b. Clinical Research

i. **Drug Development**: Assessing the efficacy of new oxytocin analogs or treatments for conditions such as labor induction or lactation issues.

ii. **Safety Studies**: Evaluating potential differences in safety and efficacy between oxytocin products.

c. Basic Research

i. **Understanding Biological Mechanisms**: Studying the mechanisms of action of oxytocin and its effects on uterine contractions, lactation, and other physiological processes.

ii. **Exploring New Therapeutic Uses**: Investigating potential new uses for oxytocin in clinical settings.

BIOASSAY OF VASOPRESSIN

The bioassay of vasopressin, also known as antidiuretic hormone (ADH), is used to measure the biological activity of this hormone, which plays a critical role in regulating water balance and blood pressure. Accurate bioassays of vasopressin are essential for evaluating the potency and efficacy of vasopressin preparations used in clinical treatments and research.

Bioassay of Vasopressin

1. Importance and Objectives

The bioassay of vasopressin is important for:

a. **Quantifying Vasopressin Activity**: Determining the potency of vasopressin preparations.

b. **Quality Control**: Ensuring that vasopressin products meet required standards for clinical use.

c. **Comparing Formulations**: Evaluating different vasopressin formulations or brands to ensure consistent therapeutic effects.

2. Types of Vasopressin Bioassays

a. In Vivo Bioassays

Description: In vivo bioassays involve testing vasopressin on living animals to measure its physiological effects.

Methodology:

i. **Animal Models**: Common models include rats or rabbits. Vasopressin's effects on water retention and blood pressure are typically studied.

ii. **Procedure**: Administer vasopressin to the animal and monitor physiological changes, such as water retention and blood pressure. This often involves measuring urine output, serum osmolality, and blood pressure changes.

iii. **Endpoints**: Primary endpoints include the volume of urine produced, changes in serum osmolality, and blood pressure measurements.

Advantages:

i. Provides comprehensive data on the physiological effects of vasopressin, including systemic interactions.

ii. Reflects the overall impact of vasopressin in a living system.

Limitations:

i. Ethical considerations and the need for animal welfare approvals.

ii. Variability in animal responses and complexity of the biological system.

b. In Vitro Bioassays

Description: In vitro bioassays are conducted using isolated tissues or cell cultures to measure vasopressin activity.

Methodology:

i. **Kidney Tissue Assays**: Use isolated kidney tissues or segments to study vasopressin's effect on water reabsorption. The tissue is placed in a controlled environment, and vasopressin is applied to observe changes in water handling or ion transport.

ii. **Cell Culture Assays**: Cultured cells expressing vasopressin receptors can be used to measure receptor binding or activation. Techniques such as radiolabeled ligand binding assays or reporter gene assays are used.

iii. **Procedures**: Assessments might involve measuring changes in water permeability in kidney cells or receptor activation in cell cultures.

Advantages:

i. Provides controlled conditions and focuses on specific cellular or tissue responses.

ii. Reduces variability and allows for more precise measurements.

Limitations:

i. May not fully replicate the complex physiological effects of vasopressin.

ii. Limited ability to assess systemic interactions and long-term effects.

c. Comparative Bioassays

Description: Comparative bioassays involve comparing the activity of different vasopressin preparations or formulations using standardized methods.

Methodology:

i. **Standardized Vasopressin**: Utilize reference vasopressin preparations to compare the biological activity of different samples.

ii. **Experimental Design**: Administer test vasopressin and reference vasopressin under identical conditions and compare their effects on endpoints such as urine output or blood pressure.

Advantages:

i. Ensures consistency and equivalence between different vasopressin products.

ii. Helps in standardizing vasopressin preparations across manufacturers.

Limitations:

i. Requires accurate and consistent reference standards.

ii. May not account for all differences in formulation or delivery methods.

3. Key Considerations in Vasopressin Bioassay

a. Calibration and Standardization

i. **Reference Standards**: Accurate and standardized reference vasopressin preparations are essential for comparing biological activity. Regulatory bodies provide standard vasopressin preparations for this purpose.

ii. **Calibration**: Bioassays must be calibrated using known standards to ensure accurate results.

b. Method Validation

i. **Precision and Accuracy**: Ensure that the bioassay method is precise and accurate by conducting validation studies.

ii. **Reproducibility**: The assay should yield consistent results across different laboratories and conditions.

c. Ethical and Regulatory Considerations

i. **Ethical Approval**: In vivo assays require ethical approval and adherence to animal welfare regulations.

ii. **Regulatory Guidelines**: Follow regulatory guidelines and standards for vasopressin bioassays to ensure compliance and validity of results.

4. Applications

a. Pharmaceutical Industry

i. **Quality Control**: Ensuring that vasopressin products meet required potency and quality standards.

ii. **Formulation Development**: Comparing new vasopressin formulations or delivery systems with established products.

b. Clinical Research

i. **Drug Development**: Assessing the efficacy of new vasopressin analogs or treatments for conditions such as diabetes insipidus or hypotension.

ii. **Safety Studies**: Evaluating potential differences in safety and efficacy between vasopressin products.

c. Basic Research

i. **Understanding Biological Mechanisms**: Studying the mechanisms of action of vasopressin and its effects on water balance, blood pressure, and other physiological processes.

ii. **Exploring New Therapeutic Uses**: Investigating potential new uses for vasopressin in clinical settings.

CHAPTER – 20

BIOASSAY – II

Mr. Abu Tahir

Assistant Professor, Rajiv Gandhi Institute of Pharmacy, Faculty of Pharmaceutical Science & Technology, AKS University Satna, (M.P.)

ABSTRACT:

Bioassays are essential tools in pharmacology, providing quantitative and qualitative assessments of drug potency and biological activity. The bioassay of Adrenocorticotropic Hormone (ACTH) involves measuring its effect on adrenal steroidogenesis, typically using in vivo assays like the increase in plasma cortisol levels in rats. The bioassay of d-tubocurarine, a neuromuscular blocking agent, is commonly conducted using its effect on muscle contraction in isolated frog rectus abdominis or nerve-muscle preparations in rats. For digitalis, used in heart failure, the bioassay assesses its cardiotonic effects by measuring the contractile force of isolated heart tissues or the ECG changes in animal models. Histamine bioassay involves its ability to induce smooth muscle contractions, with isolated guinea pig ileum being a standard preparation. Finally, the bioassay of serotonin (5-HT) is conducted using its vasoconstrictive or smooth muscle contracting properties, often measured in isolated tissue preparations such as rat fundus strips. These bioassays are crucial for ensuring the efficacy and safety of pharmaceutical preparations, guiding dosage formulations, and supporting drug development and regulatory approval processes. Each bioassay type is tailored to the specific pharmacodynamics of the compound being tested, ensuring precise and reliable measurement of biological activity.

BIOASSAY OF ACTH

The bioassay of Adrenocorticotropic Hormone (ACTH) is essential for measuring the biological activity of this hormone, which plays a critical role in stimulating the adrenal glands to produce cortisol and other glucocorticoids.

Accurate bioassays of ACTH are crucial for evaluating its potency and efficacy, particularly in diagnostic and therapeutic contexts.

Bioassay of ACTH

1. Importance and Objectives

The primary objectives of ACTH bioassays are:

a. **Quantifying ACTH Activity**: Determining the potency of ACTH preparations.

b. **Quality Control**: Ensuring that ACTH products meet required standards for clinical use.

c. **Comparing Formulations**: Evaluating different ACTH formulations or brands to ensure consistent therapeutic effects.

2. Types of ACTH Bioassays

a. In Vivo Bioassays

Description: In vivo bioassays involve testing ACTH on living animals to measure its physiological effects.

Methodology:

i. **Animal Models**: Common models include rats, mice, or rabbits. These models are used to study ACTH's effects on adrenal gland function and cortisol production.

ii. **Procedure**: Administer ACTH to the animal and measure its effects on adrenal hormone levels and physiological responses. This often involves monitoring changes in plasma cortisol levels, adrenal gland weight, or other biomarkers.

iii. **Endpoints**: Primary endpoints include the increase in plasma cortisol or other adrenal hormones, changes in adrenal gland morphology, and overall response to ACTH.

Advantages:

i. Provides a comprehensive view of ACTH's physiological effects, including systemic interactions.

ii. Reflects the overall impact of ACTH in a living organism.

Limitations:

i. Ethical considerations and the need for animal welfare approvals.

ii. Variability in animal responses and complexity of the biological system.

b. In Vitro Bioassays

Description: In vitro bioassays are conducted using isolated tissues or cell cultures to measure ACTH activity.

Methodology:

i. **Adrenal Cell Culture Assays**: Use cultured adrenal cells to study ACTH's effects on steroidogenesis. Cells are exposed to ACTH, and changes in cortisol or other adrenal steroids are measured.

ii. **Receptor Binding Assays**: Measure ACTH binding to its receptors on adrenal cells. Techniques such as radiolabeled ligand binding assays or receptor activation assays are used.

iii. **Procedures**: Assessments might involve measuring changes in hormone production, receptor binding, or gene expression related to steroidogenesis.

Advantages:

i. Provides controlled conditions and focuses on specific cellular or molecular responses.

ii. Reduces variability and allows for more precise measurements.

Limitations:

i. May not fully replicate the complex physiological effects of ACTH.

ii. Limited ability to assess systemic interactions and long-term effects.

c. Comparative Bioassays

Description: Comparative bioassays involve comparing the activity of different ACTH preparations or formulations using standardized methods.

Methodology:

i. **Standardized ACTH**: Utilize reference ACTH preparations to compare the biological activity of different samples.
ii. **Experimental Design**: Administer test ACTH and reference ACTH under identical conditions and compare their effects on endpoints such as cortisol production or receptor binding.

Advantages:

i. Ensures consistency and equivalence between different ACTH products.
ii. Helps in standardizing ACTH preparations across manufacturers.

Limitations:

i. Requires accurate and consistent reference standards.
ii. May not account for all differences in formulation or delivery methods.

3. Key Considerations in ACTH Bioassay

a. Calibration and Standardization

i. **Reference Standards**: Accurate and standardized reference ACTH preparations are essential for comparing biological activity. Regulatory bodies provide standard ACTH preparations for this purpose.
ii. **Calibration**: Bioassays must be calibrated using known standards to ensure accurate results.

b. Method Validation

i. **Precision and Accuracy**: Ensure that the bioassay method is precise and accurate by conducting validation studies.
ii. **Reproducibility**: The assay should yield consistent results across different laboratories and conditions.

c. Ethical and Regulatory Considerations

i. **Ethical Approval**: In vivo assays require ethical approval and adherence to animal welfare regulations.
ii. **Regulatory Guidelines**: Follow regulatory guidelines and standards for ACTH bioassays to ensure compliance and validity of results.

4. Applications

a. Pharmaceutical Industry

i. **Quality Control**: Ensuring that ACTH products meet required potency and quality standards.

ii. **Formulation Development**: Comparing new ACTH formulations or delivery systems with established products.

b. Clinical Research

i. **Diagnostic Testing**: Assessing the efficacy of ACTH preparations for diagnosing adrenal disorders or evaluating adrenal function.

ii. **Drug Development**: Evaluating new ACTH analogs or treatments for conditions such as Addison's disease or congenital adrenal hyperplasia.

c. Basic Research

i. **Understanding Biological Mechanisms**: Studying the mechanisms of action of ACTH and its effects on adrenal hormone production and metabolism.

ii. **Exploring New Therapeutic Uses**: Investigating potential new uses for ACTH in clinical settings.

BIOASSAY OF D-TUBOCURARINE

The bioassay of d-tubocurarine, a neuromuscular blocker, is used to measure its pharmacological activity, specifically its ability to induce muscle relaxation by blocking neuromuscular transmission. Accurate bioassays of d-tubocurarine are crucial for evaluating its potency and efficacy in clinical and research settings.

Bioassay of d-Tubocurarine

1. Importance and Objectives

The primary objectives of d-tubocurarine bioassays are:

a. **Quantifying d-Tubocurarine Activity**: Determining the potency and efficacy of d-tubocurarine preparations.

b. **Quality Control**: Ensuring that d-tubocurarine products meet required standards for clinical use.

c. **Comparing Formulations**: Evaluating different d-tubocurarine formulations or brands to ensure consistent therapeutic effects.

2. Types of d-Tubocurarine Bioassays

a. In Vivo Bioassays

Description: In vivo bioassays involve testing d-tubocurarine on living animals to measure its neuromuscular blocking effects.

Methodology:

i. **Animal Models**: Common models include rodents or rabbits. These animals are used to study d-tubocurarine's effects on muscle contraction and neuromuscular junctions.

ii. **Procedure**: Administer d-tubocurarine to the animal and monitor its effects on muscle contractions. This typically involves measuring the muscle response to electrical stimulation or monitoring the effects on voluntary muscle movements.

iii. **Endpoints**: Primary endpoints include the degree of muscle paralysis, changes in muscle contraction amplitude, and the dose-response relationship.

Advantages:

i. Provides direct data on the physiological effects of d-tubocurarine in a whole organism.

ii. Reflects the overall impact on neuromuscular function.

Limitations:

i. Ethical considerations and the need for animal welfare approvals.

ii. Variability in animal responses and the complexity of the biological system.

b. In Vitro Bioassays

Description: In vitro bioassays are conducted using isolated tissues or muscle preparations to measure d-tubocurarine activity.

Methodology:

i. **Muscle Strip Assays**: Use isolated muscle strips from animals to study d-tubocurarine's effect on muscle contraction. Muscle strips are exposed to d-tubocurarine, and changes in contraction in response to electrical stimulation are measured.

ii. **Neuromuscular Junction Assays**: Study the effect of d-tubocurarine on neuromuscular junctions by using isolated nerve-muscle preparations. The effects on neurotransmitter release and muscle contraction are assessed.

iii. **Procedures**: Measurements might involve changes in muscle tension, response to electrical stimulation, or neurotransmitter release at the neuromuscular junction.

Advantages:

i. Provides controlled conditions and focuses on specific tissue or cellular responses.

ii. Allows for more precise measurements of neuromuscular effects.

Limitations:

i. May not fully replicate the complex physiological effects of d-tubocurarine.

ii. Limited ability to assess systemic interactions and long-term effects.

c. Comparative Bioassays

Description: Comparative bioassays involve comparing the activity of different d-tubocurarine preparations or formulations using standardized methods.

Methodology:

i. **Standardized d-Tubocurarine**: Utilize reference d-tubocurarine preparations to compare the biological activity of different samples.

ii. **Experimental Design**: Administer test d-tubocurarine and reference d-tubocurarine under identical conditions and compare their effects on muscle contractions or neuromuscular function.

Advantages:

i. Ensures consistency and equivalence between different d-tubocurarine products.
ii. Helps in standardizing d-tubocurarine preparations across manufacturers.

Limitations:

i. Requires accurate and consistent reference standards.
ii. May not account for all differences in formulation or delivery methods.

3. Key Considerations in d-Tubocurarine Bioassay

a. Calibration and Standardization

i. **Reference Standards**: Accurate and standardized reference d-tubocurarine preparations are essential for comparing biological activity. Regulatory bodies provide standard d-tubocurarine preparations for this purpose.
ii. **Calibration**: Bioassays must be calibrated using known standards to ensure accurate results.

b. Method Validation

i. **Precision and Accuracy**: Ensure that the bioassay method is precise and accurate by conducting validation studies.
ii. **Reproducibility**: The assay should yield consistent results across different laboratories and conditions.

c. Ethical and Regulatory Considerations

i. **Ethical Approval**: In vivo assays require ethical approval and adherence to animal welfare regulations.
ii. **Regulatory Guidelines**: Follow regulatory guidelines and standards for d-tubocurarine bioassays to ensure compliance and validity of results.

4. Applications

a. Pharmaceutical Industry

i. **Quality Control**: Ensuring that d-tubocurarine products meet required potency and quality standards.

ii. **Formulation Development**: Comparing new d-tubocurarine formulations or delivery systems with established products.

b. Clinical Research

i. **Drug Development**: Evaluating new d-tubocurarine analogs or treatments for use as neuromuscular blockers.

ii. **Safety Studies**: Assessing potential differences in safety and efficacy between d-tubocurarine products.

c. Basic Research

i. **Understanding Biological Mechanisms**: Studying the mechanisms of action of d-tubocurarine and its effects on neuromuscular transmission and muscle relaxation.

ii. **Exploring New Therapeutic Uses**: Investigating potential new uses for d-tubocurarine or related compounds in clinical settings.

BIOASSAY OF DIGITALIS

The bioassay of digitalis, a class of cardiac glycosides used to treat heart conditions like atrial fibrillation and heart failure, is essential for evaluating the potency and efficacy of these compounds. Digitalis preparations are used to increase the force of heart contractions and regulate heart rhythm, so precise bioassays are crucial for ensuring their safe and effective use.

Bioassay of Digitalis

1. Importance and Objectives

The primary objectives of bioassaying digitalis are:

a. **Quantifying Digitalis Activity**: Determining the potency of digitalis preparations.

b. **Quality Control**: Ensuring that digitalis products meet required standards for clinical use.

c. **Comparing Formulations**: Evaluating different digitalis formulations or brands to ensure consistent therapeutic effects.

2. Types of Digitalis Bioassays

a. In Vivo Bioassays

Description: In vivo bioassays involve testing digitalis on living animals to measure its effects on cardiac function.

Methodology:

i. **Animal Models**: Common models include rats, rabbits, or dogs. These models are used to study digitalis's effects on heart rate, force of contraction, and overall cardiac function.

ii. **Procedure**: Administer digitalis to the animal and monitor its effects on heart function. Techniques include ECG (electrocardiogram) monitoring, measuring heart rate, and assessing cardiac output.

iii. **Endpoints**: Primary endpoints include changes in heart rate, force of cardiac contractions, and ECG changes indicative of therapeutic or toxic effects.

Advantages:

i. Provides comprehensive data on the physiological effects of digitalis on the entire cardiovascular system.

ii. Reflects the overall impact of digitalis on cardiac function.

Limitations:

i. Ethical considerations and the need for animal welfare approvals.

ii. Variability in animal responses and complexity of the biological system.

b. In Vitro Bioassays

Description: In vitro bioassays are conducted using isolated tissues or cell cultures to measure digitalis activity.

Methodology:

i. **Isolated Heart Tissue Assays**: Use isolated heart tissues or muscle strips from animals to study digitalis's effect on cardiac contractility.

Tissue is exposed to digitalis, and changes in contraction force or frequency are measured.

ii. **Cell Culture Assays**: Cultured cardiomyocytes or other heart cells can be used to study digitalis's effects on cellular contractility or ion channel activity.

iii. **Procedures**: Assessments might involve measuring changes in contractile force, intracellular calcium levels, or ion channel activity.

Advantages:

i. Provides controlled conditions and focuses on specific cellular or tissue responses.

ii. Reduces variability and allows for more precise measurements.

Limitations:

i. May not fully replicate the complex physiological effects of digitalis.

ii. Limited ability to assess systemic interactions and long-term effects.

c. Comparative Bioassays

Description: Comparative bioassays involve comparing the activity of different digitalis preparations or formulations using standardized methods.

Methodology:

i. **Standardized Digitalis**: Utilize reference digitalis preparations to compare the biological activity of different samples.

ii. **Experimental Design**: Administer test digitalis and reference digitalis under identical conditions and compare their effects on cardiac function or other relevant endpoints.

Advantages:

i. Ensures consistency and equivalence between different digitalis products.

ii. Helps in standardizing digitalis preparations across manufacturers.

Limitations:

i. Requires accurate and consistent reference standards.

ii. May not account for all differences in formulation or delivery methods.

3. Key Considerations in Digitalis Bioassay

a. Calibration and Standardization

i. **Reference Standards**: Accurate and standardized reference digitalis preparations are essential for comparing biological activity. Regulatory bodies provide standard digitalis preparations for this purpose.

ii. **Calibration**: Bioassays must be calibrated using known standards to ensure accurate results.

b. Method Validation

i. **Precision and Accuracy**: Ensure that the bioassay method is precise and accurate by conducting validation studies.

ii. **Reproducibility**: The assay should yield consistent results across different laboratories and conditions.

c. Ethical and Regulatory Considerations

i. **Ethical Approval**: In vivo assays require ethical approval and adherence to animal welfare regulations.

ii. **Regulatory Guidelines**: Follow regulatory guidelines and standards for digitalis bioassays to ensure compliance and validity of results.

4. Applications

a. Pharmaceutical Industry

i. **Quality Control**: Ensuring that digitalis products meet required potency and quality standards.

ii. **Formulation Development**: Comparing new digitalis formulations or delivery systems with established products.

b. Clinical Research

i. **Drug Development**: Evaluating new digitalis analogs or treatments for heart conditions.

ii. **Safety Studies**: Assessing potential differences in safety and efficacy between digitalis products.

c. Basic Research

i. **Understanding Biological Mechanisms**: Studying the mechanisms of action of digitalis and its effects on cardiac function and ion channel activity.

ii. **Exploring New Therapeutic Uses**: Investigating potential new uses for digitalis or related compounds in clinical settings.

BIOASSAY OF HISTAMINE

The bioassay of histamine is crucial for evaluating the potency and efficacy of histamine preparations and understanding its physiological effects. Histamine is a biogenic amine involved in various physiological processes, including allergic responses, gastric acid secretion, and neurotransmission. Accurate bioassays help in assessing histamine's biological activity and developing related pharmaceuticals.

Bioassay of Histamine

1. Importance and Objectives

The primary objectives of bioassaying histamine are:

a. **Quantifying Histamine Activity**: Determining the potency of histamine preparations.

b. **Quality Control**: Ensuring that histamine products meet required standards for clinical and research use.

c. **Comparing Formulations**: Evaluating different histamine formulations or brands to ensure consistent biological activity.

2. Types of Histamine Bioassays

a. In Vivo Bioassays

Description: In vivo bioassays involve testing histamine on living animals to measure its physiological effects.

Methodology:

i. **Animal Models**: Common models include rats, guinea pigs, or rabbits. These models are used to study histamine's effects on various physiological systems.
ii. **Procedure**: Administer histamine to the animal and monitor its effects on parameters such as blood pressure, heart rate, gastric acid secretion, or allergic responses.
iii. **Endpoints**: Primary endpoints may include changes in blood pressure, heart rate, gastric acid secretion levels, or symptoms of an allergic reaction (e.g., wheal and flare responses).

Advantages:

i. Provides comprehensive data on the physiological effects of histamine across different systems.
ii. Reflects the overall impact of histamine in a living organism.

Limitations:

i. Ethical considerations and the need for animal welfare approvals.
ii. Variability in animal responses and complexity of the biological system.

b. In Vitro Bioassays

Description: In vitro bioassays are conducted using isolated tissues or cell cultures to measure histamine activity.

Methodology:

i. **Tissue Preparations**: Use isolated tissues, such as the gastric mucosa or bronchial tissues, to study histamine's effects on physiological responses. Tissue preparations are exposed to histamine, and changes in parameters such as gastric acid secretion or bronchoconstriction are measured.
ii. **Cell Culture Assays**: Cultured cells, such as mast cells or histamine-sensitive cell lines, can be used to study histamine's effects on cellular

responses. Techniques may include measuring histamine release, receptor binding, or changes in intracellular signaling pathways.

iii. **Procedures**: Assessments might involve measuring changes in tissue contraction, secretion rates, or cell signaling in response to histamine exposure.

Advantages:

i. Provides controlled conditions and focuses on specific tissue or cellular responses.

ii. Reduces variability and allows for more precise measurements.

Limitations:

i. May not fully replicate the complex physiological effects of histamine.

ii. Limited ability to assess systemic interactions and long-term effects.

c. Comparative Bioassays

Description: Comparative bioassays involve comparing the activity of different histamine preparations or formulations using standardized methods.

Methodology:

i. **Standardized Histamine**: Utilize reference histamine preparations to compare the biological activity of different samples.

ii. **Experimental Design**: Administer test histamine and reference histamine under identical conditions and compare their effects on endpoints such as tissue responses or receptor binding.

Advantages:

i. Ensures consistency and equivalence between different histamine products.

ii. Helps in standardizing histamine preparations across manufacturers.

Limitations:

i. Requires accurate and consistent reference standards.

ii. May not account for all differences in formulation or delivery methods.

3. Key Considerations in Histamine Bioassay

a. Calibration and Standardization

i. **Reference Standards**: Accurate and standardized reference histamine preparations are essential for comparing biological activity. Regulatory bodies provide standard histamine preparations for this purpose.

ii. **Calibration**: Bioassays must be calibrated using known standards to ensure accurate results.

b. Method Validation

i. **Precision and Accuracy**: Ensure that the bioassay method is precise and accurate by conducting validation studies.

ii. **Reproducibility**: The assay should yield consistent results across different laboratories and conditions.

c. Ethical and Regulatory Considerations

i. **Ethical Approval**: In vivo assays require ethical approval and adherence to animal welfare regulations.

ii. **Regulatory Guidelines**: Follow regulatory guidelines and standards for histamine bioassays to ensure compliance and validity of results.

4. Applications

a. Pharmaceutical Industry

i. **Quality Control**: Ensuring that histamine products meet required potency and quality standards.

ii. **Formulation Development**: Comparing new histamine formulations or delivery systems with established products.

b. Clinical Research

i. **Drug Development**: Evaluating new histamine analogs or treatments for conditions like allergies or acid-related disorders.

ii. **Safety Studies**: Assessing potential differences in safety and efficacy between histamine products.

c. Basic Research

i. **Understanding Biological Mechanisms**: Studying the mechanisms of action of histamine and its effects on various physiological systems, such as the immune system, gastrointestinal tract, and cardiovascular system.

ii. **Exploring New Therapeutic Uses**: Investigating potential new uses for histamine or related compounds in clinical settings.

BIOASSAY OF 5-HT

The bioassay of 5-Hydroxytryptamine (5-HT), also known as serotonin, is crucial for assessing its biological activity, potency, and efficacy. Serotonin is a neurotransmitter involved in regulating mood, anxiety, and various physiological functions, such as gastrointestinal motility and vasoconstriction. Accurate bioassays help in understanding serotonin's role in these processes and evaluating the effectiveness of drugs that modulate its activity.

Bioassay of 5-HT (Serotonin)

1. Importance and Objectives

The primary objectives of bioassaying 5-HT are:

a. **Quantifying 5-HT Activity**: Determining the potency and efficacy of 5-HT preparations.

b. **Quality Control**: Ensuring that serotonin products meet required standards for clinical and research use.

c. **Comparing Formulations**: Evaluating different serotonin formulations or drugs that affect serotonin levels to ensure consistent biological activity.

2. Types of 5-HT Bioassays

a. In Vivo Bioassays

Description: In vivo bioassays involve testing serotonin on living animals to measure its physiological and behavioral effects.

Methodology:

i. **Animal Models**: Common models include rats, mice, or rabbits. These models are used to study serotonin's effects on mood, behavior, and various physiological systems.
ii. **Procedure**: Administer serotonin to the animal and monitor its effects on parameters such as behavior, blood pressure, gastrointestinal motility, or brain activity. Techniques include behavioral tests, physiological measurements, and monitoring of neurotransmitter levels.
iii. **Endpoints**: Primary endpoints include changes in behavior (e.g., anxiety-like or depression-like behaviors), blood pressure, heart rate, gastrointestinal motility, and neurotransmitter levels in the brain.

Advantages:

i. Provides comprehensive data on the physiological and behavioral effects of serotonin.
ii. Reflects the overall impact of serotonin in a living organism.

Limitations:

i. Ethical considerations and the need for animal welfare approvals.
ii. Variability in animal responses and the complexity of the biological system.

b. In Vitro Bioassays

Description: In vitro bioassays are conducted using isolated tissues or cell cultures to measure serotonin activity.

Methodology:

i. **Tissue Preparations**: Use isolated tissues, such as smooth muscle strips or brain slices, to study serotonin's effects on physiological responses. Tissue preparations are exposed to serotonin, and changes in parameters such as contraction, neurotransmitter release, or receptor activation are measured.
ii. **Cell Culture Assays**: Cultured cells, such as serotonergic neurons or cell lines expressing serotonin receptors, can be used to study

serotonin's effects on cellular responses. Techniques include measuring receptor binding, intracellular signaling, or neurotransmitter release.

iii. **Procedures**: Assessments might involve measuring changes in tissue contraction, receptor binding affinity, or changes in cellular signaling pathways in response to serotonin exposure.

Advantages:

i. Provides controlled conditions and focuses on specific tissue or cellular responses.

ii. Reduces variability and allows for more precise measurements.

Limitations:

i. May not fully replicate the complex physiological effects of serotonin.

ii. Limited ability to assess systemic interactions and long-term effects.

c. Comparative Bioassays

Description: Comparative bioassays involve comparing the activity of different serotonin preparations or formulations using standardized methods.

Methodology:

i. **Standardized 5-HT**: Utilize reference serotonin preparations to compare the biological activity of different samples.

ii. **Experimental Design**: Administer test serotonin and reference serotonin under identical conditions and compare their effects on endpoints such as tissue responses or receptor binding.

Advantages:

i. Ensures consistency and equivalence between different serotonin products.

ii. Helps in standardizing serotonin preparations across manufacturers.

Limitations:

i. Requires accurate and consistent reference standards.

ii. May not account for all differences in formulation or delivery methods.

3. Key Considerations in 5-HT Bioassay

a. Calibration and Standardization

i. **Reference Standards**: Accurate and standardized reference serotonin preparations are essential for comparing biological activity. Regulatory bodies provide standard serotonin preparations for this purpose.

ii. **Calibration**: Bioassays must be calibrated using known standards to ensure accurate results.

b. Method Validation

i. **Precision and Accuracy**: Ensure that the bioassay method is precise and accurate by conducting validation studies.

ii. **Reproducibility**: The assay should yield consistent results across different laboratories and conditions.

c. Ethical and Regulatory Considerations

i. **Ethical Approval**: In vivo assays require ethical approval and adherence to animal welfare regulations.

ii. **Regulatory Guidelines**: Follow regulatory guidelines and standards for serotonin bioassays to ensure compliance and validity of results.

4. Applications

a. Pharmaceutical Industry

i. **Quality Control**: Ensuring that serotonin products meet required potency and quality standards.

ii. **Formulation Development**: Comparing new serotonin formulations or drugs affecting serotonin levels with established products.

b. Clinical Research

i. **Drug Development**: Evaluating new serotonin analogs or treatments for mood disorders, gastrointestinal conditions, or other serotonin-related conditions.

ii. **Safety Studies**: Assessing potential differences in safety and efficacy between serotonin products.

c. Basic Research

i. **Understanding Biological Mechanisms**: Studying the mechanisms of action of serotonin and its effects on various physiological systems, including mood regulation, gastrointestinal motility, and neurotransmission.

ii. **Exploring New Therapeutic Uses**: Investigating potential new uses for serotonin or related compounds in clinical settings.

Multiple Choice Questions (MCQs)

1. What is the primary purpose of a bioassay?
    a) To measure the chemical properties of a substance
    b) To evaluate the biological activity of a substance
    c) To determine the physical properties of a substance
    d) To identify the color of a substance
2. Which type of bioassay is performed on living organisms?
    a) In Vivo Bioassay
    b) In Vitro Bioassay
    c) In Silico Bioassay
    d) Comparative Bioassay
3. What does the dose-response curve in a bioassay help determine?
    a) The color of the substance
    b) The weight of the substance
    c) The potency and efficacy of the substance
    d) The chemical composition of the substance
4. Which bioassay involves the use of computational models?
    a) In Vivo Bioassay
    b) In Vitro Bioassay
    c) In Silico Bioassay

d) Comparative Bioassay

5. What is an advantage of in vitro bioassays?
   a) They reflect complex interactions within a living organism
   b) They provide controlled experimental conditions
   c) They are ethical and do not require approval
   d) They measure qualitative responses only
6. Which hormone's bioassay is essential for determining its potency in regulating water balance and blood pressure?
   a) Insulin
   b) Oxytocin
   c) Vasopressin
   d) ACTH
7. What is a common model used in in vivo bioassays for oxytocin?
   a) Cultured cells
   b) Human volunteers
   c) Pregnant rats or mice
   d) Isolated tissue samples
8. What is a key consideration in bioassays to ensure reliable results?
   a) Variability in experimental conditions
   b) Consistency in experimental conditions
   c) Use of a single control group
   d) Ignoring dose-response relationships
9. Which bioassay type is particularly useful in early-stage drug discovery to predict biological activity?
   a) In Vivo Bioassay
   b) In Vitro Bioassay
   c) In Silico Bioassay
   d) Comparative Bioassay
10. What is the primary function of comparative bioassays?

a) To measure the biological activity of a single substance
b) To compare the biological activity of different substances
c) To evaluate the ethical considerations of bioassays
d) To determine the chemical composition of substances

11. What is a primary endpoint in the bioassay of insulin using animal models?
a) Blood pressure changes
b) Bone density
c) Decrease in blood glucose levels
d) Heart rate variability

12. Which bioassay method uses isolated tissues or cell cultures?
a) In Vivo Bioassay
b) In Vitro Bioassay
c) In Silico Bioassay
d) Comparative Bioassay

13. What is an advantage of using in vivo bioassays?
a) They provide a direct measure of biological effects in a whole organism
b) They are less variable than in vitro bioassays
c) They do not require ethical considerations
d) They are faster and less expensive than other types

14. What is the purpose of including control groups in a bioassay?
a) To increase variability in results
b) To ensure that observed effects are due to the test substance
c) To measure the physical properties of the substance
d) To ignore the dose-response relationship

15. Which bioassay is crucial for evaluating the biological activity of cardiac glycosides like digitalis?
a) Bioassay of insulin
b) Bioassay of oxytocin

c) Bioassay of digitalis

d) Bioassay of ACTH

16. What is the primary objective of bioassaying vasopressin?

a) To measure its chemical properties

b) To determine its potency in regulating water balance and blood pressure

c) To evaluate its color

d) To compare its weight with other substances

17. Which endpoint is commonly measured in the bioassay of histamine?

a) Blood pressure changes

b) Bone density

c) Muscle contraction force

d) Serum osmolality

18. What is a key consideration for ensuring the validity of bioassay results?

a) Ignoring ethical considerations

b) Using consistent reference standards

c) Avoiding method validation

d) Increasing variability in experimental conditions

19. Which bioassay method is used to study the effects of serotonin on mood and behavior?

a) In Vivo Bioassay

b) In Vitro Bioassay

c) In Silico Bioassay

d) Comparative Bioassay

20. What is the significance of establishing a dose-response relationship in bioassays?

a) To measure the weight of the substance

b) To determine the potency and efficacy of the substance

c) To evaluate the ethical considerations

d) To ignore the biological effects

Short Answer Type Questions (Subjective)

1. Define bioassay and explain its primary purpose.
2. What are the main differences between in vivo and in vitro bioassays?
3. Describe the significance of the dose-response relationship in bioassays.
4. What are the key considerations in designing a bioassay?
5. Explain the role of control groups in bioassays.
6. Discuss the advantages and limitations of in vivo bioassays.
7. How are in silico bioassays used in drug discovery?
8. What is the importance of standardization in bioassays?
9. Describe the process of bioassaying insulin using animal models.
10. What are the primary endpoints measured in the bioassay of oxytocin?
11. Explain the significance of calibrating bioassays with reference standards.
12. How do comparative bioassays ensure consistency in biological activity?
13. Discuss the applications of bioassays in drug development and testing.
14. What are the ethical considerations involved in conducting in vivo bioassays?
15. Describe the methods used in the bioassay of digitalis.
16. What is the primary objective of bioassaying histamine?
17. How do in vitro bioassays provide controlled experimental conditions?
18. Explain the significance of method validation in bioassays.
19. What are the primary applications of bioassays in clinical research?
20. Discuss the importance of bioassays in environmental monitoring.

Long Answer Type Questions (Subjective)

1. Discuss the principles and applications of bioassays, including the different types and their respective advantages and limitations.

2. Explain the process of bioassaying insulin, detailing the methods used, key considerations, and applications in drug development and clinical research.
3. Describe the bioassay of oxytocin, including in vivo and in vitro methods, endpoints measured, and applications in pharmaceutical industry and clinical research.
4. Discuss the bioassay of vasopressin, highlighting its importance, methodologies used, and key considerations for ensuring accurate and reliable results.
5. Explain the bioassay of digitalis, including the different types of bioassays, methods used, and applications in the pharmaceutical industry and clinical research.
6. Describe the bioassay of histamine, including in vivo and in vitro methods, endpoints measured, and applications in pharmaceutical and clinical research.
7. Discuss the bioassay of serotonin (5-HT), detailing the methodologies used, key considerations, and applications in drug development and clinical research.
8. Explain the role of bioassays in drug development, including screening for new drugs, determining potency and efficacy, and assessing safety.
9. Describe the importance of standardization and calibration in bioassays, including the use of reference standards and method validation.
10. Discuss the ethical considerations involved in conducting bioassays, particularly in vivo bioassays, and the measures taken to ensure ethical compliance.

Answer Key for MCQs

1. b) To evaluate the biological activity of a substance
2. a) In Vivo Bioassay
3. c) The potency and efficacy of the substance

4. c) In Silico Bioassay
5. b) They provide controlled experimental conditions
6. c) Vasopressin
7. c) Pregnant rats or mice
8. b) Consistency in experimental conditions
9. c) In Silico Bioassay
10. b) To compare the biological activity of different substances
11. c) Decrease in blood glucose levels
12. b) In Vitro Bioassay
13. a) They provide a direct measure of biological effects in a whole organism
14. b) To ensure that observed effects are due to the test substance
15. c) Bioassay of digitalis
16. b) To determine its potency in regulating water balance and blood pressure
17. a) Blood pressure changes
18. b) Using consistent reference standards
19. a) In Vivo Bioassay
20. b) To determine the potency and efficacy of the substance

www.ingramcontent.com/pod-product-compliance
Lightning Source LLC
LaVergne TN
LVHW021136160826
845679LV00023B/1923

* 9 7 9 8 8 9 6 3 2 2 2 1 4 *